BYGONE BRITAIN

AT HOME

1900–1970

LONDON: HMSO

Researched and prepared by Publishing Services, Central Office of Information.

© Selection and introduction Crown copyright 1995

Applications for reproduction should be made to HMSO

First published 1995

ISBN 0 11 701897 X

Published by HMSO and available from:

HMSO Publications Centre
(Mail, fax and telephone orders only)
PO Box 276, London SW8 SDT
Telephone orders 0171 873 9090
General enquiries 0171 873 0011
(queuing system in operation for both numbers)
Fax orders 0171 873 8200

HMSO Bookshops
49 High Holborn, London, WC1V 6HB
(counter service only)
0171 873 0011 Fax 0171 831 1326
68-69 Bull Street, Birmingham, B4 6AD
0121 236 9696 Fax 0121 236 9699
33 Wine Street, Bristol, BS1 2BQ
0117 9264306 Fax 0117 9294515
9-21 Princess Street, Manchester, M60 8AS
0161 834 7201 Fax 0161 833 0634
16 Arthur Street, Belfast, BT1 4GD
01232 238451 Fax 01232 235401
71 Lothian Road, Edinburgh EH3 9AZ
0131 228 4181 Fax 0131 229 2734
The HMSO Oriel Bookshop
The Friary, Cardiff CF1 4AA
01222 395548 Fax 01222 384347

HMSO's Accredited Agents
(see Yellow Pages)
and through good book sellers

Acknowledgments

We would like to thank the staff of the British Library Newspaper Library at Colindale for their ready and cheerful assistance and co-operation, and for their expertise in problem-solving. The staff at the British Library at Bloomsbury have also helped in turning up rare and distant journals. We are also indebted to the following, who so kindly allowed us access to their archives: the National Magazine Company (*Harpers, Queen, Good Housekeeping* and *She* magazines); the National Federation of Women's Institutes (*Home and Country*); and the Consumers Association (*Which ?* magazine). We stress that copyright in the extracts quoted belongs to the newspapers and magazines concerned, and to their successors in business. Present owners have been most kind in granting permission to quote. These include Times Newspapers Limited, Express Group Newspapers Ltd, Associated Newspapers, Mirror Group Newspapers Ltd, IPC Magazines Ltd and Condé Nast Publications Ltd. In spite of all our efforts, it has not been possible to trace all present copyright owners in some of the extracts quoted. If we have in any way offended, we invite those concerned to get in touch with us. We would like to thank our colleagues in COI Pictures Section for helping us to choose the photographs for this book. The main cover illustration is courtesy of the Trustees of the Geffrye Museum.

PREFACE

By Sir Harry Secombe

There's nothing quite like coming across a 50-year-old newspaper or magazine – when you're moving house, perhaps, or having a particularly vigorous spring-clean. The shape and size of their yellowing pages may look familiar, but their contents seem to come from another world.

The Bygone Britain series explores our past through the pages of these old newspapers and magazines, which were only ever meant to be bought, read for a day or so and thrown away, but often end up lining people's drawers or wrapped round their crockery.

I find them endlessly fascinating. On the one hand here are events familiar through the reasoned analysis of history – battles, political upheavals – reported with vivid immediacy. Yet news items such as Chamberlain's successful appeasement mission to Berlin can only be viewed through the lens of hindsight. There are also the news stories that took a long time to happen: the earliest of many items about the Channel Tunnel in Bygone Britain is dated 1907!

Quite unselfconsciously, the articles, letters and advertisements reveal completely different priorities from our own. It is quite shocking that a small and ostensibly sentimental item about the discovery of an abandoned baby finishes with the casual disclosure that the infant was then consigned to the workhouse. Conversely, the behaviour of these aliens from another age has the power to amuse us in a way that would make them quite indignant: the excruciating niceties of visiting cards are surely no laughing matter, and what on earth is wrong with attempting to banish grey hair with radium? Likewise, in these knowledgeable days of niche marketing and core business, we find it absurd to see an advertisement urging hairdressers to sell the odd bicycle on the side.

But there are many hints that the people who populate these pages are not such strangers to us after all. Get-rich-quick schemes and dubious books already feature prominently in the small ads, and the slimming advertisements seem as widespread as in our own press. Some of the ideas voiced in the articles are ones that we thought our own generation had come up with: domestic science as a subject for boys, the dangers of too much exposure to the sun. And, needless to say, affairs of the heart loom large across the pages, whatever the decade.

The things that we can recall ourselves exert their own particular attraction. Coverage of events we remember, pictures of celebrities, advertisements for objects we coveted excite a warm glow of recognition and affection. Other pictures may arouse quite opposite emotions: horror and self-loathing to think that we ever went around with lapels like that! Our reactions to our memories are as much a gauge of how we as individuals have changed as of how society has changed.

So what conclusions can we draw from leafing through the pages of the Bygone Britain books? The increasing pace of technological change is evident, as is the growing informality – in manners, in language, and in address to the readers. The problem page letters confirm this. Early in the century, the letters themselves do not appear; all we see are the replies, addressed to a mysterious correspondent with a fanciful name: Heart's Ease or Sapphire. Fifty years later many writers think nothing of revealing their true identities along with their troubles. (In passing, let us be thankful for the demise of the enterprising service offered by the *Hairdressers and Toilet Requisites Gazette*, whereby people sent in samples of falling hair – and worse – for trichological analysis.)

Does the very different look of the articles in the 1900s and those of the 1960s – tiny, dense text with small headlines giving way to more spacious type with *Sun*-style screamers – mean that our powers of concentration are declining? That papers and magazines have to try harder to wrest our attention from television is obvious, but modern technology, availability of newsprint, and more widespread literacy have all played their part in shaping our contemporary press.

Whether you have a serious interest in British history and society, or you're an avid consumer of trivia; whether you can remember most of the first seventy years of this century, or you weren't even born, you will find plenty to wonder at, to mourn and to laugh about in the Bygone Britain series.

INTRODUCTION

For an unremarkable monosyllable, the word 'home' is enormously emotive, signifying warmth, security, rest, familiarity, safety, welcome, privacy and love. These are the conditions homes aspire to, and where the reality falls short problems arise.

At Home surveys the home in the first 70 years of the century in all its guises: the centre of family life, showcase for consumer goods, a refuge in which the rites of self-improvement can take place, the housewife's workplace and, it has to be said, the site of considerable personal trauma.

The domestic interior, like clothes themselves, has been the subject of increasingly rapid changes in fashion. While no one in their right mind would mourn the passing of the craze for animal furniture, as reported by *The World and His Wife* in 1910 ('Mounted with the heads, lions make startlingly attractive floor decorations'), the wallpaper ideas offered in a 1934 edition of *House and Home* are still striking and elegant. In retrospect even the stolidness of utility furniture has an air of craftsmanship and quality. In the 1960s – starting, indeed, as early as the 1950s – the cool, clean lines of Scandinavian furniture are all the rage (though the bridge chairs featured on p. 130 are a glaring exception to this trend). The advertisements chronicle the development of cookers, heaters and cleaners throughout the period, highlighting some excellent ideas that strangely do not seem to have withstood the test of time: the electrical plug with its own on/off switch and the Newmaid non-electric vacuum cleaner in four exciting colour schemes.

First, of course, you need something to put all this decor in, and two very different stories emerge in *At Home*. By 1900 the suburbs were, so to speak, exploding and builders following the wide variety of designs in standard architectural pattern books were throwing up villas and terraces all over the place. The ranks of the middle classes were growing, and their residences grew correspondingly. By 1923 *Good Housekeeping* featured a palatial bungalow-style 'country cottage' that could be built for £1,600. A few years later, the *Daily Mirror* reported ' . . . agitation . . . growing into anger against the manner in which "bungaloid" development is spoiling the beauty of the Sussex Downs.' However, a modest semi could still be had for £675 in the early 1930s.

Many were not so lucky, though. The shameful presence of slums persists throughout the pages of the book, with the *Illustrated Sunday Herald* reporting Queen Mary's tears on visiting a Shoreditch slum in 1922. Yet a series of photographs taken over 40 years later shows derelict and dilapidated housing flourishing in Scotland and Lancashire. Even those who had been rehoused were not necessarily more fortunate: several people were killed and eighty families lost their homes with the collapse of the system-built Ronan Point tower block in 1968.

But if you were lucky enough to have some reasonably sound walls to call your own, you still had to grapple with what went on within them. There were – and still are – two main problems: dirt and people. Technology increasingly provides the answer to the former, but the latter prove more intractable.

At Home runs the whole gamut of the problems caused by other people, from the illuminating intricacies of card-leaving expounded in *Queen* in 1903, to the ridiculous excesses of the husband who slapped his wife because she squeezed the toothpaste from the middle of the tube and found himself in the divorce courts. Along the way there is firm guidance on what the maid's routine should be (from *Home Sweet Home* in 1934) and how her room should look.

The sense that there is a domestic ideal to live up to provides the inspiration for home-based self-improvement. The pages of magazines and newspapers offer endless scope for (chiefly) the housewife to better herself, though there are opportunities for men too. The lady of the house can lose 28 pounds in a month, banish grey hair, remodel her figure (perhaps with the Scheerskin 'Cinch-Waist' corselette in fabulous Lycra) and ensure personal freshness by investing in a range of products, some more plausible than others. At the turn of the century the man of the house could educate himself with Purity Books (which seemed to operate on the 'need to know' principle, with titles such as *What a Young Man Ought to Know*, *What a Young Husband Ought to Know* and *What a Man of 45 Should Know*). Later in the period, his interests are expected to tend more towards electronics and the technical specifications of household appliances.

Despite the evolution from the sentimental hearthside of Victorian songs, via architect Le Corbusier's concept of a 'living-machine' (1923) and the making do and mending of the wartime home, to the hi-tech entertainment centre that the 1950s and 1960s ushered in, and despite the pressures that often bubble up inside it, home remains one thing most of us would rather not lose.

Verity Ridgman
COI
August 1995

1900 ▰ 1909

FIND KRUGER.

£500 REWARDS.

We offer **£500** in REWARDS FOR FINDING KRUGER'S HEAD, which is concealed in this picture. Can you find it? We want to introduce **SYMONDS' TEA** in every household, and to those who help us to do so we will repay with Bicycles, Watches, Silverware, Jewellery, &c. We give real £14 14s. **BICYCLES** and other articles of true value.

NONE OF YOUR MONEY WANTED.

You will not be compelled to buy anything of us, but you can gain **Valuable Prizes** by solving the puzzle and rendering us slight home assistance (supplying addresses of friends, &c.). So any man, woman, boy, or girl can gain rich reward. You can receive **BICYCLE, &c.,** within 3 days after you answer this advertisement, providing you comply with our simple conditions. **No Hawking,** no "Snowball" scheme; but an honourable offer by a registered Company. Cut out picture with **KRUGER'S HEAD,** marked by Pencil; send to us with 6 penny stamps, for postage, advertising, &c., and we will send a beautiful piece of **Silverware or Jewellery** with our offers; so you can obtain Bicycle, &c., quickly. Be sure to write name and full address plainly. Answers to Kruger Puzzle without 6 stamps will receive no attention, therefore don't forget to enclose them.

ADDRESS—

SYMONDS' TEA CO., LTD.,

B. P., DEVONSHIRE STREET, W.C., LONDON.

Mother's Help and Little Dressmaker **1900**

OUR late beloved Queen, amidst the thronging duties, public and private, which unavoidably pressed on her, yet found time to pay attention to the arrangements for her table. It is understood that, in conjunction with her old and faithful friend, the late Lady Churchill, her Majesty herself selected the dishes and prepared the menu card for the last Christmas dinner she would ever preside over. The simple but elegant card, printed at the private press within the Royal precincts, has an illuminated ornamental border, the upper portion of which is scrollwork carrying the monogram "V.R." In the centre is a small view of Osborne House, beneath which comes the following menu :—

HER MAJESTY'S DINNER.
Christmas Day, 1900.

POTAGES.
Tortue Claire. Crème d'Orge à l'Américaine.

POISSONS.
Turbot, Sauce Mousseuse.
Filets de Sole Panés, Sauce Ravigote.

ENTRÉE.
Celestines à la Noël.

RELEVÉS.
Dindonneau à la Chipolata.
Chine of Pork.
Roast Beef.   Plum Pudding.

ENTREMETS.
Asperges, Sauce Hollandaise.
Mince Pies.
Eclairs au Chocolat.

BUFFET.
Baron of Beef.   Woodcock Pie.   Game Pie.
Boar's Head.   Brawn.

Caterer and Hotel Keeper's Gazette **1901**

THE OKTIS CORSET SHIELD.

To THOSE who have suffered—as what woman has not?—from the inopportune breakage of corset bones, the Oktis corset shield comes as an undoubted boon. It certainly carries out what it professes—namely, doubles the life of a corset by affording protection to those side bones on which the strain of any sudden movement falls most severely, whilst at the same time it cannot be accused of perceptibly increasing the waist measurement. The invention is a most simple one, consisting of a set of stiffeners attached by narrow tape bands, and has merely to be stitched firmly within the corset, one shield on each side, just where the bones are liable to break with such dire results as regards both comfort and elegance of contour. The stiffeners are made of rustless zairoid, and are capped to prevent any possibility of chafing in any way. The Oktis shields are to be obtained of all good drapers and ladies' outfitters, and can be worn with any make of corset.

Queen **1900**

No. 19925a.

HERTFORD.—Country house to be let, furnished, for a few months; seven bedrooms, bath, and dressing rooms, two staircases, three reception-rooms, kitchen, offices, servants' sitting-room, laundry; stabling for three, coach-house; garden; good water; two miles from three towns; close to golf links; shooting and hunting; rent £3 3s., inclusive of gardener's wages, garden produce, and eggs.—19925a.

The Lady **1901**

HOROSCOPE READINGS.

THIS feature of our paper will, we are sure, be appreciated by our readers, who can have advice on any subject suitable for dealing with in a column of this kind. Information will be given on Character, Health, Pursuits, Marriage, Travelling, Friends and Enemies, Lucky Planet, Gems, Day, and Colours. Readers availing themselves of this column must enclose six penny stamps with the following particulars: *Nom de plume*, for identification of answer; male or female, married or single; year, day, and month of birth, time of day (a.m. or p.m.), place of birth. All questions will be answered in rotation as received, one subject or question only will be dealt with at a time. *Note* that information will *not* be given on time of death. Address all letters to "Asturel," THE LADY'S GAZETTE Offices, Clock House, Arundel Street, Strand.

It must be distinctly understood by all subscribers to this column that "Asturel" has not the slightest intention of deceiving or misleading, and payment is accepted only upon this express condition.

BONO (Halifax).—A good time for you to make a removal will be February next, the third week if possible. You will do better in the suburbs than in the town, and to the south or south-east. Your birthplace will never be much good to you for business and progress.

INDRA (Cardiff).—If you intend marrying in the second half of October, the 21st seems a very fair day for the event. Good agreement is promised, and your partner will make headway and come to a respectable position. You will never get on well with his brethren, and the less you have to do with them the better.

X. X. X. (Exeter).—The child will be haughty and arrogant if not controlled; he should not be allowed to associate with cross or coarse people, as he will be easily impressed by those about him. Great pains should be taken with the diet and desires in early years, or the health will be damaged through over eating. Let him have plenty of fresh air and exercise; teach him to be kind to birds and animals, and to respect old age.

JET (Bournemouth).—Your lucky gems are moss-agate and emerald; the colours red and yellow. Your planet is Venus, and the lucky day Friday.

VIOLET (Leeds).—You should have no difficulty in securing a situation during the next month. Answer advertisements or apply personally in third week. You should obtain something on the 17th, 18th, or 21st. You must govern your temper or you will often find yourself out of a situation. Something more active would suit you.

M. H. (London).—For success places north-east of birthplace should be chosen, though you would do fairly well in Bristol, Taunton, Birmingham, Dublin, and the Midlands. 1902 looks a year of activity and movement for you, and a change of residence is very probable. Should choice of locality rest with you, let it be one of the places named—Bristol for preference, next Birmingham.

BRIGHT-EYES (Surrey).—Your little girl has some good influences at birth, and will be reared without much trouble. Care must be taken against infection in the early years, and of mishaps to the legs. Don't let her associate with aged and unhealthy people, for she is very mediumistic, would soon be robbed of her strength and become ill. See that she does not get playing with fire, or near explosives. She will become popular, have a large circle of friends and gain preferment.

DOUR (Yorkshire).—Love affairs will be very interesting this year. You will pay attentions to a clear-complexioned female; blue eyes and brown hair; one fond of pleasure and recreation. You would do well to marry this lady, but it looks as if you will pass her over for one of ruddy complexion, dark hair, and grey eyes; rather short, conceited, hot tempered, and very little affection. It depends on your choice as to whether you have harmony or disharmony in your married life. The one described first would be a helpmate, the second a drag to your ambitions and progress. 1904 or 1905 will bring marriage.

Lady's Gazette 1901

AN ARTISTIC WALL PLAQUE.

EVERY British subject with an atom of respect for a great woman in his composition has mourned the loss of Queen Victoria, and few are there who would not feel grateful for an opportunity to pay homage to her memory. We think, therefore, that in bringing out a faithful medallion portrait of her late Majesty in a style which suggests its introduction to the most luxurious hotel smoke room, writing room, or vestibule, Messrs. Kimball & Morton (Limited) of Bothwell Circus, Glasgow, have done exceedingly well, and we should be pleased to see their enterprise attended with marked success. These medallions, a splendid specimen of which in nickel on blue plush lies before us, are made of solid cast metal and beautifully finished, and the likeness, as may be seen from our illustration, is remarkably good. The medallions are mounted in various forms, some being on solid wooden shields and finished in nickel, aluminium, or gold bronze. The most popular mount at the present moment, however, is a wooden shield covered with crimson or blue

plush, which shows up the bright metal portrait in splendid relief. It measures over all 15 inches by 11 inches. Better qualities of medallions can be had. These are plated in copper, silver, and gold. Finished in real gold, with crown and mantilla artistically coloured, it forms a beautiful and lasting wall decoration and a constant attraction. Any of the medallions made by Messrs. Kimball & Morton will last for many years without requiring the least attention, and then, if necessary, can be replated at a moderate cost. The medallion is fixed to the shield by means of two screws at the back, so it can be very easily detached for the purpose.

Caterer and Hotel Keeper's Gazette 1901

Spirit Message Department.

EXPERIMENTAL CLAIRVOYANCE.

WE wish to call the special attention of our readers to the fact that we have arranged to conduct a series of experiments in clairvoyance for the benefit of our readers. A medium, who has been eminently successful in public, has kindly undertaken to sit weekly with us for the purpose of experimentation, which will be conducted as follows : Our readers are invited to forward us envelopes, containing a sheet of paper, on which they have written some quotation from a favourite author, or some verses of a hymn. No name should be sent or special question asked ; but in order that the answer may be identified, an initial, *nom de plume*, or number should be written on the enclosure. The medium will not open or touch the envelope, but will endeavour to obtain messages for those who have forwarded the letters.

Note.—The medium will choose the letters to be dealt with, and all others will be destroyed from week to week.

Envelopes should be addressed—

    'EXPERIMENT,'

      'TWO WORLDS' OFFICE,

        18, CORPORATION-ST.,

          MANCHESTER,

and accompanied by a coupon to be found on page iii.

We would direct the attention of our readers to the rule that all letters addressed 'Experiment' should be accompanied by a coupon to be found on page iii. of the current issue. This rule we found had been ignored by several whose letters were opened after the seance. No delineation will be published if we find the coupon has not been enclosed.

ACKNOWLEDGMENTS.

DEAR SIR, Kindly thank the medium who sent me such an excellent description of a very near relative, and also for the cheering message.—Yours very truly,

          C. G. R.

DEAR SIR,—The delineations given to Madge are quite correct. I am seeking to know more of Spiritualism and the higher life. I feel that the spirit described might be my own child, but could not be absolutely certain.—With thanks, I remain, yours,

          MADGE.

Two Worlds 1902

KING'S GUESTS.

Message from His Majesty to the Diners.

500,000 AT TABLE.

Semi-State Visits of the Prince and Princess of Wales.

To-day in every district of London thousands of the poor are dining as the guests of the King, and, excepting the Queen, every member of the Royal Family in the metropolis is paying a round of gracious visits to the festive gatherings.

The most joyful message has come to the poor diners from the King's sick room; it is the announcement by the doctors that his Majesty—on the day of the Coronation feast which he himself proposed—is out of danger.

It is impossible at this moment to state the exact number to whom the King's dinner is being served; but it is certain that the number prescribed by his Majesty—half a million—has been fully reached and most likely exceeded.

Twenty-nine districts have had to be served, consisting of the City and twenty-eight metropolitan boroughs.

No less than 350,000 lb. of meat were cooked, so that, allowing for loss of weight, each diner might be provided with ½ lb. To this has to be added:—

250,000 lb. of potatoes.
125 tons of pudding.
250,000 lb. of bread.
1,000,000 oz. of cheese.
36,000 gallons of beer.
160,000 pints of ginger beer.
75,000 pints of lime juice.

The following telegram from Sir Francis Knollys has been received by the Lord Mayor of London :—

> Buckingham Palace, Saturday,
> 11.20 a.m.
>
> I am commanded by the King to inform your lordship that his Majesty and the Queen had intended visiting some of his Coronation dinners to-day, and he deeply regrets that his illness prevents their doing so.
>
> The King has, however, deputed members of his family to represent him at as many of these dinners as possible.
>
> I am further commanded by the King to express his hope that his guests are enjoying themselves, and are passing a happy day.
>
> KNOLLYS.

Evening News 1902

Answers to Correspondents.

W. J. J. (Coventry).—*Chelsea Buns*, 1d. 4 lbs. flour, 1 oz. yeast, 10 ozs. sugar, 10 ozs. butter, four eggs, and a quart of milk. Set a bun sponge with this, and when ready weigh out and tin in the same fashion on a baking sheet as for small loaves. Prove, and bake in a good oven. Whilst they are still hot, brush over with a thin covering of water icing. The water icing is made by simply adding hot water to a little icing sugar. *Banbury Cakes*. Make a good puff paste in the usual way. After giving it the last rolling, roll into a sheet about ⅛ in. thick, and cut the sheet into squares about 3 in. each way. Lay the squares on a board, wash them over with water, and then fill them with a mixture made as follows, and which you should have ready prepared : Take ½ lb. of good butter and the same weight of powdered sugar, ½ lb. currants, ¼ lb. of citron, orange, and lemon peels in equal proportions, and finely cut ¼ oz. ground ginger and the same weight of ground cassia ; work all these together into a mass, and place a piece of it, about the size of a walnut, in each of the squares of paste, folding two corners over on it, and then turning it over with the folded parts down. Now place the cakes together on a board, flatten them, and wash them with milk ; then dust them heavily with powdered sugar, and bake in a steady heat. *Jam Sandwich*.

British Baker 1903

INSTANCES IN CARD LEAVING.

CARD LEAVING is one of those subjects so bristling with side issues that it would be difficult to exhaust the instances whence they arise. It would seem that our correspondents realise this, to judge from the questions addressed to us week after week.

Leaving cards after entertainments should offer no difficulty, but it does, nevertheless, by reason of the before-mentioned individual circumstances. After a dance given by a friend or a friend's friend, as is often the case, those invited should, as a matter of etiquette, leave cards. Then comes the question, "Whose cards should be left, and how many?" If a mother and daughter have been invited the mother should leave one of her cards, with her daughter's name upon it; if two daughters, the two daughters' names. It is now so much the fashion not to invite a mother with her daughters; to give boy and girl dances, and invite the daughters only. Still, if a dance is given by a friend or acquaintance of the mother—and it generally is so—she should, although not invited to the dance, leave her card with her daughter's name upon it. Again, if a girl friend of her daughter's gave the invitation the mother should leave a card with her daughter's name upon it for the giver of the dance; her daughter being a young girl and having her name upon her mother's cards. Such card leaving as this would not commence a calling or even a card-leaving acquaintance; it would simply convey thanks for civility shown to the daughter.

There is no question as to whether the father's cards should be left with the mother's on this occasion; he has not been invited, and he is not expected to join in acknowledging the invitation given to his daughter, consequently his cards are not left. When young married couples are invited to a dance, the wife should leave one of her own and two of her husband's cards on this particular occasion. These cards should be left within the current week.

Queen 1903

ALMSHOUSES OF THE IRONMONGERS' COMPANY : IN THE GARDEN.

Almspeople, 1903

THE PHYSIOLOGICAL NECESSITY
OF A DAY OF REST.

By Dr. Robertson Wallace.

There can be no question in the minds of all those who go about the world with their eyes open, that the old ideas and methods of Sunday observance in England are undergoing, and indeed, have undergone, a marked change. In the present article I shall briefly allude to the effect which this change has had, or is likely to have on the mental and physical well-being of the community, leaving the spiritual aspects of the question to be discussed by experts in these matters.

Human experience has shown that five-and-a-half days' continuous application, with the necessary intervals for food and recuperation, at any particular task demanding concentrated muscular or mental exertion, is about as much as the average worker can stand. This is a period quite long enough for out-door work, and much too long for a great deal of indoor work.

Rest is absolutely necessary to health ; but " rest " is one of the most elastic of all the pliable terms to be found in the English dictionary. One man's rest is another man's labour. In his definition of rest every man must be a dictionary unto himself. Rest is not simply the negation of activity, or that impossible form of inactivity known as " doing nothing." You cannot do nothing, even if you try very hard for a fortnight. A human being must either be doing evil or good, or thinking about it ; or he must be unconscious. When he has ceased altogether to employ both his mind and his muscles, he can only employ an undertaker. The healthy human animal can only rest by directing his activities into fresh channels, and not by attempting to smother or strangle them altogether.

Chic
1904

THE FOOD OF THE FAIR.

DIET plays a very large part in the production or modification of womanly beauty. A woman who eats a properly balanced diet should have a well proportioned frame and a fine complexion. The rounded outlines and soft plump cheeks of youth are due to the presence beneath the skin of just the right amount of fat to conceal the bones, and the angularities inherent in the mineral framework which is the prop and mainstay of the loveliest of our sex.

I think the finest features and complexions are to be found in those women who are the most temperate in eating and drinking, and who are fairly active in their movements. The lazy woman who eats largely, and has a *penchant* for liqueurs, is seldom the embodiment of loveliness. Briskness and beauty often appear to go together. The active woman does not become fat and heavy, nor does she lose her fine figure as soon as her more leisurely inclined sister. The women who are always putting on fat are those who are always putting off their time, and who are so much occupied in doing nothing that they never have time to do anything.

Chic 1904

MANNERS AND MORALS.

SCENE AT A DINNER PARTY.

Mrs. Annie Sinclair, who obtained a decree nisi in the Divorce Court yesterday, complained that her husband was deficient both in manners and morals.

They were married in 1892, and subsequently lived at Boston. The respondent at one time held a commission in the Lincolnshire Volunteers, but was asked to resign because he got drunk at a dance. On one occasion, at a dinner party at his house, a leg of mutton which was served up displeased him. He swore at his wife, and, declaring that he could get a better dinner at the Bull Inn, he walked out of the house, leaving his wife in tears.

Subsequently he went to Canada, and Mrs. Sinclair went to see him off, ignorant of the fact that he was taking with him a servant girl named Ruth Campling. From Canada he wrote to his wife, addressing her as "My own sweet wife." He referred to his folly, said it was all his fault, and expressed the hope that when he did return she would be able "to put her arms round his neck." The letter finished up: "Now, my love, for the present, farewell. May someone reward you for all your love and kindness to your poor old boy."

At this time the former servant girl was still in his company. He afterwards went to South Africa, and joined the Mounted Police.

Daily News 1905

Counsel and Comfort

"Is it a sin to act the fool to amuse and make other people laugh?" That is the unusual question put to me by "L. W."

Well, "L. W.," to make people laugh, of course, is not a sin, though some people make themselves very absurd, and forfeit their self-respect in trying to amuse people. The great thing for you is to avoid, in your desire to be pleasant, mere clownishness and buffoonery. When you make these mistakes people may laugh at you, and think you good company, but you are in danger, perhaps, of losing their respect. A quiet, cheerful, happy manner is much more to be desired and to be sought than a loud, blustering, "tomfooling" one. But in either case there is not necessarily any question of sin.

Sunday Circle 1904

THE TALE OF A COW

AND WHY IT WAS TWISTED.

STRANGE SCENE AT CHATHAM.

(From Our Own Correspondent.)
CHATHAM, Wednesday Night.

The exploits of a cow which entered a house in Chatham, walked upstairs, and left by the front bedroom window, were related at Rochester County Court yesterday, when James Black, a butcher, of Newington, was sued for £8 damages.

On April 18 Mrs. Dickenson, the wife of a local footballer, sent her little girl on an errand. A minute later the child returned screaming that a mad bull was after her. She had hardly said the words when a cow dashed through the open front door. Mrs. Dickenson dragged the child into a room, and had just banged the door, when the animal crashed against it. Its onslaught threatened to break down the door, so Mrs. Dickenson and a friend who was in the house with her piled furniture against it.

After a quarter of an hour the cow went upstairs, entered the front bedroom, and proceeded to demolish the furniture. The drover said he had never driven the cow before, and went to fetch the owner. Nobody seemed able to do anything until a lad fourteen years of age—who said he knew something about cows—made his way upstairs and twisted the animal's tail to such good purpose that it leapt through the window. The cow was in the bedroom over an hour.

Judgment was given for the plaintiff for five guineas.

Daily News 1905

COFFEE.—At to-day's auctions the larger supply of 5236 packages met with a good demand and nearly all sold at very steady rates.

641 bags of East India were offered as follows : 336 bags Mysore sold, small common greenish 44s 6d, low middling 46s to 47s, bold common 51s, pea-berry 52s to 54s 6d. 138 bags Neilgherry sold, small fair greenish and colory 44s 6d, middling 47s 6d to 49s 6d, bold common 52s 6d, good to fine 58s 6d to 67s, pea-berry 53s to 55s. 52 bags Nelliampathies sold, small common greenish 43s, low middling 46s 6d, common bold 49s, pea-berry 51s. 111 bags Shevaroy sold, small fair colory 44s to 44s 6d, low middling to middling 46s 6d to 47s 6d, bold fair to good 52s 6d to 55s 6d, pea-berry 52s. 4 bags native sold at 38s to 44s.

8 barrels and 100 bags Jamaica sold, good ordinary palish to fine ordinary greenish and grayish 40s to 44s.

Of 2591 bags Costa Rica 1776 sold, small common greenish to fine blue 43s to 53s 6d, low middling greenish to middling colory 52s 6d to 60s 6d, good middling to fine middling colory 63s to 69s, bold fair grayish to fine blue 62s 6d to 73s, very fine blue 77s, pea-berry 58s to 81s.

373 bags Guatemala sold, small fair to good colory 42s 6d to 45s, low middling to middling 46s to 50s, bold fair greenish and colory 50s to 51s, good blue 54s, pea-berry 52s to 56s.

Of 204 bags Vera Paz 158 sold, small fair to good blue 45s 6d to 49s, middling to good middling 55s to 76s, bold good 71s 6d to 78s, fine 103s 6d, pea-berry 61s to 114s.

54 bags Nicaragua sold, small common greenish 41s, middling 48s, fair bold 52s, pea-berry 53s.

197 bags Mexican sold, small good blue 44s 6d, middling greenish and colory 51s, bold good blue 67s, pea-berry 71s.

Of 1068 bags Colombian 433 sold, small fair grayish to good greenish 42s 6d to 44s, ordinary greenish 37s, fine ordinary to low middling grayish 43s 6d to 46s, middling grayish and greenish 47s to 49s, bold good greenish 54s 6d, pea-berry 50s to 54s 6d.

Public Ledger 1906

TOO GOOD TO BE TRUE.

LONDON, *December 30.*

Credence was given to a rumour yesterday that a "good" landlord had been discovered in a South London suburb, and that he was about to build 10,000 new houses in the neighbourhood of the Crystal Palace. Forty thousand householders left their work and searched eagerly for this *rara aris*. He was found late in the afternoon—inside a coffin at Highgate Cemetery.

Clarion 1907

The Epicure of the Fireside. There is a current phrase, an adjuration to "go and eat coke," which hitherto we believe has been considered in certain circles an infallibly crushing retort in verbal controversy. But the supremacy of the phrase is threatened. The diet ironically recommended may become ere long not only possible but popular. For if we can eat firewood, why not the other combustible as well? A little time ago a gentleman residing in a workhouse proclaimed the fact that he had discovered great dietary virtues in common deal. Working in the firewood department, he indulged now and then in minced splinters, and found them not only appetising but medicinal, far transcending the qualities of the ordinary brown loaf. And now his theory has received strong indorsement from no less an authority than the "Lancet," which declares that there is no reason why wood should not be used as a source of food. True, a certain digestive peculiarity generally only found in the horse had hitherto been considered necessary. But it is clear now that this belief must be revised. And if we can eat wood, adds the "Lancet," we may add to the menu our shirts and collars, which possess the same properties. No danger of dear food now, any way!

Evening Standard

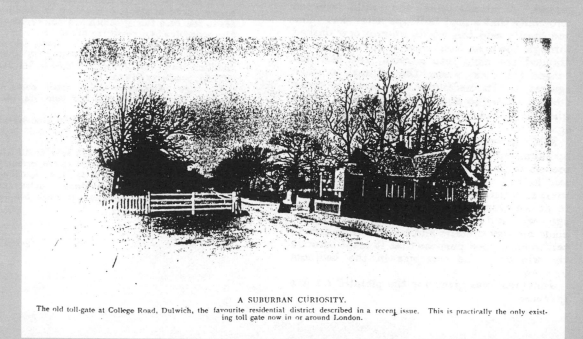

A SUBURBAN CURIOSITY.

The old toll-gate at College Road, Dulwich, the favourite residential district described in a recent issue. This is practically the only existing toll gate now in or around London.

House Property and Land Advertiser 1907

RECENT DESIGNS IN DOMESTIC ARCHITECTURE.

A HOUSE at Warford, Cheshire, designed for Mr. Ernest Agnew by Mr. Percy Worthington, is the subject of our first illustrations this month, and its general character is evident from these. The hall being the centre of life in the house, is free from all use as a service way, the passage from the servants' quarters to the door being quite independent of it, and, as a matter of comfort, the staircase is placed in a small stair-

MAIN ENTRANCE TO MR. AGNEW'S HOUSE AT WARFORD
PERCY WORTHINGTON, ARCHITECT

case hall off it. The living rooms get the sun all day, and a harmony of colour has been got in stone, small bricks, and unstained oak. The gardens lie south and east, with a fore-court formed by a yew hedge to the west, and a formal terrace-garden on the east side, enclosed on two sides by the house. The long window seen over the hall is a gallery on the chamber-floor. The woodwork throughout is wainscot oak, and the fireplace and walls of the large hall are of Bath stone, the latter panelled to a height of eight feet with oak.

Studio 1908

It is past expression deplorable that some churches of the London diocese are becoming the dumping-ground of so-called marriages, which the clergy in other countries decline to solemnise. The newspapers last week described a wedding ceremony at All Souls', Langham-place, which ceremony the rector is stated to have "most impressively conducted," amid the usual surroundings of "palms and tall white lilies," and to the strains of a "fully choral" service. One of the parties had been divorced in America, and it had been found impossible to persuade any members of the clergy of New York to take part in the re-marriage of the person in question. Rumours reached England some time ago to the effect that the venue had been changed in consequence, but the scent of the actual place chosen, and of the priest who was complaisant enough to violate the law of the Church under the shelter of the law of the land, was successfully disguised. The *dénoûment* came too late for any protest to be made. It is a matter of grave scandal and anxiety with many London Churchmen that this diocese should enjoy an unenviable notoriety for its "facilities" for the marriage of divorced persons. We cannot feel satisfied that everything has been done that is possible to prevent the scandal. It should be made perfectly clear to every priest and every layman in the diocese, that the Bishop not only regards these marriages with disfavour, but pronounces them no marriages at all in the eyes of the Church.

Church Times 1906

THE DEADLY BEDROOM CLIMATE.—We talk of unfavourable climates; but an eminent physician rightly said that the most deadly climate he knew was that of the shut-in bedroom. There can be no doubt that very much of the weakness, the "tired feeling," the sense of incapacity for exertion, from which so many suffer in these strenuous days, is due to the lack of fresh air. We turn away from nature's supreme tonic, shut it out from our houses as if it were a deadly enemy, and then rush to the chemist for bitters and pills. Could anything be more irrational?

Scottish Women's Temperance News 1908

Advice 1908

Continental Express 1908

Poultry Farming.

Poultry Farming in Rhodesia affords a
capital outlet for the energetic housewife who
is desirous of being something more than an
ornament to the establishment. Needless to say,
if run on systematic lines, poultry farming can
be assured of good local markets in any of the
Rhodesian Towns. The fast developing Mining
Centres naturally of themselves create a capital
market for both poultry and eggs.

A LIST of the present
Blue Blood. owners of the best-known
houses in Park Lane reads
very much like an extract from Debrett.
Peers, statesmen, and politicians here live
side by side, although of late a tendency
has rather manifested itself among prominent financiers and South African multi-
millionaires to take up their residence in
this erstwhile exclusive quarter as well.
It is to these latter that is due the somewhat bizarre style that has manifested
itself in some of the newer buildings.
Certainly, many of them are of a nature
that affords a very curious contrast to the
dignified simplicity of the older mansions.

Brook House, which Sir Ernest Cassel has
recently acquired from Lord Tweedmouth.

THE PASSING OF THE MOUSTACHE.

Opinions For and Against.

Shaving is generally looked upon as more profitable than haircutting. It takes a shorter time and needs less of a practised hand to perform the operation. Popular fashion decrees that man who wears hair on the upper lip is now decidedly out of fashion, and in view of the fact that there is more profit in shaving it is well for hairdressers that this is the case. There are, however, whole legions of men who still persist in being non-fashionable. Such a state of affairs has inspired the *Daily Mirror* to get up a discussion on the subject, and one might well ask " Is the clean-shaven man ousting in popularity his ' moustached ' brother ?" From all accounts it would seem so, at all events it is becoming quite notorious that ladies prefer " beardless youths " to the hairy individual.

" Very few men about town have moustaches " a representative of a Bond Street hairdresser told the *Daily Mirror*, "in fact, the moustache is almost entirely the prerogative of the soldier."

Women, for many reasons, prefer the clean-shaven man. A number, representing all ages, have expressed their views. Of ten not one was in favour of a beard.

Their decisions are as follows :—

I have a natural repulsion to seeing hair on a man's face.

All nice men, actors, clergymen, and other professional men are clean-shaven. Men without a moustache look more intelligent.

A bad-tempered, cynical, or criminal mouth may be hidden by a moustache.

I much prefer a clean-shaven man. I do not consider a moustache hygienic.

Most girls detest the dandy with the waxed moustache. I prefer no moustache. If a man, however, has a very ugly mouth, a small " tooth-brush " moustache is the least unsightly.

Decidedly give me a clean-shaven man if he has a good mouth and chin. Men with weak chins should be made to wear beards.

The remaining four ladies decided against the moustache on the score of cleanliness and neat appearance.

Eleven typical men gave their opinion. Eight were in favour of the clean shave, two against, the last wavered.

" I do not wear a moustache," said the first, "because my moustache would, when grown, have a green tomato shade. Also, I do not want to look old. I think the moustacheless man is cleaner."

The other opinions were as follows :—

A moustache is a hive of bacilli.

I do not wear a moustache because I do not wish to appear a coward. The mouth is a truer index to character than the eyes, and men can hide emotion behind a moustache. I prefer to be able to control my lips and expression.

I have no courage to go through the awful stage when a moustache is merely bristles.

I wear no moustache because I have a mouth I do not wish to hide. Only men of bad character need wear moustaches.

My wife does not like moustaches.

I never dared to risk the attempt to grow one.

Ladies tell me that a moustache does not suit me.

Two men in favour of moustaches gave as their respective reasons : (1) " I have no wish to appear womanish " ; (2) " It saves both time and money to grow a moustache." The eleventh opinion was as follows : " Looking younger than I am, I grow a moustache to make myself look older ; when older, I shall clean shave."

The Hairdresser and Toilet Requisites Gazette **1909**

North Devon Journal **1909**

DISORDERLY HOUSE AT BARNSTAPLE.

A WOMAN SENT TO PRISON.

Before the Mayor (Mr. F. W. Hunt), Messrs. H. Barrett, W. F. Gardiner, and A. Bradford, at Barnstaple Police Court on Thursday, *May Nott*, a young single woman, was charged with having on November 3rd and 4th unlawfully kept a disorderly house at 21, Zion's-place.

Accused, crying, replied. "I am guilty like this —they came and asked me to take them in."

Mr. J. Bacon, prosecuting, said proceedings were taken under the Criminal Law Amendment Act, 1885, Section 13, and the penalty for the offence was a fine not exceeding £20, or imprisonment, not exceeding three months, with or without hard labour. He gave a resumé of the case, explaining that the defendant was the tenant and occupier of No. 21, Zion's place.

P.S. Tucker said that he was on duty near the cab shelter in the Square about 11.45 p.m. on the night of November 3rd, when he noticed two men and women go across the path near the Albert clock, and proceed through Litchdon-street up the alley leading to Zion's-place. Witness went there, accompanied by P.C. Fry, and saw lights in the house occupied by the defendant. He heard voices, both male and female, in the kitchen. First the inmates talked in an undertone, while afterwards some of them went upstairs into the bedroom. They were laughing and talking, and at last someone from the bottom of the stairs shouted : "Shut up and be quiet." About one a.m. the defendant opened the front door from the inside. Witness said, " Who are those men and women you have in your bedroom ?" and she replied, " You had better go and see." Witness noticed a man standing in the kitchen, while in the room upstairs he found two men and two girls, the latter of whom were of ill-fame. One of the girls said that the reason why she was there was that she had been locked out.—Mr. Gardiner : Do you know who the men were ?—Witness replied that they were not living in Barnstaple, being strangers—service men. Witness said to the defendant, " You know you are not allowed to do this sort of thing, and I shall have to report it." She replied, " If you do I shall go and drown myself," and witness told her that if she talked in that manner he should have to deal seriously with her. The men asked him not to report the matter, as it would affect their positions, being service men. He knew the defendant, and he was sorry to say that she was not much better than the other girls. P.S. Tucker added that when defendant was served with the summons she replied, " I am very sorry that it should have happened ; there was no harm done, and there was no one drunk."

London and Provincial Magazine **1909**

❧   LEICESTER.   ❧

IT is difficult to think of Leicester as a town of considerable industrial importance. The impression remains with one of a clear and sunny atmosphere, wide streets, clean brick buildings, and a constant background of green trees. The boot and hosiery factories appear to give out little or no smoke. The gas-works on the Aylestone Road, a tree-bordered avenue, are almost picturesque ; even a foundry that we visited had at the one end of the yard a small flower and vegetable plot and a water-cress bed. The people are equally pleasant to look upon, and the girls from the factories, who fill the streets with their cycles at the dinner-hour and at closing time, are fresh complexioned and cheery looking.

London and Provincial Magazine **1909**

"On Saturday the family dined at home, and then went to a private dance at a friend's house. They returned home about half-past eleven and were quite hoppy."—*Daily Paper*.

We see nothing unnatural in this.

UNDOUBTEDLY the largest soap works north of the Tweed are those at Aberdeen, which belong to Messrs. Ogston & Tennant .td., who have also extensive works at St. Rollox, Glasgow. For many years Messrs. Ogston & Tennant have been famed for the excellence and purity of their soaps, and the increasing sales prove that the public appreciate the firm's efforts to supply only the best quality of goods. Among others of their well-known soaps are "Balmoral" Cleanser and "Balmoral" Carbolic. They are classed with the very best household soaps on the market in price and quality,

Miss Jean Aylwin.

and everywhere give uniform satisfaction. We have no hesitation in recommending them, and we have no doubt that those who use them will be thoroughly satisfied with their superior qualities, and after a first trial will continue to use them. "Bouquet" Soap is perhaps the best known of all their toilet soaps, being certainly one of the foremost of the many toilet soaps at the disposal of the public. It is a super-fatted soap, absolutely free from excess of alkali. It is matchless for the complexion, and is an excellent emollient, being perfectly harmless to the most tender and delicate of skins. It can be relied upon as the best for all toilet purposes, and when once tried will certainly be bought again. In addition to the above Messrs. Ogston & Tennant are makers of soft soap and candles—needless to say, these can be equally well recommended—and can be obtained, together with the above-mentioned articles, at any of the leading grocers, stores, or chemists. The brand "Balmoral" is only used by Messrs. Ogston & Tennant on their finest qualities of hard soaps, soft soaps, toilet soaps, and candles, and any of their manufactures bearing the brand "Balmoral" carries a guarantee of excellence.

London and Provincial Magazine 1909

LANDKEY WESLEYAN CHURCH.

RE-OPENING OF THE ORGAN.

The completion of the important extension scheme carried out in connection with Landkey Wesleyan Church was consummated on Tuesday, when the organ, the capacity of which has been practically doubled, was re-opened. The old organ, whilst very harmonious, was deficient in a number of important stops, and the new instrument contains all these necessary swell pipes, the stops being on the tubular pneumatic principle. The combined instruments, which are identical in appearance, occupy each side of the rostrum. the additional swells and stops of the new organ being connected underground. Enclosed in a wood casement, the pipes are cream coloured, artistically relieved with gold tracery. The organ previously contained the following stops : Open diapason, 8ft.; liblich gedact, 8ft.; dulciana, 8ft.; octave, 4ft.; flute, 4ft.; pedal organ bourdon, 16ft.; and the following additions have been made in the new instrument :—swell organ ; open diapason, 8ft.; hohl flute, 8ft.; viol d'gamba, 8ft.; harmonic flute, 8ft.; reed oboe, 8ft ; and the couplers swell to great ; swell to pedals, great to pedals, four composition to pedals, and two to great and two to swell.

North Devon Journal 1909

1910–1919

LA MODE ELEGANTE

1 Tea-gown of embroidered tulle. The skirt is made of three lace flounces. The bodice has two points shaped as a shawl, held at the waist by a fancy braid pattern.

2. Parma-violet crêpe-de-Chine tea-gown. The apron ends in a broad Oriental embroidery design — purple and gold. Bodice made of gold lace. Very long sleeves.

3. Tea-gown of grass-green "charmeuse," veiled with black Chantilly tulle. A cloak of tulle covers the gown. Satin sash at the height of the knees.

4. Lemon-coloured satin tea-gown, striped with insertions of white lace. Long coat of orange mousseline-de-soie, ending in two large and broad bows of mousseline.

World and His Wife **1910**

THE CRAZE FOR ANIMAL FURNITURE

How pets may be used to decorate the drawing-room

A T the moment there is a veritable craze for all kinds of ornaments, nicknacks, and furniture made out of animals. At the finish, the desire to decorate the home with these natural history trophies is a commendable one. They are at once quaint, interesting, and decidedly attractive. Then they add a dignity and grace to the drawing-room, dining-room, or hall, not associated with other furniture.

To show the demand for ornaments of this description, one has only to add that all the leading naturalists now issue pamphlets giving instructions as to the best means of preserving that portion of the animal which the owner would like converted into an ornament. Naturally, these instructions appeal to those who keep deer, horses, and other creatures, and who, at their death, would like to retain some memento of the animal they knew and petted when alive. Hence the naturalists are devoting their attention to the manufacture of these novel little articles ; and it is certainly surprising what they can do with the commonest of trophies.

One London West End naturalist is exhibiting at the present time over fifty different designs of hoof trophies. They are all registered and protected. A glance at them is a revelation of how beautiful and useful the hoof of a horse or deer may be made by those skilled in this particular profession. They can be converted into pincushions, candlesticks, letter-balances, matchboxes, inkstands, reading-lamps, calendar-holders, and a host of other useful devices. It is the same with the larger animals. To-day we can obtain the foot of an elephant converted into a liqueur-stand, umbrella-stand, a vase for flowers, &c. Recently a titled gentleman ordered one of the first-named.

Then the horns of the larger animals make pretty and effective stands for flowers. Another use to which both birds and animals are now being put is that of lampstands. Take, for instance, the monkey and swan lamps seen in our illustrations. The former was made for a society lady. For years she kept these two creatures as pets. When they died, she took them to a taxidermist and had them mounted in this way. The two little fellows are depicted in a very lifelike manner, the topmost one bearing the oil-well after the manner of Atlas, with his tail coiled around the crossbar, while his playfellow decorates the pillar of the lampstand.

The taxidermist who mounted this particular lamp declares that it has resulted in a great demand for lights of this description. For months past he has been buying up all the monkey-skins obtainable, and turning them into lamps. Already, innumerable monkeys have been sold to light up drawing-rooms and billiard-rooms, the little fellows being charmingly depicted swinging from a hoop with one hand and carrying the lamp in the other. Then, to-day, parrots and cockatoos are utilised in the same manner. A popular design is to mount the parrot on a brass hoop, with outspread wings, the creature carrying the lamp on its back. Then we have the emu and swan lamp. The last-named, of which we give an illustration, was made for a country gentleman who is a great lover of waterfowl. In this particular design, the swan—a magnificent, coal-black bird—rests upon a large mirror, so as to give the impression that the stately creature is floating on some placid lake.

Then we have the complete animal mounted, but designed for some use, such as the bear shown in one of our photographs. This creature is to be found in the hall of a titled lady in one of the West End squares. At night the apartment is flooded with a soft red light from the torch in the creature's hand. This animal is one of the largest bears ever seen in this country. It was shot during one of its fishing excursions in Alaska. The electric light can be switched on from behind.

Just as there is a craze for furniture and ornaments of this description, so there is a demand for all kinds of skin rugs. Naturally, the most prized is that of the lion ; and when mounted with a head it makes an attractive as well as a useful article of furniture for any room.

Then of late the taxidermist has introduced a new idea in skin rugs by combining two and more species together. For instance, one can obtain a tiger or a leopard rug mounted on a bearskin. Then, we have novelties in skins, such as hearthrugs made out of raccoon tails, &c.

This desirable innovation of turning all kinds of trophies into delightful and useful articles for the home is mainly due, I fancy, to us women. Till recently they were useless and often ugly horns, heads, and undressed skins. But when we discovered what lovely things the taxidermist could make of them, the sportsman was encouraged to bring them home ; and the naturalist did the rest.

A HUGE STUFFED BEAR, USED AS AN ELECTRIC-LIGHT STAND

TWO DAINTY AND DECIDEDLY NOVEL LAMPSTANDS

MOUNTED WITH THE HEADS, LIONS MAKE STARTLINGLY ATTRACTIVE FLOOR DECORATIONS

Photo by Valentine.

The old town of Aldeburgh has completely disappeared under the sea, and the Moot Hall, shown above, is all that remains of the original town.

Pearson's Magazine 1911

THIS YEAR'S "LITTLE GIRL" WOMAN

The woman who would be fashionable must also be an actress of no mean ability. At the beginning of one season she is asked to look as slim as a sylph. Later in the same year she is told that a rotund maturity is the only possible appearance for a grande dame, while at the same time it is impressed upon her that almond eyes or a retrousse nosé must be cultivated.

This year one of the features of the season is to be the "little girl" woman, who must even go to the extent of cultivating a "little girlish" toddle to match the toilette.

By the aid of the present fashion, the woman of forty is to really look twenty-five, and the woman of thirty is to have all the appearance of only twenty-two. Mother and daughter, in fact, are to seem just girls together.

Surely all these quick changes call for exceptional histrionic ability.

World and His Wife 1910

S. P.—Pusing Lamas are a very speculative purchase. Try some of the Nigerian shares.

G. L.—Rhodesians should be bought. Rhodesia Explorations, Amalgamated Properties, Shamvas and Giants are all good.

T. M.—Take no notice of the circulars. If you do you will lose your money.

VEXED.—We cannot advise you on the point raised. Consult a solicitor.

AMERICAN.—They were at 207 5-8 on the day named.

H. R. L. (Manchester).—You may safely buy Amalgamated Cinematographs. They have paid up to-day two interim dividends of 5 per cent. each.

MINING.—The property is a good one. The low price of the shares is entirely due to the fact that there is no active market in them.

INQUIRY COUPON

No. 1,580 One Coupon for each Question.

Money 1911

The Court of Nature

By E. M. HARTING.

AN INTERESTING PURSUIT that tends to what has been aptly called mind-quietness has a decided value in this age of rush. A writer in an American newspaper, *The Ladies' Home Journal*, not long ago made accurate comment on the present day tendency to exaggeration in speech :

We put the common uses of the superlative and abuse of the adjective down as matters of minor importance. But physicians are discovering that this excess in speech has a decided effect upon the nervous systems of our girls; that an exaggeration in words causes a tension, and a high-strung condition that result in an abnormal nervous state. In other words, we overlook the fact that nature makes us pay for a transgression of the vocabulary as well as for a transgression of action. We cannot be excessive in any form but that punishment follows in its wake. If any girl doubts the effect of this exaggeration of speech upon the mind and body let her repeat the words "calmness," "peace," "tranquillity," earnestly and with feeling several times, and note how soothing and calming the effect will be. Then let her repeat the words "frightful," "crazy," "killing," with earnestness and feeling several times, and note how tense and agitated she becomes.

All forms of nature study have this beneficent power to soothe, whether followed in only one direction or comprising many different branches; and the value of a taste for plant collecting or bird watching can hardly be exaggerated. There are few more restful pursuits than bird watching, which, of necessity, demands a slowness of movement, an absence of hurry, and a large supply of patience; while at the same time it cultivates keenness, alertness, and self-control.

Queen 1912

To the Spirit of Music we might propound the query—What has become of the old-time carol-singers? For of all the dismal, untuneful wailings we have ever suffered, the throaty emanations from muffled, rain-dripping figures this Christmas have been the worst; and when the carols have received the attention of a band, German or otherwise, the effect has reduced us to the verge of sympathetic tears. What agony the poor fellows must endure, we murmured, to produce such sounds! Consolation in the form of sundry pence could not be withheld, of course. Where are the tuneful "waits" of yester year? Gone, perchance, to join the robin on the spray and the church and the footprints in the glistening snow—dear emblems which adorned the cards of our childhood. Still, in spite of the waters of discord and the absence of every misbehaving snowflake, we evidently managed to keep Christmas happily at homes and at hotels—perhaps none the less happily because it came not quite in the old-fashioned manner.

Academy and Literature 1911

THE HEIR OF WYNNSTAY.

PRESENTATION OF AN ADDRESS FROM WREXHAM.

On Wednesday a deputation representing the Wrexham Corporation visited Wynnstay and presented an address on the coming-of-age of Mr. Watkin Williams Wynn, heir to the Baronetcy. The address, which was signed by Mr. W. J. Williams (Mayor) and Mr Lawson Taylor, town clerk, referred to the cordial relations which had always subsisted between the Wynns of Wynnstay and the Borough of Wrexham.

"Your ancestors were at all times in the front ranks in the public service, and your honoured father worthily maintains the traditions of his family in serving his country. We remember with pride and gratification his public-spirited work during the South African war, and the example which he has shown as Lord Lieutenant of the County of Montgomery in connection with the King Edward Memorial Fund. His work as chairman of the Denbighshire Quarter Sessions and as a member of the County Council and the Wrexham District Council is well known and much appreciated. We earnestly trust that, following the noble example of your ancestors, you will devote yourself to the public service, and will at no distant date take your place with those engaged in the work of local government."

Mr. Wynn, in acknowledging the address, said he accepted the kind remarks of the Mayor and those contained in the address most gratefully as a testimony of the good feeling which those who had spoken and the people whom they represented felt towards his family, and he hoped that it would long continue.

CHILDREN ALL TAUGHT WELSH.

Sir Watkin Wynn said that what had been said and done that day only showed that, whatever political feeling there might be between them (and political feeling ran very high in those days) he honestly believed that there was still a feeling of true friendship among the people who lived in that district and in Wrexham and his family. Sir Watkin said he had always made up his mind that his children should learn Welsh, and he was glad to say that his daughters and his boy had learnt it from the cradle. He knew what the value of Welsh would be to his son, because in some of the remote districts of Wales it was practically essential.

Mr. J. B. Bunston presented an address on behalf of the Square and Compass Lodge of Freemasons, of which Sir W. W. Wynn is a past master.

Mr. Wynn and Sir Watkin both returned thanks. Sir Watkin paid a special tribute to the value of Freemasonry, which he said served to draw the community together, and so assisted in creating friendship amongst people who were widely separated in their religious and political opinions.

Chester Chronicle 1912

MARRY OR CLEAR OUT

BACHELORS HARASSED BY LEAP YEAR OFFERS.

STARTLING EFFECT OF IRISH MAIDEN'S BITTER PROTEST.

Owing to an order recently promulgated by the rural council of Dunshaughlin, in County Meath, to the effect that all the bachelor occupants of their labourers' cottages must either get married within three months or vacate the houses, something like consternation has been caused amongst the local unmarried males. The council's "revolutionary" order was influenced to some degree by a communication received from a Miss Bridget Brannagan, an "exile living in England," who complained that the housekeeping of the bachelors spoiled the cottages. The letter was outspoken to a degree, and the reading of it caused great merriment in the council chamber. Here are a few of Miss Bridget's sentiments:—

I spent several years of my life hoping, but the new bachelor tenants locked their cottages and went to their work in the morning, and came home in the evening to boil the kettle and make their supper with a paraffin cooking lamp. (Laughter.) Bad luck to the cooking lamps, but they were the curse of the country. (Loud laughter.) From the way you are going on, the squall of a child will never be heard in the deserted houses of Dunshaughlin. You talk about the scarcity of labourers in harvest time, but devil mend you. I say for one I don't know what you were elected for, at all, at all, to throw the ratepayers' money away on the worst men in the crowd, while there are honest men not afraid to marry a woman and rere a family of labourers still without houses, though I suppose I may never expect to see my native place again, for I can marry a decent hard-working Englishman any time I like—not a lazy boxxy too common in Ireland.

The upshot of the publicity given to the Council's edict has been a regular deluge of letters addressed to the clerk of the Council from various places in England, some from ladies wishing to be placed in communication with eligible Dunshaughlin bachelors, and others inquiring for the address of Bridget Brannagan. One letter, addressed to a resident, asked if it were of any use "offering four girls from Bristol as likely candidates," adding that they "would be very pleased, owing to the dreadful state of the country at present, to settle in the apparently peaceful village of Dunshaughlin with good husbands." A Bayswater letter ran: "I am an English girl, aged 29, anxious to settle down to matrimonial bliss." A letter signed "Iris and Doris," which came from Portsmouth, with a photograph of a very pretty maiden, stated that the writers, who were sisters, had a little income of their own, and would be obliged for photos of "two nice young men, and they must be in a decent position." A correspondent from Kent described herself as "quite domesticated, musical, tall and slight, and dark." Another letter purports to come from a widow in Leytonstone, who "is a cook in service, but is anxious to settle down." The communications from aspirants for the hand of Miss Brannagan present the other side of the picture. One is from Stoke Newington, and depicts the writer as "only a poor labourer, but thoroughly domesticated." He "can wash clothes, cook, and scrub." It was decided to leave the letters in charge of the clerk, so that any interested parties can see them.

News of the World 1912

HIGHBURY FURNISHING CO., Ltd.

Directors—L. SIEGENBERG & SON.

A HOME OF YOUR OWN FOR £10.

6/- monthly. SITTING ROOM comprises:— Massive Couch, Spring Seat Easy Chair, 5 Upholstered Small Chairs, Centre Table, Overmantel, Fender and complete set of Implements, Cornice Pole and Fittings, and Floor Covering. BEDROOM comprises Strong Double Bedstead with Bedding, all complete, Washing Stand, Chest of Drawers, Toilet Glass, Cane Seat Chair, Yard of Carpet, and Cornice Pole and Fittings complete.

DON'T DELAY YOUR MARRIAGE

because you do not possess the required capital necessary for the purchasing of home. Ready money is none too plentiful therefore you will appreciate the advantages of our NEW BONUS INSTALMENT SYSTEM which enables you to furnish out of your income without any fuss or trouble. You select the Furniture you require and easy payments are arranged to suit your convenience. You have the use of the furniture while paying for it.

GENERAL TERMS.				
£5 worth £0	4	0	per month
10	0	6	0	„
20	0	11	0	„
30	0	17	0	„
50	1	8	0	„

NO SECURITY, NO FUSS or TROUBLE. STRICT PRIVACY.

NO HARSH DEALINGS. We do unto others as we would be done by.

FREE LIFE INSURANCE. FREE FIRE INSURANCE.

Send for our illustrated Catalogue and Furnishing Guide, containing over 600 illustrations, post free.

Business Hours: Open every day, including Saturdays, 7 till 8. We close Thursdays at one.

The "HOMELAND" Dining Room Suite.

In Leatherette, well made and finished complete. Comprising: Couch, Large Gent.'s Easy Chair, Lady's Easy Chair and 4 Small Chairs. £5 17s. 6d.

The "CARLTON" Bedroom Suite.

Light or dark Walnut, comprising: Plate Glass Door Wardrobe with drawer at bottom, Full Dressing Chest with large mirror door and 2 side mirrors, Washstand, marble top and china tile back, fitted cupboard and towel rails. £8 17s. 6d.

UPPER STREET, ISLINGTON, LONDON, N.

Telephone 807 North. (EXACT CORNER PARK ST.) Telegrams "Obligebury," London.

AVOID GETTING TOO FAT.—This is an easy matter when the famous Antipon treatment for the permanent cure of obesity is adopted. Thousands of men and women have regained a correct figure, with improved health and increased strength, through this simple, harmless, and in every respect irreproachable home treatment, without troubling about any rigorous dietary rules. Antipon, indeed, gives tone to the digestive system, promoting a keen appetite and aiding assimilation. Nutrition and weight reduction thus work together in the lasting recovery of beauty and form and normal vitality. Antipon overcomes the obstinate tendency to grow too fat. The cures it effects are therefore enduring. Once symmetrical proportions are restored there is no further need for the treatment. This cannot be said of any of the old-time treatments, which had to be persisted in, at the expense of health and strength, in order to keep down the weight as long as possible. Antipon brings about a reduction of 8oz. to 3lb. within twenty-four hours, and the subsequent daily decrease is highly satisfactory. Antipon is a liquid, containing only the most harmless vegetable substances. Antipon is sold in bottles, price 2s. 6d. and 4s. 6d., by chemists, stores, &c., or, in case of difficulty, may be had (on remitting amount), carriage paid and privately packed, from the Antipon Company, 13, Olmar-street, London, S.E. The *Graphic* says: "A wonderful specific in the treatment of corpulence is Antipon, which causes a daily diminution of fat until normal weight is attained. The cure is lasting, and the treatment is harmless. The tonic effects of Antipon are wonderful; the appetite is increased, digestion promoted, the blood purified, and the muscles strengthened."—[ADVT.]

A Labour-Saving Device for the Home

A very useful little invention which will specially appeal to mothers of vigorous boys and girls who, when they leave the garden invariably bring some of it indoors, on their boots is the "Standalone" Foot Scraper and Brush. It is a scraper combined with brushes and a pole, it scrapes and brushes off the dirt from the sole and upper of the boot rapidly and with little effort of the user. The pole supports one while using it, making it so simple that a child will find it easy.

The "Standalone" scraper brush may be kept indoors or out, can be moved from place to place, and since in its simplest form it costs only 2s. 6d., it is certainly cheap enough. The illustration gives a good idea of its shape, but there are many styles at various prices from which to choose.

It may be mentioned that these scrapers are of British manufacture and can be obtained from any ironmonger or from the Gripper Mfg. Co., Clarendon Park, Leicester.

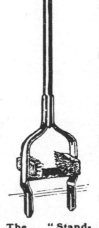

The "Standalone" Foot Scraper and Brush (Bi-Prong Pattern)

Hearth and Home 1913

RISKS RUN BY THE WOMAN WHO WALKS BY HERSELF IN LONDON

To the Editor of the Daily Sketch.

My wife was looking in the windows in High-street, Kensington, when a man, apparently well dressed, stood at her side and said, "Yes, they do have a fine show in these windows, don't they?" My wife replied, "How dare you address me?" I particularly call attention to his reply, "How dare you accost me in the street like this?"

The accusation was a thunderbolt, and my wife collapsed; but it is easy to imagine what might have happened.

My wife will be in the neighbourhood every afternoon with me and a big stick in attendance, and if we can see the man I shall not ask for the interference of a policeman.

London, E.C.   W. E. R.

Daily Sketch 1914

Daily Mirror 1913

HOUSE THAT WILL CLEAN ITSELF.

Mr. Arnold Bennett to Realise His Dream of a Perfect Home.

AUTOMATIC PARADISE.

When Mr. Arnold Bennett, the distinguished author, takes up a permanent residence in his native England—he has grown tired of Paris and the Parisians—he will live in a house that might be called " The Housewife's Paradise."

Two years ago Mr. Bennett imagined such a house in his novel, " The Card." Now, as nearly as they can be, his dreams will be realised.

The hero of " The Card " is a self-made man who cannot help feeling ashamed of the humble cottage in which his mother insists on remaining, refusing to move into a larger house because she could not bear to have servants about her.

So The Card uses his ingenuity and builds a house so cleverly fashioned that the work of keeping it clean can be done in a quarter the usual time, and then, by strategy, makes his old mother move into it.

Now The Card's ingenious labour-saving appliances, most of which have never gone past the author's imagination, are to be tested, and those of them that prove practicable will be installed in the house in which Mr. Bennett will live.

MR. ARNOLD BENNETT.

First, the author bought a house at Thorpe, near Colchester, and then he persuaded Mr. Rickards, the artist who illustrated his book on restaurants, to get out plans for its reconstruction and improvement. "And put in all the labour-saving appliances you can," said Mr. Bennett.

WHY MEN GROW BALD

Damaging Effect on the Hair of Constant Hat-Raising.

PENALTY OF POLITENESS.

Every time a man lifts his hat in politeness he is making himself more liable to baldness.

Why men go bald sooner than women has hitherto been explained in the first place by the fact that they usually wear a hat more than women, and secondly the hard bowler and airless silk hat conduce to baldness.

Now, however, a new theory is propounded by a clever West End specialist in hair culture, who states that men attain baldness by degrees through continually raising their hats.

" The reason why men go bald," he said, " is because their heads are subject to such violent atmospheric changes. A man is always lifting his hat, and each time he does so his head experiences a sudden change of temperature.

" People nowadays see in microbes the cause of many diseases, when in many cases there is a much more simple solution of the problem.

EFFECT OF TIGHT COLLARS.

" It is very seldom that soldiers get bald early, for they do not raise their hats, but salute.

" Women, too, never go bald so soon as men; that is because their hats are retained on their heads when they are out of doors and are only taken off when indoors.

" Another reason why men go bald is because they so often wear their hair clipped close to the head.

" I let my hair grow longer in the winter than in the summer, and keep it so.

" My assistants do the same. It helps to keep the hair healthy and is a preventive against baldness."

Another cause of baldness a doctor told *The Daily Mirror* is the wearing of tight collars.

" Tight collars prevent the proper supply of blood going to the head and the roots of the hair," he said.

Daily Mirror 1913

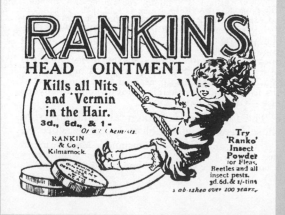

SOCIAL SNARES OR TRIALS IN TACT
For Rules see previous issue

TRIALS IN TACT PROBLEM (NEW SERIES) No. 21.

TENTH OF THE QUARTER.

(*Answers to be posted on or before September 16th.*)

Miss A meets two sisters called C at a mutual friend's house. They make friends, and on parting, Miss C says if ever Miss A comes to Harrogate, where the C's live, they hope she will let them know. They give their addresses and letters are exchanged from time to time. After about a year Miss A goes to Harrogate and writes to tell the C's and suggests a meeting. She gets no answer, although she knows the C's are at home. What course should she take?

(SUGGESTED BY " OXFORD.")

ANSWERS

TRIALS IN TACT PROBLEM (NEW SERIES), No. 18.

Mrs. C. was going upstairs one day, when from the staircase window she saw Mrs. D coming to call. Mrs. D was a new acquaintance who was always coming to call and whom Mrs. C did not care for, and so she told the servant to say " Not at Home." A few minutes afterwards a friend of hers arrived and asked Mrs. C to go out with her, which she did, and outside the door she found Mrs. D talking to someone. Mrs. D must, of course, have seen the other lady admitted. Should Mrs. C say anything to Mrs. D ?

I see no reason why Mrs. C should say anything to Mrs. D. She has nothing to apologise for, as " Not At Home " is understood to mean not visible or not at home to visitors, and Mrs. D will probably conclude that Mrs. C had an appointment to go out with a friend, and that that was the reason why she said" Not at Home." She should therefore bow and pass on. To enter into needless explanations is always foolish, especially in a case like this, where Mrs. C is anxious to discourage rather than encourage Mrs. B's visits.

Marks have been awarded as follows :—
Adline, 4 ; Angélique, 3 ; Auntie Fluff, 3 ; Banksia, 6 ; Banshee, 6 ; Confido, 5 ; Green Shamrock 6 ; Le Chat Bleu, 6 ; Mac, 5 ; Moonbird, 5 ; Naillil, 5 ; Oxford, 6 ; Punnlea, 6 ; Skye, 4 ; Yatti, 2.

The following are two of the best answers received :—

I do not think Mrs. C need say anything to Mrs. D. " Not at Home " often means engaged or just going out, and as Mrs. D sees Mrs. C in a few minutes with a friend, she will interpret the formula in both these ways.—BANKSIA.

Certainly not. Mrs. C had a perfect right to say " Not At Home," and it is an understood thing that one may be at home to one person and not to another, on any given day, so that she owes no apology to any one. As a matter of fact, if she is seen to go out with a friend who has just arrived, it would be natural to assume that she expected the friend, and was therefore not at home to anyone else.—GREEN SHAMROCK.

The following is taken at random from those answers which have failed to score :—

I think under the circumstances Mrs. C might just say in passing :" Good afternoon I am sorry I could not see you when you called just now." Z.Y.X.

Hearth and Home 1913

A COOK AS SHE PREPARES TOBY, THE PET GOOSE, FOR THE TABLE.

OH who has slain my gentle dear ?
    Oh where has little Toby gone ?
Alas ! his corpse is lying here
    So haggard and so woe-begone.

All callously I took his life,
    Nor boggled at the squeal of him
What time I slew him with a knife
    And meant to make a meal of him.

Oh let a tear bedim your eye,
    A prayer be wafted rafter-wards.
It is a dreadful thing to die
    And to be eaten afterwards.

Granta 1914

CHESHIRE WOMEN AND WAR WORK.

A meeting of the Cheshire County Committee for promoting the employment of women in agriculture and horticulture was held at Crewe on Friday. Lord Newton was in the chair, and the following members amongst others were present: The Lady Egerton of Tatton, Lady Sheffield, Lady Forbes Adam, Mrs. Johnson, Mrs. Young, Miss Greg, and Messrs. Henry Tollemache, Speakman, Allen, Clarke, Bainbridge, Longe, etc., and the hon. secretary, Hon. John E. Cross. It was reported that the training schemes in the public gardens were progressing favourably, and that women were being trained in the parks at Crewe, Heaton Park, and Birkenhead. Lady Sheffield and other members of the committee reported that the students taken to train in their private gardens were doing very satisfactory work. It was further reported that nine students had been received for a month's training in milking and light farm work at the Worleston Dairy Institute owing to a grant received from the Board of Agriculture. These students will be available for work with farmers on October 30th, and it is hoped that situations may be found for them where they will not only be of use on the farms, but where they may also acquire further experience. The statistical returns for the month ending October 15th were read. These showed that 107 vacancies for women farm workers and women gardeners had been filled during the month, and that 66 vacancies (included in the above figures) for women for potato picking had been filled. Mr. F. Clarke gave an interesting account of the success he had had in employing women for potato picking in the Wirral district, and assured the committee that they had been of the utmost service to farmers.

Crewe Chronicle 1915

ROYAL PAGE'S STORY.

Woke to Find Man in His Bedroom.

BUCKINGHAM PALACE CHASE.

Intruder Charged at Bow-street.

"I done it out of bravado. I heard of the suffragettes trying to get into Buckingham Palace, and I wondered if it could possibly be done. It was purely a drunken freak."—George Henry Pike at Bow-street.

The man who broke into Buckingham Palace and disturbed the servants of the King was in the dock at Bow-street to-day.

His name is George Henry Pike, and he is described as a motor fitter, of Moreland-terrace, Pimlico.

"On Enclosed Premises."

He looked a very inoffensive and contrite Palace-breaker as he stood before Mr. Hopkins. He was wearing an old grey suit, the coat much tattered, and a dirty linen collar.

The charge against him was of being a suspected person found on enclosed premises—to wit, the servants' apartments at Buckingham Palace—for the supposed purpose of committing a felony.

To the Top Floor.

It was shown, in the course of the evidence, that Pike had wandered from the basement to the top floor of the Palace, trying 'many doors—most of which were locked—and that when found he was wearing a morning-coat and vest which he had discovered in one of the rooms.

Mr. Muskett, who prosecuted, stated that accused, hitherto a respectable young man, had given way to drink owing to domestic trouble.

Accused, who made the statement set out above, was remanded for a week.

READERS of Miss Braddon are to be found in unexpected quarters. I have heard her praised by a novelist who rather prides himself on his artistic conscience, and I have also been present when a group of Georgian young men, who in the days before the war did not balk at Futurism, were not ashamed to confess their liking for her work. The truth is that, like Alexandre Dumas, she was a born story-teller, and she told her tales with so much zest that the reader never thinks of applying critical standards. Her plots are all ingenious and carefully constructed. As to which of her three score and ten novels ought to be placed first, I find great difference of opinion, though " Ishmael " and " Joshua Haggard's Daughter " would each get a large number of votes. People who care for literary anniversaries may like to be reminded that the year of Miss Braddon's birth—that of the accession of Queen Victoria—saw the publication of Carlyle's " French Revolution," Lockhart's " Life of Scott," Prescott's " Ferdinand and Isabella," and Dickens's " Pickwick," while in the same year Cruikshank was at work on the illustrations to " Oliver Twist."

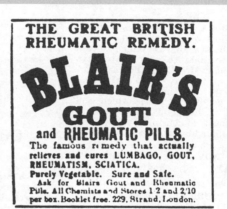
MY DEAR MOTHERS,

I want to say a word to-day about Plain Daughters. Some mothers labour under the foolish delusion that if a girl is plain it doesn't much matter what she wears.

Now, this is absolute nonsense, and the reverse of the truth. If a girl is pretty she will look pretty no matter what she wears, but if she is plain, her dress matters quite a lot. You can't make a pretty girl ugly by dressing her badly, but you can make a plain girl look ever so much plainer than she really is by clothing her unbecomingly.

Every girl should have her chance, while she is young, of making the best of herself. I think it was Sydney Smith who said that many a future was made or marred by a Hat ! There is truth in it.

Because a girl is plain there is no need to make her look plainer. It is her mother's duty to try and make her prettier, and she can do it if she will cheer her up by showing her what she can do to improve herself.

Dowdiness and depression are unbecoming things. Cheeriness is beautifying, like sunshine. It is the Sunshine of the Soul.

Your well-wisher,

FLORENCE STACPOOLE.

DOMESTIC TROUBLES OF A NANTWICH COUPLE.

HUSBAND'S APPEAL AND WIFE'S SAD STORY.

The domestic troubles of a Nantwich couple again occupied the attention of the magistrates at the Petty Sessions on Monday. The defendant was Wm. Binnersley, of Stapeley, who was summoned by his wife for persistent cruelty.

The wife asked for a separation order, a weekly allowance, and the custody of the children. She said she was married 27 years ago. Her husband was cruel to her three months after their marriage took place and he had been more or less cruel to her ever since. On the 23rd July last he came home drunk, knocked her about, chased her out of the house, and then dragged her back again. She left him that night and she and her little boy wandered about more or less for a week. Her boy for three nights slept in a shed belonging to Mr. Hollyse, she staying with him. She had maintained herself for six or seven weeks by taking in washing. She did not know what her husband's earnings were. Sometimes he gave her a sovereign and sometimes less, and out of that she had to keep him, herself, and two children. She had not received anything from him since she left him. She had worked hard to maintain herself and her two children, and upon what she earned and what the little boy had earned they had lived.

In cross-examination by Mr. J. P. Whittingham, who again appeared for the husband, the wife said that was the third time she had been to the Court.

Mr. Whittingham: On the first occasion you told the magistrates that you struck him with a basin on the head and cut it open.

Witness: Well, I was like to do that in self-defence when he beat me. She denied that the trouble arose through her wanting to go and live in Nantwich. She could not afford to bring witnesses to the Court.

Mr. Whittingham: There is no corroboration of your story?—The Wife: Well, I leave you to judge whether I deserve it or not.—On the first occasion Mr. Tollemache and other magistrates dismissed the case?—Yes, because I could not afford to bring witnesses.—The case on the second occasion was adjourned for three months?—It was (said the wife), who added, "I sent a letter to my husband asking him if he would give me food and a bed to sleep on."

Mr. Whittingham elicited that last week she had also received a letter from her husband, which she handed to the magistrates.

Crewe Chronicle 1915

Sunday Pictorial 1916

Her Husband Wounded.

Lady Mildred Follett, who is, of course, a sister of the Earl of Dunmore, V.C., has, I am informed, a special bit of war nursing on hand just now. Her husband, Captain Gilbert Follett, M.V.O., of the Coldstream Guards, is at home recovering from a rather serious wound. Here's wishing him luck and quickly well again.

VOLUNTARY FOOD RATIONS.

By MRS C. S. PEEL.

THE FOOD CONTROLLER has issued an appeal to the people of this nation to limit their consumption of meat, sugar, and bread to the following quantities :

Bread	4lb.	per head per week.
Sugar	¾lb.	,, ,, ,, ,,
Meat	2½lb.	,, ,, ,, ,,

These quantities of these special foods are quite sufficient for the needs of normal persons, indeed without any real hardship in well-to-do households where the bills of fare include some fish and eggs, vegetables and fruit, cereals, pulses, and nuts, the allowance of bread might be cut down for adults to 3lb. or 3½lb. per head, of sugar to 8oz. or 10oz., and of meat to 2lb.

Were this allowance of meat adhered to it would mean roughly that meat (including bacon, ham, poultry, and, of course, game) was eaten once a day only, or if the persons to be catered for preferred two meat meals, that at the greater number of them a very small quantity of meat would have to suffice. I have already in these pages (Jan. 20 and 27) endeavoured to show that the average well-to-do person eats more food than is necessary to keep him in health, and that he could adopt a diet less rich in protein without detriment to health.

I give to-day some recipes for semi-meatless dishes, and these will be followed by recipes for pulse, cereal, vegetable, cheese, and nut dishes.

Queen 1917

When "He" Returns

LITTLE wives who are making new, cosy homes for the happy day when "He" returns for good should bear in mind that "He" has become intolerant of all fripperies.

Air, space, and the simplest of utensils will suffice for him, be he officer or "Tommy."

This ought to be a relief now that money is scarce.

The wife whose man has left an over-crowded home need have no pangs at making a wholesale clearance of useless articles. "He" will probably not miss "this" or "that," but will be thankful for extra room to stretch his weary limbs. He has become so accustomed to the simple life, and the advantages that follow in its wake—health, appetite, and the power to sleep o' nights.

Mother and Home 1916

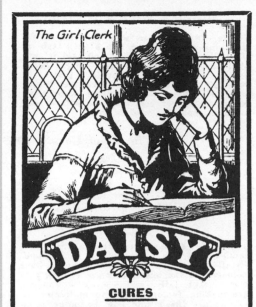

The Girl Clerk

"DAISY"

CURES

HEADACHE & NEURALGIA

The strain consequent on physical and mental exertion can scarcely fail in numerous cases to undermine the nervous systems of girl war-workers. A remedy should be taken to check the first symptoms, which are usually severe headaches or neuralgia.

The proved remedy for Headache, Neuralgia and all nervy pains is "Daisy." The most severe pain from whatever cause arising can be cured, the nerves soothed and refreshed, by taking a single "Daisy." These wonderful little powders are so easy and pleasant to take in a cup of tea or hot water. "Daisy" acts so quickly and effectively that headache and neuralgia pains are cured in a few minutes as if by magic.

A packet of "Daisy" is a household necessity—never be without one in the house. Remember, too, that there is no better remedy for soldiers' and sailors' headaches. Send a packet to-day to your friends at the Front, on the high seas, and in the training camp.

"Daisy" is sold by Chemists and Stores everywhere in packets containing 20 powders, price 1/1½d. Single "Daisy," 1d.

THE RELIABLE CURE

— One of the proudest and happiest women in England to-day is Mrs. Hanscombe, who lives in Kimberley-road, Beckenham. Her eight sons have been fighting on the various battle fronts since the beginning of the war, and her ninth son is also in khaki. Mrs. Hanscombe says: "I never believed they would all come back. Yet here they are all home again or on their way home."

British Weekly 1918

IT is with some relief that the nation heard from Mr. Bonar Law the announcement of the new decision to keep the food supply first, and to notify the War Office of the change in policy. It is the worst kind of foolishness to make a mistake and then to hold to it. But the foolishness of asking ordinary folk to dig all they could, and labour in the fields Sabbath and week day, and, at the same time to withdraw and still withdraw those already labouring there, struck most people as peculiarly gratuitous. The farm labourers are to remain, and more are to return. There is one other matter, however, that needs attending to, before the country will be really convinced of any peril to its food, and that is the waste on Drink. If there really is a grain shortage, barley in beer is criminal. Mr. Runciman said, the other day, he had told the Cabinet he would never be a party to rationing the people while there was no drastic action on the waste in Drink. There are a great many people asked to ration themselves who resolutely take the same attitude. We are supposed to be eating too much bread. We are even directed to turn our attention a little more to meat. In the meantime the waste of barley, and all manner of farinaceous foods, goes on in the breweries. There is a storm coming up. Let there be no mistake about that. The indignation is immense, if suppressed. It is not a matter of teetotalers and organised Temperance. These are as one man, unashamed. But all common sense people are behind them; and they are getting ready for the first indubitable sign, other than is found in mere words. The Government is playing a very dangerous game indeed.

At Home:

Methodist Recorder 1917

WAR BREAD.

PROSPECT THAT SITUATION WILL BE RELIEVED.

Mr. Alan G. Anderson, vice-chairman of the Wheat Commission, received at the Ministry of Food last evening a number of journalists, and made a statement on war bread, and the criticisms that it is unpalatable and indigestible. He stated that the public must be educated to look upon bread as the staff of life, not as dainty food with which their appetite is to be tickled.

At the invitation of the Food Controller a committee of scientific experts are engaged in experiments on the digestibility of war bread, and the advantage of milling to various standards. Certain millers had not yet succeeded in properly adapting their organisation and machinery to existing requirements, with the result that badly made flour has been used in certain districts, but the general standard of milling will, no doubt, improve in future. The suggestion that the mixture of flour should be standardised is impracticable. It is necessary that each centre shall consume the grain most convenient to it, and the Food Controller, owing to the lack of supply of any substituted cereal obtainable throughout the United Kingdom would be unable to supply the same grain for admixture to all mills.

The disease "rope" has made its appearance sporadically throughout the country. It is caused by a germ generally present in any dirt or dust usually found on the outer husk of wheat. The germ is almost always present in flour. Milling to a higher percentage of extraction, and the use of wheat of lower grades such as is now coming into the country tend to increase the risk. The bacillus is normally quite harmless, but when conditions are favourable it causes fermentation. Conditions tending to fermentation are warmth and excessive moisture, and the recent trouble is probably partly due to the exceptional weather.

Generally speaking Mr. Anderson thought bakers had done their best, and would do better. He hoped later on the situation would be relieved by abundant supplies of maize.

Nottingham Evening Post 1917

A SPLEN-
DID
SERIAL.

Her Mother-in-Law.

By H.
ST. JOHN
COOPER.

NEW READERS START HERE.

SYLVIA LINWOOD, *the pretty and loving little bride of*
HOWARD LINWOOD, *a poor and stern parson, has just come to
her new home, which is ruled by*
MRS. LINWOOD, *Howard's mother, a cruel and uncharitable
woman who poses as a Christian. She hates Sylvia, and wanted
Howard to marry his cousin,*
ROSA, *who lives with them, a girl as cold and cruel as herself;
and Rosa and she take care to make Sylvia's life a misery.
So Sylvia only enjoys the time she spends away from the home
with Howard's Rector and his nephew,*
JACK REDWAY, *a nice young man who becomes very infatuated
with Sylvia. Mrs. Linwood tells Howard about this new
acquaintanceship, and Howard sternly forbids Sylvia to see
Jack any more. He now leaves her in Mrs. Linwood's charge,
and, brokenhearted through his unfair treatment of her, Sylvia
allows herself to be ordered about by Rosa and Mrs. Linwood,
who work her to death, hoping to drive her away by their cruel
treatment. One day Howard catches his mother closing the
door against a poor woman who only wants a permit to see her
dying son who is in a reformatory; for the first time his faith
is shaken, and he promises to help the woman. However,
when he speaks to Mrs. Linwood about it, she says the woman
is a drunkard, and it is no use noticing what she says. So
Howard, with his faith in his mother restored, breaks his
promise to the woman and leaves the matter alone. Two days
afterwards, as Howard is returning from his work, he is stopped
by the woman in the street. 'You lied to me," she says.
" You said you would come, and you did not. It is too late
now !" " Why too late !" he asks, touched by her misery.
"See, I am here now !" " My boy died yesterday," she
answers, and turns suddenly away.*

Home Companion 1919

MINER'S WIFE'S WASTE.

Mrs. Ada Lawrence, who was fined £5 for
throwing 4lb. of bread into a swill tub at
Walsall, is a miner's wife, and said it was
dirty bread her husband had brought home.
The magistrate remarked that the
woman's husband was on strike, and it was
a serious thing when strikers were going
about asking for help that the wife of one
of them should be wasting bread.

Tavistock Gazette 1919

*Cornish
Guardian
1919*

"WAR-RICH" BUSINESS MEN'S
ESTATES.

Very quickly and very thoroughly a new
landed gentry is being created in England.
Estates which for hundreds of years have
belonged to the one family are coming into
the market daily, and leading auctioneers
are making fortunes hitherto undreamt of.
Who are the people now becoming land-
owners? Inquiries show that about half of
the estates are passing to business men who
have made fortunes during the war and that
the other half is being bought by tenant-
farmers.
"The great demand to-day is for small
estates with easy accessibility to the large
towns," said Messrs. May and Rowden,
estate agents of Maddox Street, W., who
dispose of many large properties. "Ten or
fifteen years ago such places were extremely
difficult to purchase; to-day they are coming
into the market in dozens.
"Farm land is being bought by the tenant-
farmers. Most of these people have done
well during the war, and are now able to
realise their long-cherished ambition of buying their land.
"England is changing hands, it is true,
but the change is to the good when it brings
about the sub-division of the land for farming purposes. In the next couple of years
the country will see still more significant
changes in the ownership of land. The present Budget is merely transitory; when we
get the peace Budgets proper and people see
what financial burden they have to bear
there are likely to be still more radical
changes."

Nottingham Evening Post 1917

WHAT TO DO.
PROBLEMS OF CONDUCT.
No. 355.

Dolly Travers goes to lunch at a West-
end restaurant alone. To her surprise she
perceives her brother-in-law, Tim Moly-
neux, at another table, lunching with an
unknown and charming lady. Presently
Tim comes over to Dolly, and says in an
embarrassed voice, " I say, Dolly, I shall be
obliged if you will not mention to Florence
that you saw me to-day." Florence is
Tim's wife and Dolly's sister. What
should Dolly do?

A copy of "Flames in the Wind," by
Helen Hudson, will be given for the best
solution. Solutions, on postcards only,
should be as short as possible, and
addressed to Problem Editor, British
WEEKLY Office, St. Paul's House, War-
wick-square, E.C. 4, and should arrive not
later than first post on Tuesday morning,
February 26. The prize award will be
made in the issue of March 7. No reader
to send in more than one solution. We
invite readers to send us war problems.
No competitor winning a prize is eligible
for another until three months have
elapsed.

British Weekly 1918

HAUNTINGS.

Fancy sketch of any lady who when applying for jamming sugar made false returns regarding
her 'orchard' !

A careful record is being kept of the names of the persons to whom sugar has been issued.

1920–1929

– Let this stove do the work

Let the new improved Valor-Perfection Oil Cooking Stove give you time for the better things in life — and better cooking too.

The new 1926 Models are 17% faster and more efficient, because the new double wall chimneys concentrate a pure flame of intense heat just where it is needed. Saves hours of toil and enough money on the fuel bill to pay for itself. And there's more room too. That lower shelf provides a place for heavy utensils.

It is just the right height to prevent backaches, and the oven has glass panels in the door for watching all within.

Strength, rigidity and long life are combined with a lightness which makes it easy to move to the right and light place.

The 1926 Model cabinet top, with porcelain enamelled back, is as fine in appearance as it is useful in service.

Buy a Valor-Perfection to-day. "Let this Stove do the work."

Sold by all Ironmongers and Stores
from
29/6

Look for the Valor Shield without which none is genuine.

Valor-Perfection
OIL COOKING STOVES

Write for Illustrated and Descriptive Folder to
ANGLO-AMERICAN OIL CO., LTD.,
(462) Stove and Heater Dept., 36, Queen Anne's Gate, London, S.W.1

Always use **ROYAL DAYLIGHT OIL** *for best results*

MR. ROBERTSON KEENE is open to accept one or two Pupils in Actual Conjuring, Stagecraft, Elocution, &c. Acts invented and arranged. Sole right tricks invented and patter written to order. 18, Woburn Place, Russell Square, W.C. 1. 'Phone: 7384 City.

Magician Monthly 1920

WHAT IS WORN.

THE question whether necks will be high or low has not been determined, and is not likely to be—for the simple reason that both will be worn. And an equally obliging

The Lady 1921

A useful coat-frock

attitude seems to have been adopted in regard to the width of the early spring gowns—in other words, our "silhouette" may be quite slender and narrow, or else there is a widened overskirt or tunic over a narrow underdress to give an outspreading effect.

IN DEFENCE OF THE COAL FIRE.

WOMAN EXPERT'S TESTS

PRACTICAL ADVICE ON GRATES AND FUELS.

In the last report of the Fuel Research Board, reference was made to a research carried out by Dr. Margaret W. Fishenden for the Manchester Corporation Air Pollution Advisory Board, with the assistance of grants from the Department of Scientific and Industrial Research, the results of which indicated that the open coal fire is not so wasteful and inefficient as it is sometimes painted. A full account of this research has now been published as a special report by the Fuel Research Board (Stationery Office, 4s.).

The heat generated in a coal fire is said to go in three directions—(1) heat is radiated into the room ; (2) heat is carried up the flue by the warm air and gases, part escaping through the chimney, while part, heating the walls of the flue on its passage, is gradually conducted through the walls to the outside or to adjacent rooms ; (3) heat is given up to the walls and from them passes into the room or is conducted elsewhere.

The heat which is completely wasted from a heating point of view is—(a) that which escapes from the top of the chimney, though even this is doing useful work in causing ventilation ; and (b) that which is conducted through the walls at the back of the fire to the outside. When the chimney is in an inside wall, a part of (b) heats adjoining rooms.

While it is difficult to define satisfactorily the efficiency of a coal fire, it is clear that the efficiency is much greater than has been generally assumed. With an inside chimney, the only final loss is the heat in the gas escaping from the top of the chimney. When the draught is only just what is necessary for hygienic purposes, this also is doing useful work, so that there is no loss as regards the heat actually generated by the coal, and the efficiency may fairly be said to approach 100 per cent. There is, however, always a certain loss in unburnt products in the form of ash, soot, or gas.

The Times 1920

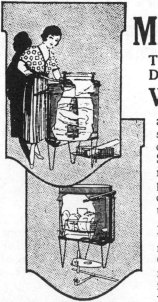

Discussion Class.

LADY SPEAKER AND SOVIET RUSSIA.

The speaker at the Accrington Discussion Class on Sunday evening was Miss Ellen C. Wilkinson, M.A., of Manchester, who gave her impressions of Soviet Russia, gathered from a visit to the country from the beginning of June to the end of August of this year. The chair was occupied by the president, Mr. J. R. Emmett, J.P.

Miss Wilkinson declared that there had perhaps never been any movement which had received such misrepresentation in the Press as the Russian revolution. She described at length the ideas which underlay the Bolshevist revolution, spoke of the great achievements of the Red army, and quoted extensively from Trotsky to show that the Bolshevists believed that they were holding the front trenches for the world revolution. In the middle of 1919 the fate of the capitalist world was in the balance, and all the cards for the moment were in the hands of the workers. It was possible then for the working classes in every country to have seized power and no one could have stopped them. But the leaders of the working classes in the various countries, instead of concentrating on a working class policy for re-construction, were concerned with the restoration of pre-war conditions as the idea of getting back to prosperity, and this gave the employers time to re-establish themselves. At the conference she attended the workers were told they had thrown away their chances as workers because they had followed the will of the wisp. Dealing with the famine in Russia, she declared that it was not the International Relief Committee, not even the Friends, in spite of their magnificent work, which was saving the famine stricken districts, but the organisation of the Bolshevics who had simply turned their army automatically into a great famine relief organisation. During her stay in Russia she was the guest of the Government and the house where she lived was under the charge of a lady whose husband had been executed by the Bolshevists. This lady, although an anti-Bolshevist, declared that there was no question of any alternative Government to the Bolshevists for the present, and that if any change were made the only result would be chaos, re-action and murder. The lady simply voiced the general opinions of the people of Russia. If the Bolshevists could get machinery and food to the country—and this was the reason she assigned for the recent concessions by Lenin to the capitalists—their regime was sure. They must not imagine that the Bolshevists were going to make peace with capitalism. If they were forced to pay the Czar's debts it was in order to get food, and whatever concessions they gave were just so that they might get on their feet. Their chief concern was to hold on until they got a revolutionary organisation in some of the other countries of the world.

Accrington Observer 1921

COFFEE POT NEWCASTLE-ON-TYNE

Coffee Pot, 1737

A responsibility devolves upon the possessor of old Silver, but in the care of this, and in fact all silverware, a great help is found in the modern Liquid Silver Polish,

SILVO

This is just as effective in cleaning and polishing the every-day articles of silver and plate as the more cherished pieces.

RECKITT & SONS, LTD.
HULL & LONDON.

Silvo is guaranteed non-injurious. Use it with an old soft cloth.

SILVO
SILVER POLISH

QUEEN'S TEARS IN THE SLUMS.

Seeing for Herself How the East End Poor Live.

TENEMENTS INSPECTED.

Pearly King and His Children Introduced to Her Majesty.

There were wonderful scenes in the East End yesterday when the Queen paid her promised visit to Shoreditch.

Every thoroughfare along which it was hoped the Queen would pass was packed with a dense throng, and some were impassable.

Many carried flags, and nearly every house was decorated in some way.

When the Queen arrived at the Shoreditch Town Hall, where Rose, the 12-year-old daughter of the Mayor, Mr. W. H. Girling, presented her with a bouquet of red carnations, the crowd broke the cordon of police, and hundreds of children dashed towards the Royal car.

There was only a short ceremony of welcome to delay the actual tour, upon which the Mayor and his little daughter accompanied the Queen.

"WHAT WRETCHED ROOMS."

Tale of Struggle to Live.

A halt was called at the ex-service men's club, where the enthusiasm was indescribable, and at the missions at Hoxton Hall and in Harman-street.

There was another stop when the Pearly King of Shoreditch, with his little son and daughter, one on each shoulder, were introduced to the Queen.

Then came Ware-street, a row of decaying tenements with scarcely one whole window pane in the whole length, the landlords of which are unknown.

The Queen's Tears.

Not even the warm, spring sunshine could make it anything but unsightly, and there were tears in the eyes of the Queen as she looked around.

By chance her car had to pull up outside No. 13, occupied by Mr. and Mrs. Gosling and their seven children, and the Queen got out.

"They're coming in here," cried one of the girls, and the family at once stampeded.

"Oh, what wretched little rooms," exclaimed the Queen as she looked round the poor home. There were beds in all three rooms, which were very crowded, but the children looked well and happy.

The Queen noticed that as she shook hands with them all, and said so.

"I told her it was a hard struggle to live," Mrs. Gosling said to the *Illustrated Sunday Herald* afterwards, "and her Majesty said she knew it must be.

"Something Ought to be Done."

"She was crying, I'm sure, when I said I would rather pawn than borrow, and she said something ought to be done to get me a respectable home to live in."

It was in Wilmer-gardens that the crowd was thickest. Here the people live six families, often 30 people, in a house, in what was once one of London's roughest streets.

The Queen looked sad as she gazed around.

It was not until she reached the infirmary, however, and visited the babies' ward that the sad mood was dispelled.

"Anyone could see she loves the babies," a sister said. "She spoke to them all, and put her arms round one."

Illustrated Sunday Herald 1922

"A year ago, at Baste's summer home at Oberwartha, near Dresden, when the boy entered the room Herr Baste heard a visitor sy, 'He rmoceoseybwJnpu-e pi2srly. Here comes young Auguste.' The statement was repeated till he was forced to take action."
Morning Paper.

A hateful thing to repeat.

Punch 1922

Everywoman's Weekly 1922

Frocks & Frills

Cause and Effect.
by Maxine.

IT is the longer skirt that is responsible for the very large and shady hats that most women are wearing these hot and sunny days. And the effect is certainly most charming and graceful.

Shapes are irregular and trimmings varied. Drooping effects are most popular, particularly when carried out with bunches of grapes. A pretty trimming for a piquant face is one I saw at Ascot where a softly drooping crinoline hat sported a half-blown rose beneath the brim and just above the left ear.

Quills are a fashionable trimming if somewhat hard, unless you are the right type, when they are absolutely the smartest thing going.

There is certainly this one advantage

Plain ivory spun silk is the material for this smart jumper. Lines of silk machine stitching ornament the vest, otherwise the jumper is left severely unadorned. Material required, 2¼ yards 40 inches wide. Pattern No. 447, price 1s.

Pattern No. 450 combines these two dainty garments, camisole and underskirt. The former needs 1½ yard of yard wide material and the latter 2 yards, 40 inches wide. Both patterns are supplied for 1s.

about broad brims and that is they save us from that harassed and screwed-up expression that marks the unshaded face on a sunny day.

* * *

A Pretty Trimming.

Quite the simplest and incidentally the most charming mode of trimming a leghorn or other soft straw is by appliqued flowers or fruit. Designs cut from chintz or printed silk or satin are appliqued to tulle of the same colour as the hat. The whole thing is then very easily adjusted.

DIED AGED 102.

While Taking Her First Medicine.

Mrs. Mary Ann Spencer, of Thurnscoe-lane, Rotherham, Yorks, died yesterday, aged 102, after 12 hours' illness.

She was just partaking of the first dose of doctor's medicine she had had in all her long and active life.

Her surviving brother, aged 96, resides at Crookes, Sheffield, with his family of four generations.

Illustrated Sunday Herald 1922

Everywoman's Weekly 1922

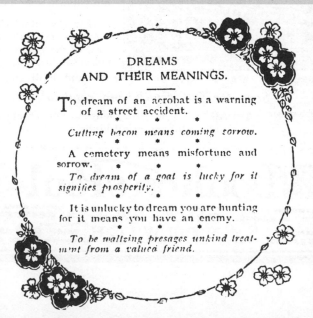

DREAMS AND THEIR MEANINGS.

To dream of an acrobat is a warning of a street accident.

* * *

Cutting bacon means coming sorrow.

* * *

A cemetery means misfortune and sorrow.

To dream of a goat is lucky for it signifies prosperity.

* * *

It is unlucky to dream you are hunting for it means you have an enemy.

* * *

To be waltzing presages unkind treatment from a valued friend.

SEX EQUALITY IN DIVORCE.

M.P.'S DISCUSS ONE LAW FOR ALL.

Whether a wife should have the right to divorce her husband on the ground of adultery alone—a right which the husband now possesses—was the question debated in the House of Commons when Major Entwistle moved the second reading of the Matrimonial Causes Bill.

Major Entwistle said the time had gone by when the wife could be regarded as her husband's chattel, and when marriage was regarded more as a matter of purchase. He thought it was high time the House should put an end to such anomalies and anachronisms.

The present state of the law gave a husband complete license to commit adultery with impunity, and that was scandalous. There were many cases where husbands lived notoriously in continuous adultery with another woman, and the wife had no remedy.

A trenchant speech in opposition came from Mr. Dennis Herbert.

"This Bill would give a woman the right to dissolve marriage because of one single act of misconduct by the husband. Divorce should not be possible except for repeated or habitual misconduct," he declared.

Mr. Hemmerde said that if men and women were put on an equality in respect of divorce it would get rid of the intolerable humbug of the procedure for the restitution of conjugal rights.

Mr. Bridgeman said the Government would not oppose the Bill, and would support it if it did not go any further.

The Bill was then given a second reading.

The People 1923

A Louis XV model gramophone, with electric equipment and turntable lamp.

Ideal Home 1923

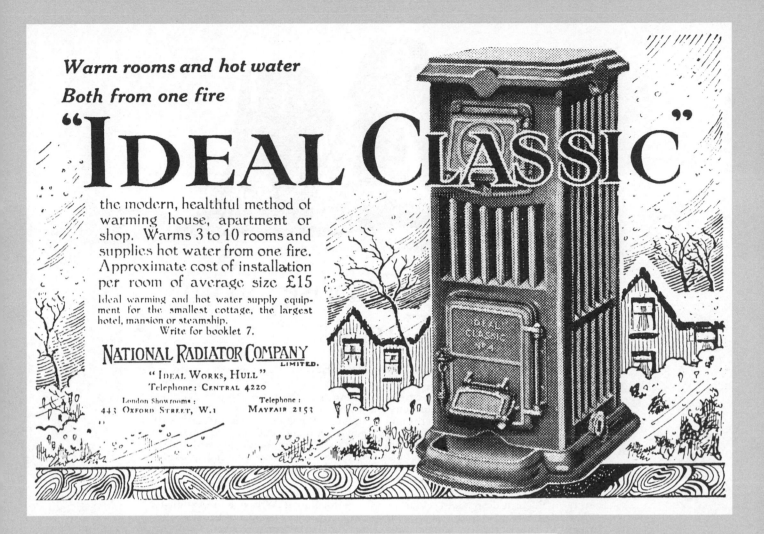

Warm rooms and hot water
Both from one fire
"IDEAL CLASSIC"

the modern, healthful method of warming house, apartment or shop. Warms 3 to 10 rooms and supplies hot water from one fire. Approximate cost of installation per room of average size £15

Ideal warming and hot water supply equipment for the smallest cottage, the largest hotel, mansion or steamship.

Write for booklet 7.

NATIONAL RADIATOR COMPANY LIMITED.

"IDEAL WORKS, HULL"
Telephone: CENTRAL 4220

London Showrooms:
443 OXFORD STREET, W.1

Telephone:
MAYFAIR 2153

"I could never make out why they were called 'servants.' They seemed to me much more like rulers"

DORIS PAILTHORPE

Good Housekeeping
1923

A group of Wilton rugs in exclusive designs.

How to Choose your Carpet

by G. B. HUGHES.

WHEN furnishing, carpets should be chosen before anything else, the covers and curtains being selected to harmonise with them. The carpet development of the past few years has been simply wonderful, many of the machine-made reproductions of Oriental carpets giving the rich and subtle effects of Eastern design and colouring.

The most beautiful and best wearing carpets in the world are emphatically those of Persian origin, although some copies I have just seen are of surpassing grace and elegancy. For hitherto uncaptured loveliness and soul-enchanting colouring there is nothing to compare with them, yet they were manufactured in England. No pre-war carpet can rival such matchless charm and texture, even to the deep lustrous silk-like sheen that was once the hall-mark of the genuine Persian article. Kidderminster is manufacturing reproductions of Turkey carpets. Such carpets beautify and dignify the average home beyond all reckoning, and cost very little more than the usual inharmonious floor-covering.

The best carpet is invariably the best investment, both artistically and financially. With the economy stunt so much to the fore it is not everyone who can afford the best. Then try a square of golden-brown art felt with small corners cut off to make it octagonal, and bordered with black felt. Such a floor-covering, provided the colour scheme of the room harmonises, is a delight to the eye and a joy to the senses.

Self-coloured Wilton and Axminster carpets are very popular because they may easily be repaired when worn.

One great drawback to such a carpet is that it stains easily. A good quality Brussels carpet is durable, and ofttimes has excellent patterns, particularly in floral designs, many of which are intricate and beautiful combinations of conventional floral forms.

Colourings of soft tones of rose, pale blue, cream, or green are especially delicate and worthy of the praise of lovers of the beautiful.

For staircases, carpets without borders are ideal. A good underfelt and a pad on the tread are necessary if the carpet is expected to wear any length of time. The carpet should also be moved up and down every few months to ensure that certain spots will not get shabby and worn before the remainder.

In bedrooms adults invariably prefer soft, thick carpets; therefore texture is more important than pattern, so long as regard is given to tone and harmony.

Chinese carpets are now very much in popular favour. Here are some exquisite designs.

A TURN OF THE TAP

Brings Unlimited Hot Water

at as many points as you like in the house in a few seconds. When you have a CLARKHILL it's just like having Hot Water laid on at the main.

Fitted in the kitchen or the scullery, the Clarkhill leaves your bathroom clear of apparatus, and being entirely automatic, it only burns gas whilst you are actually drawing water. Directly you turn off the hot-water tap the burners are automatically extinguished, leaving a separate tiny by-pass ready to ignite the burners the next time Hot Water is required.

Wonderful economy—and no other work to do than just turn on any hot-water tap to obtain as much or as little Hot Water as you want.

You will know more about this modern system by reading "Years Ahead," a folder which we shall be pleased to send you by return of post on receipt of your request.

'CLARKHILL'
AUTOMATIC WATER HEATERS

CLARKHILLS, LTD.
13 Albemarle Street, London, W.1
Gerrard 1988

Good Housekeeping 1923

WIFE THROWN FROM A WINDOW.

TIED TO A BEDPOST AND THRASHED.

"A BLACKGUARD."

Mrs. Lilian Linton, of Upper George-street, Portman-square, who was granted a decree nisi in the Divorce Court yesterday, stated that shortly after the marriage her husband tied her to the bedpost, beat her "dreadfully," and then threw her out of the window and injured her spine.

"My only regret is that such brutality cannot be punished criminally," said Mr. Justice Hill in granting the decree. "The man is a horrible blackguard."

Mrs. Linton petitioned for divorce owing to the cruelty and misconduct of her husband, Mr. Percy Francis Linton, a coal merchant at Bexhill.

The marriage was in Colombo in September 1920, and Mrs. Linton stated that on one occasion her husband tied her to the bedpost and threw soda-water bottles at her.

NAUTCH DANCES.

One struck her. He kicked her when she was expecting to become a mother, and the child was born prematurely.

"In December 1922," she added, when he had been drinking heavily, "he had nautch dances and debauches in the house. He threatened to kill me, and when I went to the telephone to ask for help he cut the wires.

"I asked a neighbour to come into the house, and at dinner my husband threw a tureen of hot soup over me. A day or two later he held me down and tried to kill me."

Mrs. Linton added that her husband afterwards became friendly with a nurse named Lucy Dorborne.

Daily Express 1924

A country cottage of the bungalow type with upper story, designed on entirely modern lines, which, at prevailing prices, it is estimated could be built for about £1,600, apart from the cost of the land

Granta 1924

Cats and Mice.

St. Catharine's College appears to be over-run with mice. A friend of mine who lives there told me that last Saturday he caught five mice in one mouse-trap. The trap used was a Little Nipper, but this will be but a poor testimonial for the firm, as after the fifth mouse the spring of the trap broke.

NEW EXECUTIONER.

"KINDLIEST MAN ALIVE."

"Daily Express" Correspondent.

MANCHESTER, Wednesday.

William Willis, of Ardwick, Manchester, is to be the new public executioner to succeed Ellis, who is retiring. Willis has been assistant hangman for twenty years. He was at the execution of Crippen, and he hanged Bywaters.

"You would never guess that my husband was a hangman," said Mrs. Willis to me to-day. "He is the kindliest man alive."

Willis, who is a native of Manchester, works here as an engraver. Most of the executioners of recent years have been Lancashire men. The two Billingtons, father and son, kept a barber's shop at Bolton, and Ellis is a Rochdale barber.

Daily Express 1924

ECONOMY OF MEANS.

EDITOR OF ENTERPRISING PERIODICAL IN HIS FRONT COVER MAKES THE MOST OF THE SPACE AVAILABLE.

Punch 1924

Bees which had swarmed in the roof of Dunton Parish Church, Norfolk, were disturbed by the playing of the organ at a funeral. They promptly attacked the undertaker's men, some of whom were badly stung.

Northern Daily Telegraph 1925

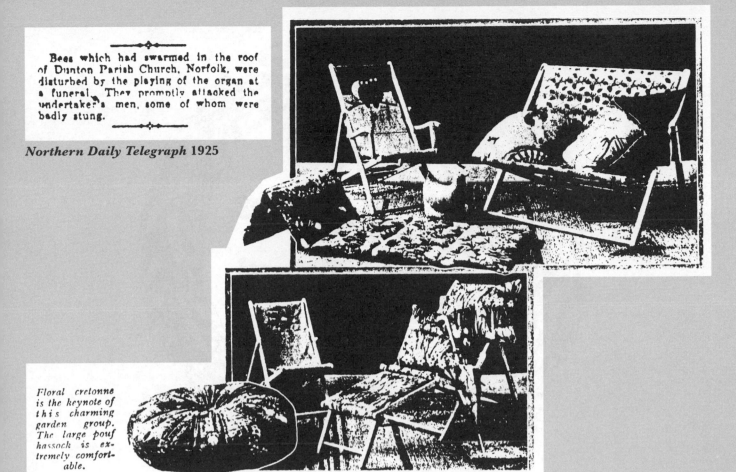

Floral cretonne is the keynote of this charming garden group. The large pouf hassock is extremely comfortable.

Ideal Home 1923

"The large beams have broken near the centre of the floor at No. 10, Downing Street. The accident is attributed to the recent visit of the Glasgow Orpheus Choir."—*Daily Paper.*

It will be remembered that:—

"Orpheus with his lute made trees
Bow themselves at his command."

Punch 1924

Let us build your New Home

THE ABOVE HOUSE SUBSTANTIALLY BUILT ON YOUR OWN SITE FOR THE MODERATE PRICE OF

£1,075

INCLUDING ALL FITTINGS (no extras)

FOR FULL PARTICULARS OF THIS AND OTHER DESIGNS APPLY TO THE ACTUAL BUILDERS,

SANTILS LTD., 74, NEWMAN STREET, OXFORD STREET, W.1.

(*Near C.L.Ry., and buses*). 'Phone: *Museum 7634*

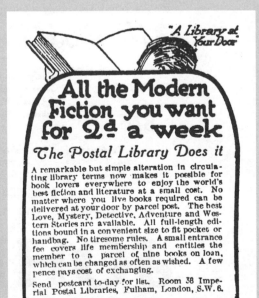

"A Library at Your Door"

All the Modern Fiction you want for 2d a week

The Postal Library Does it

A remarkable but simple alteration in circulating library terms now makes it possible for book lovers everywhere to enjoy the world's best fiction and literature at a small cost. No matter where you live books required can be delivered at your door by parcel post. The best Love, Mystery, Detective, Adventure and Western Stories are available. All full-length editions bound in a convenient size to fit pocket or handbag. No tiresome rules. A small entrance fee covers life membership and entitles the member to a parcel of nine books on loan, which can be changed as often as wished. A few pence pays cost of exchanging.

Send postcard to-day for list. Room 38 Imperial Postal Libraries, Fulham, London, S.W. 6.

A Gift Every Woman will Welcome

NO other gift will yield such a measure of helpfulness to the woman of the house as the new Johnson Floor Polishing Outfit—the new easy, liquid way of cleaning and polishing linoleum and floors. It eliminates the old method of getting down on one's hands and knees.

Just pour Johnson's Liquid Wax on the Lamb's-wool Mop and apply a thin, even coat to the floor. A few brisk strokes with the Johnson Weighted Brush will quickly bring it to a beautiful, durable, glass-like lustre that is not slippery or greasy. It's much quicker—only a few minutes required.

31/- Floor Polishing Outfit for 22/6

This Offer consists of

A SAVING OF 8/6	1 Quart Johnson's Liquid Wax 7/6	A SAVING OF 8/6
	1 Johnson's Lamb's-wool Wax Mop 7/-	
	1 Johnson's Weighted Floor Polishing Brush .. 15/6	
	1 Johnson's Book on Home Beautifying.. .. 1/-	
	31/-	

This Outfit is obtainable at Ironmongers, House Furnishers, Stores and Grocers. If any difficulty in obtaining, write us direct.

THIS XMAS GIVE A JOHNSON FLOOR POLISHING OUTFIT.
A WELCOME GIFT IN EVERY HOME.

S. C. JOHNSON & SON, LTD. (Dept. G.H.), West Drayton, Middlesex
"The Wood Finishing Authorities."

JOHNSON'S LIQUID WAX

All advertisements in GOOD HOUSEKEEPING are guaranteed.

BACK TO THE HOME.

LADY NOVELIST ON MAN'S FAILURE.

WOMEN AS RULERS OF THE WORLD.

Miss Rebecca West, the novelist, lecturing in aid of King Edward's Hospital Fund at the London School of Economics on "Is Woman's Place the Home?" launched a withering attack on "Oxford bags," the new fashionable flowing trousers.

"There has been a curious change come over the male species," she declared. "They like the home, and they are becoming more like women in the way they address you. I don't think those modern trousers do really mean anything very profound, because I have known women, quite often, so feminine that they wanted to wear the skirt, but I never came across a woman who wanted to wear two skirts—which is practically what the Oxford trousers are.

Failure of Man.

"Nearly all men admire Napoleon because he was a colossal failure—because at his death not only had he lost everything but he had shorn his country of all its power.

"Virile failure is the symbol of the career of man," she continued. "You will get that in modern politicians. Who is the most popular politician? Winston Churchill, who keeps on being popular, no matter what he does. One can hardly think of a Cabinet of any party that would not include Mr Churchill. That is because he has been so wretched a failure in everything he has done.

"I am surprised that there has not been a riot over the scandal of the way in which Mr Churchill proposes to give pensions to widows, but the House of Commons has taken it lying down. Has ever anything been so absurd as the pensions proposed for 'childless widows'? By having a quick fatal effect on a husband the widow is to get ten shillings a week!

Further Change Predicted.

"The only reason the proposal has been listened to is that man is throwing up his hands in the sphere of politics. He wants to go back to the home, and I do think really we ought not to oppose him. If men want to go back to the home we should be sympathetic to them. The species has changed enormously, and there is going to be a further change in that direction very soon. Men have been running the world for centuries, but woman is seen to be a more satisfactory article than man."

Mr Alfred Duff Cooper, M.P. (husband of Lady Diana Cooper), in a counter-lecture, expressed himself as all in favour of women enjoying themselves up to their bent. "But," he said, "when Miss West goes so far as to say that it is a proof of femininity that we wear two skirts, then one remembers the abomination of the hobble skirt, which almost prevented women walking at all."

Northern Daily Telegraph 1925

COOLERS THAT NEED NO ICE

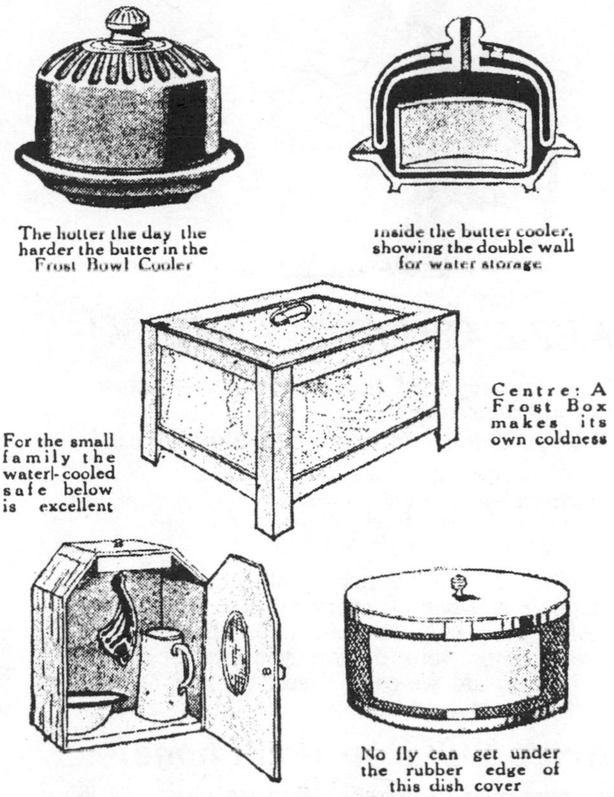
The hotter the day the harder the butter in the Frost Bowl Cooler
Inside the butter cooler, showing the double wall for water storage
For the small family the water-cooled safe below is excellent
Centre: A Frost Box makes its own coldness
No fly can get under the rubber edge of this dish cover

Modern Woman 1926

☛ THE ☚
MARVELLOUS GAS SAVER

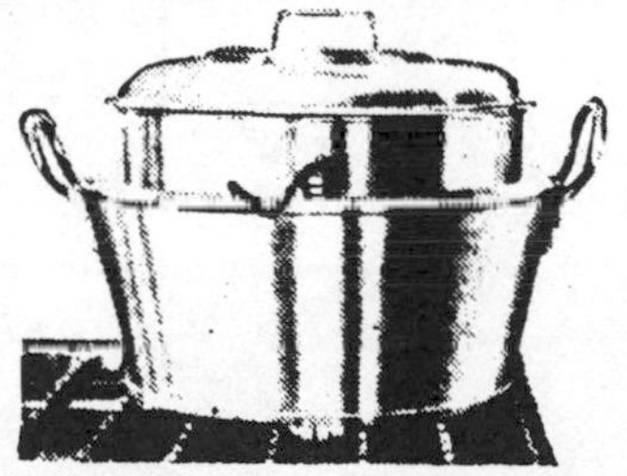

THIS INVENTION is far ahead of ALL other COOKERS or OVENS for Saving the Ga For Example. In a No. 2 Oval Boilerette, holding three gallons, you can place a dinner consisting of Two Fowls, a piece of Ham and Two Vegetables, or a dinner consisting of a Leg of Mutton, a Suet Pudding and Two Vegetables. This dinner can be cooked on the Small Simmering Burner on the top of a Gas Oven (see Illustration above) consisting of only SEVEN Jets and the Gas not turned on full.

FULL PARTICULARS POST FREE FROM
D. L. WELBANK, DUPLEX WORKS. BANBURY.

HOME MADE LUNG TONIC

How to Prepare It

Two pints cost 3s. (sugar extra).

Cough medicines are often spoken of as lung tonics, and such, in a sense, they are. After you have taken a dose of a good cough mixture you feel your chest braced up.

The following formula is given for the sake of those who like to make their own "lung tonic." They will find it equal to anything they have ever tried, and the cost is comparatively small. Thus:

CONCENTRATED CHEST MIXTURE OR LUNG TONIC
(Prescription 617)

Tartarated Antimony ..	1⅜ *grains*
Morphia Hydrochloride ..	3⅜ *grains*
Menthol	6⅜ *grains*
Oil of Cloves	16⅜ *drops*
Oil of Peppermint	16⅜ *drops*
Fluid Extract of Ipecacuanha	20 *drops*
Vinegar of Squills	2½ *ounces*
Chloroform Water to make ..	3 *ounces*

Price 3s. per bottle, post free. Sufficient to make 2 pints.

Directions.—Add 1 lb. of sugar to 1 pint of boiling water, and stir until the sugar is dissolved. When this syrup is cool add the Concentrated Chest Mixture made from the above formula, and mix thoroughly. Finally add sufficient water to make total quantity up to 2 pints. Honey or treacle may be used instead of sugar if desired.

P.S.—Must not be given to children. Supplied without the morphia, *on request*, if desired for children.

This preparation is labelled "Poison" to meet the requirements of the Pharmacy Act, but when taken in the proper doses is harmless.

Health News 1925

FOR HALF-A-CROWN A WEEK!

Perhaps you've always regarded the telephone as an expensive luxury—beyond your means?

Perhaps you'll be astonished to know how little it costs?

NOTHING—to instal.
NOTHING—for the calls you receive.
ONE PENNY—for each local call you make.
RENTAL – 2/1 to 2/6 a week.

Is that too much to pay for the luxury of being within a few seconds' talking distance of everyone else who is on the 'phone? After all, nearly *everyone* is on the 'phone—your friends, your shops, your doctor, your theatre, your office . . . . A luxury, did we say? Isn't the telephone a practical need of modern life?

Why aren't YOU on the 'Phone?

Write your name and address in the space below, post the coupon (½d. stamp only if envelope is left unsealed) and you will receive a free booklet which will tell you everything you want to know about getting the telephone into your own house, also particulars of £100 Prize Competition.

Please write clearly.

NAME ....
  (Mr., Mrs., Miss, etc.)

ADDRESS ....

  ("F." April 1926) ....

Post to The Telephone Development Association, 10, Bedford Street, London, W.C.2

MARLBOROUGH DECREE

BRIDE FORCED INTO MARRIAGE.

VATICAN EVIDENCE.

"MOTHER TORE ME FROM MY SWEETHEART."

Publication of the evidence submitted to the Sacra Rota Romana, the Supreme Court of the Vatican, which recently upheld the decision of the Southwark Diocesan Court annulling the marriage, in 1895, of the Duke of Marlborough and Consuelo Vanderbilt, has aroused renewed interest in the case.

As will be seen from our Rome correspondent's message below, the definite statement is now made that Consuelo Vanderbilt was forced by her mother, "drawn by her desire for a title of nobility," to marry the duke.

Consuelo Vanderbilt was then 17, and, according to her evidence, her mother first tore her from the influence of her sweetheart, Mr. Rutherfurd, made her leave the country, and, in "a terrible scene," threatened her that, if she escaped, she would shoot Mr. Rutherfurd.

Consuelo Duchess of Marlborough. · Mrs. W. K. Vanderbilt.

Daily Mail
1926

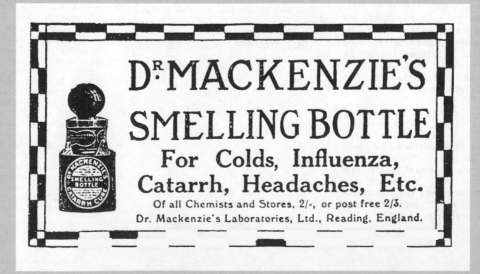

DR MACKENZIE'S SMELLING BOTTLE

For Colds, Influenza, Catarrh, Headaches, Etc.

Of all Chemists and Stores, 2/-, or post free 2/3.
Dr. Mackenzie's Laboratories, Ltd., Reading, England.

A formal room demands full-length curtains, lined, and headed with a decorative pelmet

YOUR HOME

There is no phase of home-making on which we cannot give you practical help by letter. Write to

WILMA BLOOD,

the well-known consulting decorator, about your furnishing and decoration difficulties

FLORENCE B. JACK,

the famous writer on cookery and housecraft, conducts the cookery section and will answer inquiries from readers for new recipes and cookery methods

GENERAL HOUSEKEEPING

Questions will be answered promptly and expertly. Readers are requested to enclose a STAMPED SELF-ADDRESSED ENVELOPE *with their inquiry, which should be sent to* "*Your Home,*" MODERN WOMAN *Offices,* 18, *Henrietta St., Covent Garden, London, W.C.2*

Making Curtains at Home

THE woman who can successfully upholster a chair or sofa will find no great difficulty in making new curtains. It is mainly a question of taking trouble over things that are apparently simple—being careful not to let the seams "pucker," when machining them up; using suitable material both for the curtains themselves and for the lining; and judging the length correctly.

The best length for curtains depends partly on the general character of the room. A "cottagey" room with casement windows should have curtains reaching to just below the window sill. The material should be gay but not costly. Cottons or ginghams look very well, and striped check or trellis patterns are most suitable. A formal drawing-room should have full-length curtains, and a narrow, low room will usually look best with the curtains reaching to the top of the wainscoting, or even to the floor.

The first pitfall for the inexperienced occurs when estimating the amount of a patterned material that will be required. It is important to place the main feature of the design in a good position, and to keep it at the same level in all the curtains throughout the room. Where more than one width is required for a curtain the pattern must meet exactly at the joins. This usually necessitates cutting to waste a good deal, but the stuff that is cut away will be useful for the pelmet or valance. It is usual when estimating to allow a full "repeat" of the pattern for every length required, but if several lengths were needed it would be safe to allow less.

Curtains will both hang and wear better if they are lined. Very good, heavy curtains for drawing or dining rooms should also be interlined with a thick soft material known as "bump." This makes the folds hang gracefully and gives a very rich effect. All materials used should, of course, be fadeless.

Modern Woman 1926

Daily Mail 1926

PRINCESS ELIZABETH.

CHRISTMAS WITH HER PARENTS.

ROYAL TOUR PLANS.

This is a busy Christmastide for the Duke and Duchess of York.

In addition to completing their preparations for their journey to Australia and New Zealand—which begins on January 6—they are also making arrangements for their visit to Sandringham, where they will spend Christmas with the King and Queen and other members of the Royal Family.

It will also be the first Christmas shared with them by their baby daughter.

The necessity for leaving the little Princess Elizabeth at home when they leave for their Dominions tour is keenly felt by the Duke and Duchess.

To watch the growth of a child's intelligence—in the homely old phrase, the "taking notice"—is one of the greatest joys of parenthood, but the Duke and Duchess have readily sacrificed something of that happiness to visit those over-seas subjects of the King who have prepared for them a welcome which will show how much their visit is appreciated.

When the Duchess returns to England after her six months' journey she may expect to find her daughter toddling to meet her with the uncertain steps of babyhood, and greeting her with those first efforts at words which no mother ever forgets.

A ROYAL SEND-OFF.

It was officially announced yesterday that the King and Queen will be at Victoria Station when the Duke and Duchess leave at 11.5 a.m. by a special train which will take them to Portsmouth. There they will board the battle-cruiser Renown, which will sail about 1.30 p.m., being given a naval send-off. The Prince of Wales, and possibly other members of the Royal Family, will travel to Portsmouth with them.

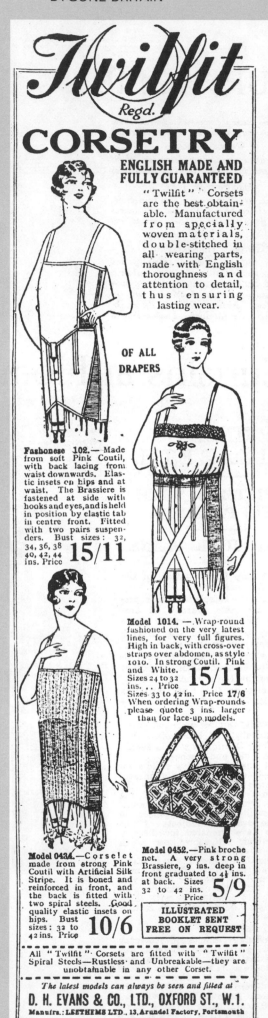

Twilfit Regd.
CORSETRY

ENGLISH MADE AND FULLY GUARANTEED

"Twilfit" Corsets are the best obtainable. Manufactured from specially woven materials, double-stitched in all wearing parts, made with English thoroughness and attention to detail, thus ensuring lasting wear.

OF ALL DRAPERS

Fashonese 102.—Made from soft Pink Coutil, with back lacing from waist downwards. Elastic insets on hips and at waist. The Brassiere is fastened at side with hooks and eyes, and is held in position by elastic tab in centre front. Fitted with two pairs suspenders. Bust sizes: 32, 34, 36, 38, 40, 42, 44 ins. Price **15/11**

Model 1014.—Wrap-round fashioned on the very latest lines, for very full figures. High in back, with cross-over straps over abdomen, as style 1010. In strong Coutil. Pink and White. Sizes 24 to 32 ins. .. Price **15/11** Sizes 33 to 42 in. Price **17/6** When ordering Wrap-rounds please quote 3 ins. larger than for lace-up models.

Model 0434.—Corselet made from strong Pink Coutil with Artificial Silk Stripe. It is boned and reinforced in front, and the back is fitted with two spiral steels. Good quality elastic insets on hips. Bust sizes: 32 to 42 ins. Price **10/6**

Model 0452.—Pink broche net. A very strong Brassiere, 9 ins. deep in front graduated to 4½ ins. at back. Sizes 32 to 42 ins. Price **5/9**

ILLUSTRATED BOOKLET SENT FREE ON REQUEST

All "Twilfit" Corsets are fitted with "Twilfit" Spiral Steels—Rustless and Unbreakable—they are unobtainable in any other Corset.

The latest models can always be seen and fitted at

D. H. EVANS & CO., LTD., OXFORD ST., W.1.

Manufrs.: LEETHEMS LTD., 13, Arundel Factory, Portsmouth

FLOOR COLLAPSE.
THREE PEOPLE DISAPPEAR INTO A CELLAR.

As she walked across the kitchen of her home at Ashburner-street, Bolton, shortly after midnight yesterday, Miss Mary Lofthouse, aged 25, felt the floor collapse and she, with all the furniture, disappeared into the cellar.

Hearing her cries, her father and mother, who were in bed, went downstairs and, walking into the dark room, also fell into the cellar.

When the three were rescued, they were all suffering from injuries to their legs and the two women had to receive hospital treatment. The house is in one of the oldest parts of the town.

Daily Mail 1926

KEENLY INTERESTED

DUCHESS OF YORK AT A COOKERY EXHIBITION.

LIKES THE CURRANT BREAD.

BIG BILL THE TURTLE TAKES NOTICE.

"This is excellent," said the Duchess of York, as she ate a slice from the winning loaf of currant bread at the stand of the Central Currant Office at the Cookery and Food Exhibition in London to-day.

The Duchess spent an hour at the Exhibition viewing the exhibits with the practised eye of an experienced housewife.

"I know from experience that English canned fruit is better than foreign," she told an attendant at one of the stands.

Some white rats in two cages attracted her attention, and she asked what they were doing in the Exhibition. She was interested to know that they demonstrate the value of milk as food, one group of rats being supplied with milk and the other with water. The former, of the same age as the latter, weighed five ounces more.

At the stand of a turtle merchant the Duchess paused to look at "Old Bill," a great turtle weighing three cwt.

"Will he move?" she asked.

"Perhaps he will if you touch him."

"Old Bill" was roused with a slight tap and obligingly lifted his head and looked at the Duchess, who was delighted.

She closely examined the winning entries in the bread competitions, and had a chat with Mr. J. J. Mackman, known as "the wizard baker of Hull," who had been judging the currant bread. She congratulated him on being the winner of 4,000 prizes for bread in various exhibitions.

Bath and Wiltshire Chronicle 1927

ECONOMICAL PERMANENT WAVING

IF your hair is-shingled, you will be specially interested in the offer of a really first-class permanent wave for 4 guineas at the Maison Rammelt, 3, Beauchamp Place, S.W.3. This special price is for shingled heads. Rammelt's charming salons, by the by, are only a stone's throw from Harrods.

The great point about this 4 - guinea offer is that Mr. F. C. Rammelt's permanent waving is acknowledged to be exceptionally good. Indeed, it transforms a rather ordinary shingle into a thing of beauty.

The Lady 1927

Here is a perfect example of permanent waving by Mr. F. C. Rammelt, who recently won a much-coveted trophy at a championship competition for permanent waving by the Gallia Boncelle process

THIS is a type of jumper suit very much favoured in Paris. The original was made of the new silk and wool kasha in black and white. The all-black skirt was pleated, and the jumper, made rather on the lines of a Russian blouse, trimmed with rows of the black material.

Home Fashion 1927

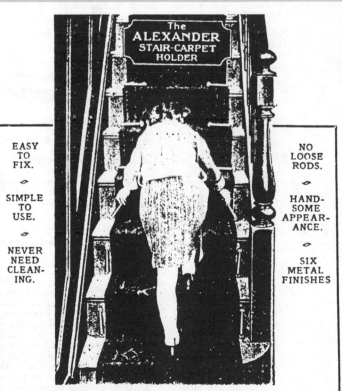

Photo by ELWIN NEAME.

THE CI-GAR-OUT

(Pronounced CIGAROUT)

The most Perfect Ash Tray yet Produced.

(Patents applied for throughout the world)

PROTECTION

Danger from Fire eliminated through using Ci-gar-out Ash Trays, which save your Tables, Carpets, and Furniture from the careless individual who drops lighted cigarettes about the room.

AN INVESTMENT

Nothing is more unpleasant than a smouldering cigarette or cigar. It can be immediately extinguished with the small Stopper attached to the spring, in any part of the tray, without soiling the most delicate gloves or fingers. A loose pin is also in the stem to loosen a cigarette in a tube or holder, or a pipe that is choked or packed too tight.

Manufactured by

HAMMERSMITH FOUNDRY & METAL WORKS

1A, WESTVILLE ROAD, LONDON, W.12

Tel.: Hammersmith 728.

Sole Manufacturers of the world-famous W.A.S. Benson Table-Ware, etc., in Electro Plate, etc. (late of Bond Street).

In Satin Finish 5/6
Nickel or Bronze 6/6
Electro Plate or Antique Silver 10/6
Solid Silver from £2 10s.
Names embossed or engraved at slight extra cost.

Obtainable at Harrods, Barkers, Selfridges, Derry & Toms, Civil Service, and other leading Stores, Jewellers, etc.

Triumph of Cigarettes.

Tobacco Trade Review 1928

A striking feature in the United Kingdom has been the change in recent years from pipes to cigarettes. In 1907 cigarettes accounted for 23·8 per cent. of the total, as against 71·1 per cent. pipe tobacco and 5·1 per cent. cigars; in 1924 cigarettes had risen to 58·5 per cent. and pipes and cigars fallen respectively to 40 per cent. and 1·5 per cent.

"The evidence we have received from trade sources," the Committee adds, "is to the effect that the trend to cigarette smoking has continued since 1924 and some witnesses considered that pipe tobaccos now account for only one-quarter of the consumption in the United Kingdom. It is, we think, probable that pipe tobacco does not now form more than 35 per cent. of the total tobacco consumption of the United Kingdom."

The advance of the cigarette in popular favour in recent years is not confined to the United Kingdom. Throughout Europe consumption now inclines towards cigarettes and the milder varieties of pipe tobaccos.

Even in Germany where pipe tobacco still predominates, a marked increase in the consumption of cigarettes has taken place. In the United States, pipe and chewing tobacco still is the greater part of the consumption but the proportion of cigarettes is increasing. Even in India the annual consumption of cigarettes is now about 6,500 million as compared with an annual figure of somewhat under 1,000 million pre-war. The cigarette is thus at present advancing in world-wide favour, but the consumption per head appears to be highest in the United Kingdom.

Scottish Village Migration.
Mr. and Mrs. John Scott, of Torphicken, with their family of ten, who recently sailed with the
Harthill contingent for Canada on board the Canadian Pacific Liner "Montcalm."

Colonizer
1928

THE ZOO DIETARY.

The annual report of the Council of the Zoological Society for 1927 gives some details as to the consumption of food by the animals in the Gardens. During the year 143 tons of hay, 133 tons of clover, and 96 tons of straw were used. No fewer than 435 horses, weighing approximately 216 tons, and 256 goats were required for the carnivora. Fifty tons of herring and whiting, nearly 2,000 pints of shrimps, 10,656 tins of condensed milk, 7 tons of apples, 2 tons of grapes, 175,704 bananas, 16,246 oranges, 32 tons of potatoes, 23,800 eggs, and 19,391 lettuces were used. Among the smaller items 7cwt. of currants, 20cwt. of rock-salt, 175lb. of "ant-eggs," 295lb. of mealworms, and 52lb. of dried flies show the odd constituents of the dietary.

Conditions suitable for exhibition of animals are not the best for breeding, and the weather in 1927 was unpropitious. There were some successes, however. Among the mammals one East African buffalo, one American bison, a Grévy's zebra, a kiang, two baboons, two Indian wild dogs, six wolves, one reindeer, eight other deer, four antelopes, 18 wild sheep and goats, 11 coypus, and 56 gerbilles were bred and reared. Among birds the most interesting successes were the breeding and rearing of three peacock pheasants, two wild turkeys, 17 blue and two white budgerigars.

Times Educational Supplement
1928

Poverty in the Manses.

An organisation exists in Scotland the need for which should make Scotland ashamed (writes the Rev. Dr. Fleming, of St. Columba's Church of Scotland, London). It mainly exists—to put the matter quite bluntly —to supply ministers of the Church and their families with cast off clothes. The report of this modest organisation (which pursues its quiet way attempting to succour lonely and needy souls who, " in their turn, are spending and being spent in seeking to succour their fellow-men ") tells of parish ministers who are finding it beyond their power to feed, clothe and educate their children. " A packet of tea "—thankfully received : a disused overcoat arriving just in time, for the old one was " refusing further renovation " : a cosy blanket : " my husband and I had just been feeling we must not spend anything on clothes this winter " : " I hardly know how to write—the Manse Auxiliary box came last night " : " I often wonder where we would all be if there had not been the Manse Auxiliary to help us " : " we had just paid 10s. to the chemist here for drugs, and could not afford tonics "—and so on, endlessly, from the beneficiaries of this noble society. It has been caustically said by a Roman Catholic writer that the Church of England does not believe in the celibacy of the clergy ; but that it largely enforces celibacy by making their marriage financially impossible. Many, many manses other than Anglican could supply material for a similar jibe. Miss Stevenson, 9, Oxford Terrace, Edinburgh, will tell any correspondent where to send gifts of clothing, scholarly books, household requisites, or money, and how to send them. The names of the recipients are, of course, kept strictly private.

Highlander 1928

MR. BERNARD SHAW AS SUN-WORSHIPPER.

INVITATION TO "JOY OF LIFE BALL."

Mr. George Bernard Shaw may appear as the High Priest of Sun-Worshippers at the "Joy of Life Ball" organised by the People's League of Health, to be held at Covent Garden on Thursday.

Miss Olga Nethersole, the founder and honorary organiser of the People's League of Health, told a reporter yesterday that she had asked Mr. Shaw to lead the Lido section of the pageant, which will depict sun-worshippers from the earliest times to the present day. It is suggested that Mr. Shaw should appear in his own wonderful sun-bathing costume, and act as the High Priest of these seekers after health.

Mr. Shaw has not yet replied to the invitation, but the prospects of his appearance are regarded as good.

Observer 1929

BEAUTY RUINED BY BUNGALOWS

Anger at the Spoiling of the Sussex Downs

SHACK HOMES

Minister of Transport Appeals to Authorities to Act

Agitation is growing into anger against the manner in which "bungaloid" development is spoiling the beauty of Sussex Downs.

Unsightly railway carriages, sheds and jerry-built so-called bungalows stand against a background of wonderful rural scenery.

No attempt is made to blend their often glaring colours with those of the country-side.

The Minister of Transport on Saturday appealed to local authorities to exercise their powers to protect England's "green and pleasant land."

Daily Mirror 1929

1930 – 1939

Queen 1930

Queen 1930

THE AUSTRALIAN XI VISIT MR. BEN TRAVERS IN SOMERSET

Samuel Wyatt

Having finished their match against Somerset in two days the Australians went to play golf at Burnham, as the guests of Ben Travers, on the third day, Friday, August 1. This group was taken at the Burnham and Berrow Golf Club at Burnham, Somerset, and the names, left to right, are: Standing—D. G. Bradman, A. Hurwood, P. M. Hornibrook, E. L. a'Beckett, T. W. Wall, Colonel Kyngdon (secretary of the club), C. V. Grimmett, C. W. Walker, W. H. Ponsford; sitting—S. McCabe, A. Kippax, Ben Travers, V. Y. Richardson, A. A. Mailey. When Mr. Ben Travers is not writing one of those sparkling plays which make the Aldwych quite unconcerned about theatre slumps, there is nothing he likes better than playing cricket, and he and our friends the enemy are old pals, as he went to Australia the last time, when Chapman and Co., the famous dustmen, were so busy sweeping up the Ashes

Tatler 1930

Northern Echo 1931

AN OUT-OF-DOORS DIARY.

30 SEPTEMBER.

The swallows have tired of their lingering. They have gone in the wake of that other hawker, the nightjar. The only hawkers remaining are the bats, still active at twilight, but thinking, with other hibernators, of the day immediately ahead when they shall retire into winter drowsiness. There is evidence in the morning that the hedgehogs have been busy in the night, doing good work in the garden and feeding fat before they seek the hole in the hedge bottom into which they will retire.

Winter has already thrust out fingers in the shape of light night frosts. Hence many insects are seeking the wall growths and particularly the ivies, the flowers of which in a short time will come to their peak and offer the last nectar feast of the year, open to all and sundry. It is about the ivies that to-day you will find the green-bottles and the bluebottles and such bees as have stuck so far through the year. Smaller fry you can count by the hundred, as you can the autumn midges in the soft noonday sun.

OUR FREE GIFTS

We have decided to give our readers the opportunity of obtaining useful articles for the home at a minimum of cost and trouble to themselves.

Here is the Scheme:—

At the top of Columns 5 and 6 on Page 2 will be found Two Coupons; all that is necessary for a reader to do is to cut these Coupons out and save them. If you wish get your friends to give you Coupons from their papers if they do not want them.

This Offer will be made until the end of April, 1931.

These Coupons may be sent in at any time, and the gifts will be forwarded.

Any number of Coupons bearing the same date may be used.

Two Coupons are published every week.

Here are the Gifts:—

25 Coupons	... ...	E.P.N.S. Jam Spoon.
50 "	... ...	E.P.N.S. Jam Spoon with Pearl Handle.
75 "	... ...	E.P.N.S. Bread Fork.
100 "	... ...	Cake Knife.
150 "	... ...	E.P.N.S. Nut Crackers.
200 "	... ...	Case of Fruit Spoons.
250 "	... ...	Sugar Scuttle and Scoop.
300 "	... ...	Oak Biscuit Barrel.
350 "	... ... Queen Anne Design Plated Candlestick.	
400 "	... ...	Salad Bowl and Servers.
500 "	... ... Case of Six Tea Knives and Forks.	
750 "	... ... Case of Fish Servers, Pearl Handles.	
1000 "	E.P.N.S. Combination Breakfast Cruet, cut glass.	

— RULES. —

1.—Pin the Coupons together in 25's.

2.—Place in envelope and enclose name and address.

3.—Send by post to

COUPON,
" NORFOLK CHRONICLE " SERIES,
HOLT, Norfolk.

4.—No correspondence can be entered into with any reader regarding this offer.

5.—Gifts cannot be exchanged.

6.—The Editor's decision is final in all matters relating to this offer of Gifts.

JOHNSON'S HOUSE FOR THE NATION.

GIFT OF MR. CECIL HARMSWORTH.

The famous house in Gough-square, London, which Dr. Johnson occupied for over ten years, and in which he compiled the greater part of his dictionary, is to be preserved for the nation. It was purchased many years ago by Mr. Cecil Bisshopp Harmsworth, and he has now formed a body of Governors to hold the property in trust for the nation.

At a dinner in the historic building on Wednesday, Mr. Harmsworth will hand over to the Governors the trust deed and the documents relating to the securities with which he has endowed the trust.

The deed sets forth that:—

The name " Dr. Johnson's House " shall never be changed.

The architectural features of the house, external and internal, shall be preserved intact.

Dr. Johnson occupied the house, which is 17, Gough-square, during the years 1748 to 1759. It is the only one of his many London residences known to be still in existence.

Mr. Cecil Harmsworth, in a booklet he has written, says that the decorations of the house, the carpets, and curtains, have been chosen with a view to wearing qualities, to simplicity, and, above all, to cheerfulness. The attic, in which Dr. Johnson compiled most of his dictionary, is to be available for social gatherings. By special permission, small parties may be served with Dr. Johnson's favourite beverage, " the cup which cheers but does not inebriate," in one or other of the smaller rooms. The house is not to be converted into a kind of museum. Mr. Harmsworth writes:—

"In this Johnson house we have the stout chain at the hall door with which, as we cannot doubt, he often barred out furious publishers and importunate duns; the staircase, intact in every particular, that has so many times creaked to his footstep as he made his way up to the Dictionary Attic; the panelled walls that have resounded to his laughter and to his prayers—what more, or better, can his most enthusiastic follower desire? "

Observer 1930

CHRISTMAS SHOPPING CHART
FOR BUSY HUSBANDS

IF YOUR WIFE IS A BLITHE YOUNG GIRL

—the kind that never should be chained down to dreary household drudgery ★

IF SHE IS AN EXCELLENT HOUSEKEEPER

—finding the utmost joy in a lovely home exquisitely kept ★

IF YOUR WIFE IS A BUSY YOUNG MOTHER

—with her time and energy taken up by the care of lively youngsters ★

IF YOUR WIFE IS NONE TOO STRONG

—a woman who finds heavy work much too fatiguing for her fragile strength ★

IF YOUR WIFE IS JUST ONE OF THE BEST

—who cares for her home and family wholeheartedly and uncomplainingly, no matter how hard the tasks, but would like to do her housekeeping the quickest, easiest way ★

GIVE HER A HOOVER AND YOU GIVE HER THE BEST

Prices from £10.18.0.   Write to Hoover Limited, Dept. A, 1, Hanover Street, Regent Street, London, W.1

Advertising is the consumer's guarantee of merit.

Everybody agrees that **THE NEW "EAVES" HOUSE** is the BEST VALUE at the Price offered in Blackpool.

These new type Dwellings are of Beautiful Design, Semi-detached. First class Materials and Workmanship on Sandy Sub-Soil, in the best Residential part of South Shore. Near the Bus, Schools, etc.

Just the House for the HOME-BUYER or the INVESTOR.

PAY A VISIT. Open all day for your inspection. Take No. 5 Bus to Ensleigh Gardens stop.

PRICE £675. No Conveyance Charges. Roads made. Mortgage arranged.

BUILDERS— **WM. EAVES & CO., LTD.**

DAGGERS HALL SAWMILLS, MARTON.

Agents on the Site: W. HOGARTH & A. COMSTIVE, or 388, CENTRAL DRIVE.   Phone 42088.

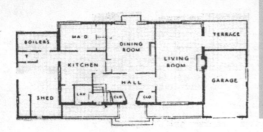

Harper's Bazaar 1931

Described by Baseden Butt

Dreams of a modern home designed "from the inside out" have come true in this unique and strikingly beautiful house at Newbury in Berkshire. Designed by Mr. Thomas S. Tait, F.R.I.B.A., the exterior shape of the house has resulted entirely from the interior plan, and the whole forms one of the most satisfying expressions of twentieth-century horizontal architecture in existence. It is walled with eleven-inch cavity brickwork, cement-rendered on the exterior and textured with semi-circular sweeps

An Idea for a Log Basket—

Logs are money-savers because they make your coal go twice as far, so if you have not bought any yet, you would be wise to get in a store for the winter months. And when you have them, here is the solution to the problem if you have no log basket in your sitting-room—an ordinary vegetable basket such as greengrocers have. They are cheap to buy, and when they are painted inside and out, in a colour to tone with your room, they give an attractive look to your hearth.

MISPLACED INGENUITY.

There is a Heath Robinson world in London, this week, at the Central Hall, where the Inventions Exhibition was opened to-day. Here, by the most elaborate and tormented ingenuity the stallholders have produced fantastic apparatus to make the simplest action difficult

Do you wish to have a morning cup of tea? Here is a strange electrical machine with an alarm clock which can be set overnight, and will boil water and make the tea at a certain hour in the morning, giving a signal when the process is completed. Or, by some similar contrivance, you may be waked up to soft gramophone music.

A tube like an oxygen container with a handle and feeder is to assist in filling pepper pots, and mustard can be served by an intricate fountain pen arrangement. On the whole, however, this is trouser year at the show, presumably as England's answer to Mr. Gandhi, and trouser presses of every kind are the leading exhibits.

* * * *

Northern Echo 1931

Modern Marriage 1932

A WONDERFUL MEDICINE THAT COPIES NATURE

Valuable Vegetable Extracts In Famous Pill Soon Conquer Disorders of the LIVER, STOMACH & BOWELS.

MEDICAL SCIENCE has given to the world a remedy that owes its success to the remarkable way in which it copies Nature's own methods. Instead of two or three common drugs, this remedy — Bile Beans — contains several valuable vegetable extracts which act on each organ in turn and thus produce lasting good health.

Purgatives (usually containing one or two ingredients) act on one portion of the

bowel only; many of them act violently —they engage in 'shock tactics' at one point. Regular doses of salts weaken the bowels and are of no lasting value, even though the dose be increased.

Here is the secret of the exceptional merit of Bile Beans. The aim of Bile Beans is to do as Nature does—secure the right kind of action in the right places by a gentle stimulation of the whole alimentary tract. Bile Beans give the nearest approach to Nature yet devised.

This highly prized formula contains a liver stimulant, a valuable extract to prevent griping, two carminatives to soothe and warm, and no less than six separate and distinct laxatives to ensure an even action in different parts of the bowel.

Wonderful Results

The stomach, liver, and the upper and lower bowel receive from Bile Beans exactly the precise help they respectively need. Take a nightly dose of Bile Beans. You will soon begin to enjoy your food, sleep well, say good-bye to the old pains, look and feel robust, and experience a new joy in living.

Home Prices: 1/3 & 3/- box. All Chemists.

BILE BEANS

Send For a Free Sample

We invite you to try a sample of Bile Beans Free. Send a postcard (stamped 1d.) with your name and address to C. E. Fulford Ltd. (Bile Beans), Leeds. Mention "Good Housekeeping," Dec. '30.

Halifax Courier and Guardian 1931

The Maid's Room.

A CONTENTED maid makes a good maid. The woman who can manage her servants will be the first to admit this. Some maids, of course, are perpetually discontented. No amount of thought or kindliness seems to have the slightest effect in altering their point of view. In such circumstances, the wisest course is—a change. No woman is justified in keeping on a maid who is sullen and "difficult" in the face of kindly treatment and comfortable housing.

But supposing your maid is a sensible girl who realises that the majority of the world, whether high or low, has its share of work to do, and is therefore prepared to labour cheerfully. She is a treasure worth an adequate setting. You will want to treat her with that courtesy that is her right as a human being.

You can best do this by helping her to develop her individuality. Though she lives in a home that is not her natural one, she must feel that she is not fettered at all hours of the day and night, but, just as any business woman works for so long and then takes her free time, she also must have the feeling that she is her own mistress on occasion. To strive after this atmosphere is better for all concerned—for maid, for mistress and for home. That is why it is worth while working to create it.

One of the best ways of beginning to achieve this desirable atmosphere is to make her room as comfortable and charming as you can. Modern taste in furnishing is all towards simplicity and bright colours. This means that the maid's room may be decorated with perfect taste at a reasonable cost.

Colour does wonders in creating a cheerful personality. Study colours which stimulate—and use them here accordingly. If it is impossible to secure a room which gets a good deal of sun, choose "sunny" colours. If it not desired to use really bright colours on account of impracticality, consider a shade like a warm beige for the walls. One or two "flower" or "garden" pictures on the walls would add a further touch of sunniness.

There are very few floor coverings that can beat the good appearance of stained boards. Wood stains are to be obtained in all colours. The only point to keep in mind is that the floor of the room should bear the darkest colour, in order to effect a well-balanced appearance. For a hard-wearing carpet that may be used in strips as rugs over a stained floor or linoleum-covered floor, hair cord carpet is to be recommended. It is inexpensive, and not difficult to brush or shake. It keeps its surface for years. It is plain, and sold in a few plain colours or in an attractive "natural" grey.

Let the furniture be as simple as possible, with plenty of drawer space. You will be but keeping up with the mode if you use simple furniture for the maid's room.

Rector and His Wife

The Rev. William Rees Jones, formerly Rector of Philleigh, was at Truro this week, fined £10 for leaving his wife chargeable to the rates since 1928. It was stated that efforts to trace him failed until last week.

Mr. Jones alleged that at Llanberis, where he was curate 25 years ago, and also at Philleigh, his wife scandalised him, caused congregations to dwindle and made his position intolerable.

He was ordered to pay 5s. a week towards his wife's future maintenance.

Caernarfon and Denbigh Herald 1932

'Skippers' are tasty for Tea

"Skippers" are delicious—and they never "repeat." For these plump, specially selected little fish are packed in the purest olive oil or the finest Tomato Purée. No hard bones, no tough skin.

IT'S THE PURE OLIVE OIL —THAT'S THE DIFFERENCE

Angus Watson & Co. Ltd., Newcastle-upon-Tyne. England.

Skn. 24·22

Success Of Rat Week In Cheltenham

Gloucestershire Echo 1932

The public is taking a greater interest in rats, said Mr. F. R. Jefford, the Borough Sanitary Inspector, of Cheltenham, in conversation with an "Echo" reporter on the success of Rat Week in the town.

By means of the Press and the cinema, he said, public interest had been re-kindled with the result that his office had received notifications that would keep the staff busy for a long time. He hoped that the people would get into the habit of notifying cases of rat destruction not only during or before Rat Week, but throughout the whole year.

Pinner.

Is a name which is thought of in connection with Harrow and to-day, with its accessibility to town because of its favourable railway facilities, rivals Harrow as a residential district. It is less than 12 miles by train and we have very great pleasure in calling attention to the merits of the houses on the Buckley Estates.

These Houses are in Eastcote Road and very handy for the Metro. and L.N.E.R. trains.

One of the points which appealed to our building expert on viewing the Estate was the variation in the style and finish of most of the houses, and to mention only one feature—the roof-tiles—on all the houses are the best hand-made Leicestershire tiles, and we invite your attention to the model of one of the houses at the Bureau, and we think all who visit Pinner and look over the houses which are ready will not look beyond the Buckley Estates for their future residence.

Until the coming of the Metropolitan Railway, Pinner was just a sleepy little village, living a secluded life of its own, and devoted to agricultural pursuits.

With the coming of the railway, Pinner began to grow with great rapidity and it is still spreading fast.

Pinner Park, between Nower Hill and Hatch End, has retained its ancient name from the time when it was forest land belonging to the Abbot of Westminster. Only one large farm-house has stood upon it from time out of mind and now the whole estate of 251 acres has been secured as an open space by the Hendon Rural District Council at a

At Pinner.

cost of more than £80,000, which it shares with the Middlesex County Council.

The most picturesque feature of the little town is the High Street, containing several half-timbered and gabled houses and cottages and an old inn, which is dated by its gaudy signboard of Queen Anne. The High Street broadens at the top where stands the parish church, a flint building with a good Perpendicular tower.

Household Gazette and Estate News 1932

"A MOTHER'S APPRECIATION."

" I honestly believe," writes a Depôt Reader, " the best work is done on the bed-cot in the men's rooms.

" A mother of one of the men came to see him a few days ago, and he introduced me to her, and she said :

" ' I do thank God that there is someone to look after the spiritual life of these boys.'

" I often meet mothers, or other relations, of the men in barracks, and without exception they express their gratitude to God for the Army Scripture Reader.

" I know that the work is telling on the lives of the men, and especially on some of the N.C.O.'s."

British Flag and Christian Sentinel 1932

BACHELOR GIRLS— ENTERTAIN!

WHEN the working woman of to-day emancipates herself from club and hostel (and the house agents will tell you how many single women are taking flats) and sets up in her own "flatlet," what is the first thing she wants to do ?

GIVE A PARTY

I have just been to one in a tiny flat in a little mews where a young woman lives very happily alone (writes a *Sunday Dispatch* woman representative).

She has not much money but, like everyone else, she was touched by the hospitable spirit of the season, and just had to give a party.

No men were invited, and although the uninvited ones (with masculine conceit) prophesied a dull evening, the eight women guests were anything but that.

They began to arrive at seven—just the right time for people who have to get home from offices.

WARM FLAT

The three-roomed flat had been well warmed for them, and some sherry helped to thaw the cold ones and make the silent ones talk.

A girl who works all day cannot be at home to prepare hot food, so everything to eat was all ready beforehand.

Here is the menu :

Cipalata (little Italian sausages) fried very brown and crisp and eaten cold from cocktail sticks. When you live alone you do anything to avoid washing up.

Bridge rolls split and buttered.

Cheese wafers.

Toast (made at the 11th hour) and spread with "Gentleman's Relish."

Dishes of small cakes from a French bakery.

Sweets.

After the initial glass of sherry, the guests drank white wine; a rather dry Macon for those who like their wine dry, a sweet Barsac for the others.

A SURE SIGN

One bottle of sherry and three of white wine did easily for eight, and everyone talked a great deal and stayed much longer than she meant to—always a good sign of the party's success.

At about 11 o'clock we drank China tea and lemon before saying good-bye.

The whole party, including a new gramophone record for the occasion, flowers, and cigarettes cost just under £1 10s.

And there were no piles of plates to wash up next morning before rushing off to work.

The same party, with less good wine, could be done for a good deal less.

So, bachelor girls, why not give that party you have been thinking of for so long? There is no greater fun in the world than being a hostess in your own domain.

Sunday Dispatch 1933

The Builder 1933

A MODEL VILLAGE

We have received from the Railway Benevolent Institution particulars of a charming model village which has been built at Beaconsfield from the designs of the owner, Mr. Callingham, of Chiltern Lodge, Ledborough-lane, Beaconsfield. It is situated in a beautiful rock garden covering an area of roughly 1,000 sq. yds., and consists of a village, with church, shops, hotel and other public buildings, 1,200 ft. of railway line with five stations complete with rolling-stock and other accessories, fields, water-courses and woods.

The railway, which is electrically controlled, has three main platforms at the terminus, double lines of rails passing along deep cuttings spanned by bridges, and an intricate system of points and electric signalling. Its engines and rolling-stock are of the most modern type. It is, in fact, a reproduction to the minutest detail of the modern railway system.

The village is electrically lit, and in the evening forms a charming picture with its illuminated streets and buildings. The buildings are of brick, stone and timber. In the fields cattle graze and the whole pastoral setting is typical of the unspoiled country-side.

The village is open to public inspection every Sunday, and the proceeds are given to charities in which the owner is interested.

Montgomery County Times 1933

EX-KAISER SILENT ON HITLER

Welsh Clergyman At Doorn

The Rev. J. Llewelyn Thomas, Vicar of Aberpergwm, near Neath, Glamorgan, returned to Croydon by air from Holland, after his annual holiday visit to the ex-Kaiser at Doorn.

"I found the ex-Kaiser in excellent health," he told a reporter. "We had many interesting talks, mostly about old times in Palestine. It was there that I first met him 32 years ago.

"During our conversations I asked him what he thought of Hitler. The ex-Kaiser merely shrugged his shoulders and made no comment."

Mr. Thomas went to Doorn last Saturday. From Amsterdam he was taken 30 miles to Doorn in the ex-Kaiser's car, which had been sent specially to meet him. He did not sleep at Doorn House during the visit this year. He was accommodated nearby, but took all his meals at the house and spent each day with the ex-Kaiser.

Reynolds Illustrated News
1933

NEARLY WED TO BEST MAN

Thought It Was "Only a Rehearsal"

"YES" THREE TIMES

"Reynolds's" Correspondent

It has just been revealed that a Walsall bride was nearly married to the best man

COMPLICATIONS began when the clergyman originally selected for the ceremony found that he had more marriages arranged than he could carry through.

Accordingly, a number were transferred to an adjacent church, the people concerned being informed. All approved the new arrangements.

The clergyman began to perform the last marriage. He asked the bride if she was prepared to take the bridegroom for her lawful husband, and received a " Yes."

Then he turned to her companion, inquired for his assent, and received a bewildered stare. The clergyman repeated the question. Instead of answering the man regarded him with a stupefied gaze.

The clergyman was patient. Slowly he again read out the procedure, telling the man what to do, and what to say.

WRONG MAN!

Receiving the bride's assent for the third time, he put the formal question to the man once more. This time it brought him to life.

"Hi," he exclaimed, "I'm not the fellow. I am not marrying her."

The clergyman was then horrified to learn that the bride's companion was not the bridegroom, but the best man!

A rush was made for the missing groom. He was found outside the church originally selected for the ceremony. At last the service was completed in its proper form.

As the party were leaving, the clergyman asked the bride for an explanation. She replied that she thought the ceremony in which the best man was acting as groom was merely a " rehearsal of the real thing."

Manchester Guardian
1933

COLOURED PEOPLE IN ENGLISH SOCIETY

A South African's Protest

Condemnation of coloured peoples being received into society and fêted in this country was made by Mr. James Stuart, formerly Assistant Secretary for Native Affairs in South Africa, in a lecture at the Royal United Services Institution, London, yesterday.

Lord Ampthill, who presided, said that Mr. Stuart in the days of Queen Victoria brought to England a deputation of Swazis, and was an interpreter of the Zulu language, a rare accomplishment for an Englishman.

Mr. Stuart said that the native problem was a serious, menacing, and virtually world-wide affair. "Imagine, then, my feelings," he said, "on seeing what goes on here in London, though not only here—how coloured people from all parts of the world are, in ever increasing numbers, received in society, welcomed into the bosoms of English families, and publicly fêted and entertained by philanthropic and other bodies.

"There are, of course, different types of African men and women, some more educated and civilised than others, but even of those few are as yet eligible to be introduced into European society. It is not a matter merely of colour and racial prejudice, but one of wisely upbringing and uplifting the man in the midst of the snares and the dangers of a civilisation alien to his own.

"I do wish to sound a note of warning," continued Mr. Stuart, "for I am afraid that unless something be done, some closer supervisory responsibility accepted and exercised, the relations between the Dominions and colonies and the Mother Country will not be all that they ought to be, nor in the long run, I fear, will the interests of the natives in those Dominions be much improved."

PRIMARY CAUSE
OF
'FLU ISOLATED

A FILTER-PASSING VIRUS

ANIMALS RENDERED IMMUNE

BRITISH DOCTORS' DISCOVERY

That the primary cause of influenza is a filter-passing virus is the conclusion reached as a result of striking experiments carried out by three British doctors—Dr. Wilson Smith, Dr. C. H. Andrewes, and Dr. P. P. Laidlaw—at the National Institute for Medical Research and described by them in to-morrow's issue of the "Lancet."

They discovered that ferrets, which were used for the first time in this line of research, are susceptible to infection with human influenza. In this way the virus of the disease was isolated.

It was also found that ferrets which had recovered from the disease were thereafter immune from it, and that the serum of human convalescents was capable of neutralising the virus of the ferret disease.

A medical correspondent, in the article which appears on Page Ten, regards these discoveries as of the greatest importance. He suggests that their significance, in combination with results recently arrived at in America, may well be that mankind will not again find itself a helpless victim to a great influenza epidemic.

Daily Telegraph
1933

MISUSED COMMON WORDS AND PHRASES

Sir—The number of things commonly likened unto the nether regions is remarkable. I have heard the expression "As cold as hell" used in all seriousness.

Other abused words and phrases are: "Boiling," "dying" (for a drink), "to hate like poison" (there is nothing to hate about poison in its passive state) and "as drunk as a lord" (an absurd expression today).

But, undoubtedly the most abused word of all is "perfection." It indicates a quality which does not exist in this world. Perhaps that is why imperfect humanity uses it so often.—Yours, &c.,
NORMAN HAMBER.
West Hampstead, N.W., Aug. 17.

VERBAL MONSTROSITIES

Sir—Like many other American residents in this best of all countries, I have to watch myself lest I, too, slip into the prevalent slovenliness.

Why do not some of your purist readers start a campaign against verbal monstrosities like "However could you?" "Whyever did you?" and "Wherever have you been?"—Yours, &c.,
BETTINA VON HUTTEN.
Strand, W.C., Aug. 17.

"PRETTY FOUL" NOT SLANG

Sir—Some correspondents are not conversant with the full meanings of words they say are misused.

"Pretty" as an adverb means "moderately, tolerably." Thus, "pretty foul," "pretty crowded," and "pretty brisk" about which they complain, are correct.

"Funny" has "queer" as one of its meanings. Thus, one who is ill, and looks "very funny" is obviously very queer.—Yours, &c.,
MARGERY SYKES.
Bletchley, Aug. 17.

SHOCKING HER UNCLE

Sir—"It was frightfully jolly of you: I was terribly thrilled. Thank you most awfully."

This was the acknowledgement received by a Victorian bachelor from a niece to whom he had sent a little present. I am afraid the stupid girl will not get another.
—Yours, &c.,
M. A.
Shrewsbury, Aug. 17.

Daily Telegraph
1933

SAVED!

*A panel treatment in which two different
types of paper are used.*

*A rather more elaborate treatment making use of an
applique corner decoration, narrow stile, textured filling
and, for the corners, an ombre or shaded paper.*

House and Home 1934

ELECTRICITY IN THE HOME.

A NEW SCHOOL OF DOMESTIC SCIENCE.

A new school of electrical domestic science, which claims to be the first of its kind in the country—was opened in London to-day. It has been started by a self-possessed, business-like young woman who knows all there is to know about the use of electricity in the home. She is Miss M. M. Minoprio and believes that the ignorance among women as regards electricity in the home is astonishing.

When a reporter called at the school in Basil Street, Knightsbridge, it was to find Miss Minoprio directing the final touches which were being put to the lecture rooms. She led the way into a large room, all white enamel and shining fittings.

"This is the kitchen where students will have practical lessons," she explained. "We like to think of this as the ideal all-electric kitchen. It contains nothing which is not worked by electricity, even to the clock and the towel-roller, which is electrically heated."

The planning and equipment of the school are thoroughly up-to-date and the students will carry out their studies in a specially ozone-purified atmosphere, while on dull days their surroundings will be brightened by artificial sunrays.

The object of the school is to train young women in modern household domestic science, particularly in all branches of electrical housecraft, and to train demonstrators for supply authorities, manufacturers and exhibition work.

Birmingham Mail 1934

BETTER HOUSE for the WORKING CLASS

Re-housing Britain's Slum Dwellers

COMPENSATION ON "REFUND" BASIS

The outstanding recommendation of the Departmental Committee on Housing, under the chairmanship of Lord Moyne, which issued its report, Wednesday, is the establishment of a Central Public Utility Council to supervise and co-ordinate the various schemes for rehousing the slum-dwellers of Britain.

It is recommended that the utility council should consist of not more than five (including the chairman), should be paid on a part-time basis, and should include at least one member with special financial qualifications. The staff should be appointed by the Minister.

Close co-operation with the Garden Cities and Town Planning Association would be necessary, and co-operation would be encouraged between local housing authorities, public utility societies, and private persons interested in voluntary housing activities.

Local authorities should be given compulsory powers and encouraged to acquire for reconditioning working-class houses, which are not in all respects fit for human habitation, but can be made fit, and to which a probable life of at least 20 years can be given.

Exeter Western Mail 1933

Home Sweet Home 1934

The Day's Routine

The maid should rise not later than half-past six or a quarter to seven, so that she can start work punctually at seven. She should open up the house, drawing blinds and curtains and opening the windows.

Her work should then be arranged more or less as follows:

Lay the fire in the dining-room.
Sweep and dust room.
7.15. Light gas stove, fill kettle and put on stove to boil for early tea.
Continue dusting of dining-room, and commence sweeping and dusting of hall and passage.
7.30. Call master and mistress.
Complete dusting of hall.
8.0. Lay table and cook breakfast.
8.30. Dining-room and kitchen breakfast.
9.0. Clear away, wash up; tidy and sweep kitchen. Clean front door-step, etc., if not done before breakfast.
Assist mistress make beds, sweep and dust bedroom. Clean bath-room and lavatory.
Sweep and dust lounge, if this is not undertaken by mistress.
11.0. Special work.
12.45. Lay the luncheon table.
1.0. Lunch.
1.45. Clear away lunch, wash up; clean and tidy kitchen.
2.30. Free time until 4.30, to go out or stay in as she pleases, but in any case not on duty.
4.30. Prepare and take in afternoon tea.
5.0. Wash up; commence preparations for dinner.
7.0. Lay table for dinner.
7.30. Dinner. Wait at table.
8.0. Bring coffee into sitting-room. Clear away and wash up. Turn down beds and fill hot-water bottles, if required.

This young lady is demonstrating the simplicity of the new Collaro playing desk—a useful attachment that will convert a table set into an efficient radio gramophone.

House and Home 1934

Gas and Home Refrigeration
By Marcia Molesworth

FIFTY YEARS AGO the house with a bathroom was a rarity; to-day, in even the smallest homes, we expect to find proper provision for bathing.

Fifty years hence some writer on domestic subjects may say the same thing about the home refrigerator. Nowadays, in spite of the fact that refrigeration is still considered a "luxury," the sale of refrigerators is increasing steadily. There is no doubt that eventually the refrigerator will become a standard appliance in the home just as the bath is nowadays. In fact, it may be called the "twentieth century larder."

Some Home Truths About Larders

The truth has at last been brought home to us that the ordinary larder, however well placed and constructed, cannot be considered as an entirely safe method of food storage. Harmful bacteria can gain a footing in food at quite a low temperature—even in muggy winter weather.

An air-cooled, gas-operated refrigerator can be built into a cupboard fitment in the kitchen. The lower cupboard can be used as a dry vegetable bin for potatoes, carrots, and so on.

Many larders, too, by their position in the house of which they are a part, cannot have a north aspect, while in flats the space for storing perishables is often inadequate and unhygienic. Health, as well as comfort, demands some better method. The answer is the refrigerator.

House and Home 1934

The Most Dangerous Place in the World

SAFE AT HOME! Which of us has not used the phrase? We always feel better satisfied when the children are " safe at home." Nothing can harm them there.

Some of us have been hearing on the wireless or reading in the papers what the Minister of Transport has been saying about the awful dangers of modern traffic. He said the other day that if we were to read of an industrial tragedy where twenty people were killed in one day we should shudder at the thought and call for some greater care in management.

Yet 7,100 people were killed on the roads of Great Britain in 1933, of whom half were children. One organisation has been blaming the way houses have been built on the sides of the existing traffic roads—they call it " ribbon development "—for this sort of thing. And it would appear to be true that a very large proportion of these children are killed within sight of their own homes.

Worse Still

Bad as all this sounds, there is an even more dangerous place for the children than playing out in the road.   And this— you may find it hard to believe—is in their own homes. It has been shown that the road tragedies are substantially exceeded by the fatal accidents in the home itself, where we have been so pleased to think that we should find safety.

Road fatalities numbered 7,100, but home fatalities numbered 7,800 in the last completed year.

Think of it!

One hundred and fifty people killed in each week in the homes of Britain.

Ten per cent. of the number—nearly 800—were due to scalds and burns to little children.   And it is safe to add that some ninety odd per cent. of this eight hundred were the direct outcome of carelessness or lack of attention.   Yet even here one hesitates when one remembers the home conditions of so many people—not the state of the home, but the absorption of so many mothers in the cares and work of the home, and some-times of earning a living as well.

Other Causes

Other causes are stairs without a handrail, which are happily rare except in slum areas, extra high (or low) windows, high cupboards and shelves which woman or child must climb to reach, lack of proper space to do necessary work, dark or awkward stairs, and of course open fires.

Then come the many things which cause fire, to which the prevalence of the cigarette and the readiness with which petrol can be obtained (leading to its use indoors) are high amongst contributors.   The stimulation of a fire by adding paraffin or " drawing it up " with a sheet of paper follows.

Education, better conditions in the home, better planning of the house—these are amongst the possible remedies.   But, of course, we can all arrange the world so much better than the world arranges itself, or at least we think we can.

But whatever may be the remedy, it is surely inadmissible that conditions are tolerable which make the home the place where three times as many people are killed as there are in industry, and some ten per cent. more are killed than by even the juggernaut of modern traffic.

House and Home **1934**

Edinburgh Evening News **1934**

WEDDED TO BEAUTY

by Ruth Murrin

BEING a mother is a full-time job. So full, it sometimes seems, that there is little time left over for being a wife. You who wake at 2 a.m. and again at 6 to satisfy the infant clamour for another meal don't need to be told. And you who mince the carrot and mash the potato and put beans through a sieve know how hard it is to save a little time to lavish on yourself. It is so easy to be swamped in the routine of feeding, bathing, dressing, training, and the everlasting washing that it is a wonder any girl ever manages to combine the business of being a Parent with that of being a Person.

Yet, if she is to be a successful wife, that is exactly what she must do. She must be well up in vitamins and child training, of course. That is her job. But at the same time she must keep in practice that knack she has of tilting a smart new hat at exactly the right angle on her head. She must keep her mind swept and aired, her conversation bright, and her complexion fresh. In a word, she must somehow be a wise, modern mother and still be the girl her husband fell in love with.

It takes effort and time and money? Of course it does. Everything worth while is costly in one way or another. But the cost of being attractive is minute in comparison with its importance. You owe it to yourself, for when you know you are pleasant to look at, your confidence soars, and everything seems to come your way more easily.

You owe it to your children. I remember a charming woman who told me she seldom used a lipstick until one day her four-year-old son remarked, " Mother, why don't you have red lips and look *new* like other ladies?" Children are keen observers, and from the time they practise their first steps until they are old enough to make their own way in the world, they love to show off a pretty mother.

You owe it to your husband. Though he may seem merely amused at the vagaries of fashion as you adopt them, he is secretly proud of your looks. He, too, likes you to appear new and different even to his familiar eyes. Also it is part of your responsibility as a wife to put your best foot forward, for the world always will judge a man's success, in some measure, by the appearance of his wife.

In these days of excellent cosmetics at small cost, even a skimpy budget can make room for the few necessary ones, and the busiest mother can squeeze in fifteen minutes a day plus a half-hour once a week for face treatments. Odd moments well used with hand lotion, nail cream, emery boards and nail white will do worlds to keep your hands worthy of your nicest parties. Your hair will respond beautifully to brushing if you have only two minutes night and morning to give to it, besides the weekly washing and a really good permanent twice a year. If you find yourself resisting changes in make-up and coiffure, if you have lost your fashion sense, quiz your unmarried friends until you are again up-to-date. They will enjoy advising you; for once they will have a

QUESTIONNAIRE FOR WIVES

How much more do you weigh than the day you were married?

Can you still get into your wedding dress?

How long is it since you have changed the way you do your hair?

Do people tell you that you have nice hands?

How many times a day do you use hand lotion?

Do you use up a box of powder even if you don't like the shade?

Does your husband still praise your complexion?

Does he notice when you change your lipstick? Your perfume?

Do you like the new tones of nail polish?

feeling of superiority over women with husbands and babies and homes of their own.

The hardest thing is to keep from sinking into the easy habit of making excuses for yourself, then gradually becoming blind to the way you really look. Your skin, for example. How does it compare with the complexion of the girl you were five or ten or fifteen years ago? Even if you have taken pretty good care of it, it is probably drier, not so smooth, not so fresh and luscious, marked by little lines which that young face did not know. Cream used oftener, and a wisely selected powder-base and smart make-up, will do a lot to make it appear young and lovely. But if you have neglected it sadly, and it is now coarse-textured and murky, only the most persistent pampering can bring it back to a semblance of what it once was. It is never possible to undo damage like this in a few weeks or months. I wish I could make every woman understand that every day of neglect must some day be paid for with interest, and since one's skin naturally becomes drier and loses some of its bloom as one grows older, it really should have better and better care as the years pass.

There are still young women who don't take seriously that first thickening of the waist and hip line that makes the difference between a youthful figure and a matronly one. It should send you to the scales immediately to check-up your weight. It should stiffen your will power to say "No, thank you," to rich foods and second helpings. It should make you critical of the way you sit and stand and walk. It should inspire you to do some snappy exercise every day. An easy exercise to fight that broadening is this: Lie on your back on the floor, knees bent and arms outstretched, and flop your legs first to the right and then to the left. You will be thrilled at the prompt way bulges flatten out.

Do you remember how, in the days when you had nothing on your mind but school and clothes and dances, you used to sit in front of a mirror and do your hair endlessly in one fashion after another? You will find it fun even now. First, make a collection of coiffures you like on other people. Clip out the pictures of stage and screen beauties, that new photograph of smart Mrs. Somebody, the illustration you like so much in a current magazine. Then with comb and brush try to get an idea of what each coiffure will do for your face. The process will be good for you if it does nothing more than show you that your hair is chopped off too short at the back or would look sweet with the new upward roll in front.

Don't tell me that your husband does not want you to change—that he forbids you to diet, that he hates cream on your face, that he thinks halo curls are silly, that he regards robin-red nail polish as improper. He may think he thinks so. But, remember, a husband is human. What he really in his heart expects of you is that you should continue to be the leading lady of his life, the heroine of the domestic drama, and that every now and then you should spring on him a new act. In that light, look at the woman you see in the mirror and ask yourself to-day.

" Is she slipping or is she still a star?"

AN OLD IRISH CUSTOM.

EGLINTON TENANT'S CLAIM.

At Eglinton Petty Sessions on Tuesday, before Mr. J. Steele Hanna (chairman), Miss Wallace, Messrs. P. S. Bell, R.M., J. A. Lamberton, and Connolly Patchell,

Charles Brown summoned Charles Carton, Brockagh, for possession of a dwelling-house held under tenancy at 1s 11d per week.

Mr. John A. Hamilton, who appeared for the plaintiff, said the rent was not being paid.

Defendant said he was willing to give up the house, but it was very difficult to get one at the present time. He contended that he was entitled to get "firing," as he had got it from the previous landlord.

Mr. Bell—According to the defendant's attitude I might refuse to pay my rent unless my landlord supplied me with coal.

The Chairman—Oh, no, this is different. There is an old Irish custom that where a house is near a bog the tenant is by the bargain to be given "firing."

The sub-sanitary officer, when asked by Mr. Hamilton if he considered the house habitable, said the roof was waterproof. There were big stones on the earthen floor, however, and he considered it insanitary.

Mr. Bell—It seems curious that if this is so you served no notice.

The Chairman—He makes his report to the authorities, and a good many of them who represent us rather block him instead of assisting him in putting some of these houses in repair. "I know," he declared, "from my own knowledge of people in this district living in houses not fit for pigs, and if he (the sub-sanitary officer) reported on them I know how he would be received." Later the Chairman said—"I have been fighting all my life to get the poor man a better house than he has."

Londonderry Sentinel 1935

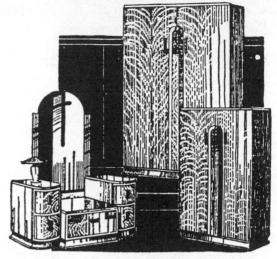

FLASHMANS
FINE FURNITURE.
New Stocks. Distinctive Designs.
Reasonable Prices.

THE WINCHESTER SUITE
comprising :
4ft. Figured Oak double door Wardrobe, divided and fitted interior, carved decoration ; Dressing Table, sunk centre, cheval mirror with copper tinted glass supports and carved drawer front, size of mount 44″ × 19″, polished edge ; Man's 'robe fitted with three shelves and two drawers. Finished in Hazel and Jacobean.

£26:15:0 Full size Bedstead to match
£5:15:0.

All kinds of Axminster and Wilton Carpets and Piece Goods.
Down Quilts, Cushions, Soft Furnishings.

Convenient Easy Payment Terms.

FLASHMAN & Co., Ltd.
Market Square, Dover.
And at Folkestone.

Cardiff and Suburban News 1935

AN ALMOST HUMAN METER.
Blind people are reckoned to be very skilful in detecting the value of coins merely by touch, but at the British Industries Fair, Castle Bromwich, there was an electricity meter that could distinguish between shillings, sixpences and pennies and also alter the recording mechanism to suit. It performs this almost human action by applying calipers to the coin when it is inserted. The next step in meter invention, perhaps, will be to devise an arrangement which, when a dud coin is used, will cut off the current and call in the police.

Runner Beans

A HOARD FOR THE WINTER

One of the main preoccupations just now in the village is how to circumvent the climate and avoid another famine in greenstuff next spring. The villages suffered even more than the towns. The English vegetables were so much discouraged by all they had to undergo that they had entirely disappeared by April, and what foreign produce was admitted never got as far as the country places.

This year everybody has crammed his garden with little cabbages of all sorts, and brussels-sprouts, cauliflowers, curly kale, and all the rest of them; but so we do every year, and this spring nothing came of it. There is, however, nearly always one week in the late summer when there is a glut of runner beans, and when it comes they shall be put down for the spring.

Each time there are beans for dinner we cut up more than we need and put the surplus down in salt. It is best to put them in an earthenware crock, like a small bread bin, but it has been done successfully in large, wide-mouthed sweet-jars, and even in three-pound jam-jars. First we sprinkle salt at the bottom of the jar, then put in sliced beans about an inch deep and cover them with salt. We go on doing this till the jar is almost full. A good inch of salt at the top completes the process. If the crock is a big one it may take weeks to fill it; but no matter, so long as the salt is kept dry. In a damp autumn it is worth while to cover the crock closely with a thick cloth folded several times while the filling is going on. Or, of course, one can buy (or pick) an enormous quantity of beans and give up a day to the business, as they do in Germany.

Manchester Guardian 1936

REAL-LIFE BUDGETS

collected from among interested readers during the past year

A Business Man's House

Income: £263.
Family: Two adults, two children.

Our income is not large, we are of those who have suffered and had to "mark-time" during the industrial depression, but we hope that my husband's position and income will improve in time to give the children the higher education and start in life they may need.

We live on one of the housing estates and have a good house of three bedrooms, bathroom, 2 living-rooms, scullery and garden. There is a good elementary school on the estate. I do all my own work, cleaning, cooking and washing (all with the aid of as modern equipment as I can afford), and knit and sew for myself and the children and still have time to read and keep up-to-date so as to be a companion to my husband.

Yearly Budget

	£	s.	d.
Rent and rates	35	0	0
Coal and logs	10	0	0
Electric light and power	5	0	0
Housekeeping	117	0	0
Insurances	26	0	0
Subscriptions	3	10	0
Clothes and renewals	30	0	0
Holidays	20	0	0
Doctor and dentist	4	0	0
Husband's pocket expenses	12	10	0
	£263	0	0

Weekly Budget

	£	s.	d.
Grocer	0	16	0
Greengrocer and fruit	0	6	0
Butcher	0	8	0
Milk and eggs	0	8	0
Fish	0	2	0
Laundry	0	1	0
Newspapers and library	0	2	6
Chemist	0	1	6
	£2	5	0

Good Housekeeping 1936

Bleaching Before Tinting

" Dear ' Midlander,'—Sample enclosed treated with Inecto. Which number has been used? Client's hair is naturally very thin, but she says during the last few months it has gone thinner. Do you think it is strong enough to stand the bleaching before applying Inecto? If not, do you advise me to tint without bleaching?—' South.' "

[If the hair is 75 per cent. to 100 per cent. white at the roots, it will be quite in order to apply the tint direct to the hair without bleaching, as the hair is very fine and should take the dye satisfactorily. If the roots are dark, bleaching will be necessary before the tint is applied, but if on each occasion it is kept strictly to the regrowth only, it should not affect the hair. Do not add too much ammonia to the peroxide, and dry off as quickly as possible.—" Midlander."]

* * *

Hairdressers' Weekly Journal 1936

OUR SHOPPING SERVICE
CHRISTMAS GIFTS

WE are not all as methodical as Queen Mary, who buys Christmas presents all the year round ; far too many make a hectic dash about three days before the festival to the detriment of our friends' pleasure and our own purses. Crowds of others all on the same quest—the " ideal gift "—shorten tempers and often lead to the purchase of the first thing that comes to hand. Then, too late, it is realized that someone quite important has been forgotten and we blame everything and everybody but ourselves !

A glance through the illustrated Christmas catalogues may be fruitful of ideas, and it is as well to make a list of friends to whom gifts are to be sent and the kind of present considered suitable. If a friend living at a distance is to be the recipient, do not let enthusiasm involve you in buying something, however charming it is, if it will not pack easily.

Among presents that are very easily packed is the wide range of synthetic jewellery, in which are included clips, brooches, ear-rings, bracelets, watches, rings and cultured pearls. These are always acceptable to recipients of the feminine gender ; no woman can have enough of such fantasies. For men, be cautious in giving cuff-links ; most men have sufficient of these articles, but seldom enough dress studs or tie pins. Beautiful workmanship and the very latest designs lift this type of gift out of the ordinary.

There is an unlimited range of exquisitely woven silk and soft woollen scarves from which to choose, and sets of scarves and bags of original design, to match, can be bought for a few shillings. Bead necklaces and theatre wraps of soft silk that fold up into a moderately sized envelope are other suggestions, while the range of artificial flowers—now so real that one instinctively stoops to smell them !—is another acceptable line to be investigated.

Fresh flowers and fruit are appreciated at all times and they can now be " wired " to any part of the world.

If you live in the country and find it difficult to come to London to shop, you are invited to write to our Shopping Expert and ask her advice. Better still, get her to do your shopping for you and save yourself all the trouble of finding your way about crowded shops. There is no charge for this service and it costs you no more. Catalogues and ideas will be sent willingly.

Inquiries should be addressed to Miss Barbara Budden, Shopping Service, Thos. Cook & Son, Ltd., Berkeley Street, London, W.1.

Traveller's Gazette 1936

Model of the
CORONATION CHAIR IN OAK

CAN you think of anything more in keeping as a model for the Coronation than the actual chair in which the King is crowned ? It is one of historic importance used in Westminster Abbey on such occasions as these, and which lends itself fortunately to the user of the fretsaw frame and a very few tools.

We give herewith a picture of the actual chair, and the model which almost anyone can make up, and are very sure it will be one of the most popular set of patterns we have ever published. Complete full size details are given in the centre pages of this issue, and it is a simple matter to paste them down to the wood supplied or to the thickness mentioned, and cut them out to complete the construction.

Hobbies Weekly 1937

NORFOLK HOUSE SALE

FAMOUS DUCAL HOME

By A SPECIAL CORRESPONDENT

During the last few days thousands of people have been visiting Norfolk House, the eighteenth-century London home of successive Dukes of Norfolk, which is shortly to be demolished.

The sale of the contents of the mansion begins to-morrow, and for three days the auctioneers will be busy dispersing the Louis XV and Louis XVI gilt-wood furniture, Chinese and old English porcelain, Italian mirrors, caskets, and cabinets, old French candelabra, brocade curtains, and silk damask wall hangings —in fact, everything on the premises down to the coal buckets and hot-water cans in the basement.

All the beautifully carved wood-work of the doorways and windows, as well as the ornate mantelpieces designed by Matthew Brettingham, the architect, 186 years ago, are to be sold out of the principal apartments, with the exception of the Music Room, which is to be removed in sections and reconstructed in the Victoria and Albert Museum.

A WONDERFUL ROOM

The most sumptuous of the great apartments is the Long Drawing Room, illustrated in Mr. Hanslip Fletcher's drawing on this page. It has six spacious windows looking out over a balcony into St. James's Square, two lofty doorways with heavily carved mahogany friezes, the hangings of walls and windows are of floral crimson silk damask, and the cornice enrichments and panelled ceiling, elaborately gilded, are in the massive style much favoured in Brettingham's day.

Each of the eighty diamond-shaped panels in the ceiling carries a separate electric light, reflected in the thirty mirrors that fill the greater part of the wall space. In this room is the finest of Brettingham's mantelpieces, carved with the head of Mercury.

The State coach and barouche used 100 years ago by the twelfth Duke are included in the sale, and later on Christie's will also sell the pictures and silver-plate, which have been removed from Norfolk House to their auction room.

Three little portraits of the Duke's ancestors are attributed to Holbein and another to Van Dyck. Among the silver are no fewer than 140 candlesticks.

Sunday Times 1938

Distance from London—10 miles.
Population—45,374. (58,000 estimated.)
Altitude—Approx. 250 ft. above sea level.
Subsoil—Gravel.
Birth Rate—13.3 per 1,000.
Death Rate—9.5 per 1,000.
Rates—9s. 5d. in the £ for the year.
Water—(Metropolitan Water Board) 6 per cent. on rateable value per annum.
Gas—(South Suburban Gas Co.) 9¼d. per therm.
Electricity—(Bromley Corporation) Lighting, 4¼d. per unit ; Heating and Cooking, 1¼d. per unit ; All-in tariff, 7 per cent. on rateable value of house and 1d. per unit.

Bromley is known to be very healthy, and is fortunate in possessing all the amenities which are essential to a popular residential district. There are many good shops, excellent schools, churches of every denomination, fine recreation grounds, and sports facilities of the very best. Hayes Common, Wickham Woods, Keston Lake and Common, Chislehurst Caves and Petts Wood are in the near neighbourhood, providing delightful country rambles amongst beautiful rural scenery.

Homefinder Small Property Guide 1937

Population—45,000 (estimated). Sutton and Cheam 82,000 (estimated).

Altitude—120 to 250 ft. above sea level.

Subsoil—Mainly chalk.

Rates—9s. 6d. in the £ for the year.

Water—4½ per cent. on gross assessment

Gas—9.2d. per therm.

Electricity—Two-part Tariff : Fixed charge, according to area of house : September-March, charge per unit, ¾d. ; two summer seasons, ½d. per unit.

Cheam is a quiet residential district in the most charming part of Surrey. On the borders of Cheam Village is Nonsuch Park, once the Royal domain of Henry VIII. There are excellent schools, good shops, and a fast and regular service of trains to the City and West End. The sanitation is up to date, there is a pure water supply, and the roads are clean and well lighted. All kinds of indoor and outdoor amusement may be had, either in the village itself, or at Sutton, which is near by

Homefinder Small Property Guide 1937

Private House Opposition

"DEAR 'MIDLANDER,'—I have cut-price opposition. The young lady responsible is dressing hair after business hours at her lodgings. Could you advise to whom I could write, or what lawful steps I could take to curtail this?—' Reader.' "

[If the house is situated within a Town Planning Scheme, under which businesses are restricted, the practice is illegal, and can be stopped by reporting it to the local Housing Committee. In the event of no protection being afforded in this way, you may report the matter to the landlord. He may take steps to stop it or increase the rent. If he refuses to take notice, you may approach the local Assessment Committee with a view to the premises being assessed as a business instead of a private dwelling.—" MIDLANDER."]

Hairdressers' Weekly Journal 1938

Gramophone **1939**

IDEAL HOME EXHIBITION

One of the many sights of the Ideal Home Exhibition now drawing to a close at Earls Court is the huge Kaleidakon, a white and silver tower which raises its head almost a hundred feet above a pool of rippling water. Here, with the aid of Quentin Maclean, at the console of a Compton organ, and an expert on a light console, duets in sound and light are given daily. As the sound of music emerges so the tower is lit by an ever changing harmony in colour in bright and pastel shades closely allied to the humour and the mood of the music being played. Apart from this, the light orchestra in the lounge on the first floor, one or two piano exhibits, the Keates-Hacker stand with its luxurious recording radiogram and the Marconiphone exhibit, music plays an insignificant part in the exhibition.

All credit to Marconiphone for providing an al-fresco lounge in the form of an old-world garden complete with rose covered pergola, summer house, gaily coloured umbrellas, tables, etc. Here one can rest tired feet and aching limbs and at the same time see and hear television programmes on Marconiphone television receivers. The setting is admirable and the viewing conditions are ideal. In the intervals between the Alexandra Palace transmissions the summer house is pressed into service as a cinema where, from the " garden," visitors can see a film show. The commentary to the film is spoken by Leslie Mitchell.

NORTHOLT Briarhill Estate. A select estate now commenced in a really fine position. Several attractive designs from which to choose, all having large airy rooms, tiled bathroom and labour-saving kitchen, large garden and garage space. Prices range from £660 to £680 Freehold, repayments from 16s. 2d. weekly according to price, rates from 5s. 6d. weekly. Book to South Harrow Piccadilly Tube Station, then Bus 140, alight at Briarhill Estate, Carr Road, or turn left from station. Cliffords Offices at 225, Northolt Road. 'Phone: Byron 2921.

Homefinder Property Guide **1937**

Buttoned or Unbuttoned

The Editor.

SINCE, in your May issue, you recklessly bid readers to come forward with suggestions, I have the temerity to raise the issue of the last and lowest waistcoat button, now left with studied carelessness unbuttoned in some circles. How did this curious habit, fashion or affectation arise and do the best-dressed men and their tailors regard it as a refinement deserving of perpetuation and imitation?

Registered Reader.

———

Mr. Henry A. Rogers, the Eton tailor, confirms our view that the practice originated at Eton College.

" I have cut clothes for Eton boys and for Old Etonians for a period extending over 42 years and never once cut a waistcoat for either except on these lines, and I may say it was the custom to do so long before I started there." Tailors like the practice, as it allows the waistcoat points to spread when sitting, so avoiding the crease that would otherwise form.

Monthly Miscellanea **1939**

Rationing

It is now almost certain that meat, as well as bacon and butter, will be rationed in the new year. It is high time. The months of hesitation which preceded the decision to begin rationing have cost the country dear. The ordinary housewife will welcome a measure which offers her the certainty of a regular supply, if limited, of these foodstuffs in place of the unlimited uncertainty which has made Friday's shopping a burden in many areas. Nothing could have been more irresponsible than the campaign against rationing in certain newspapers which boast of their patriotism, except perhaps the way in which Mr. Morrison has permitted himself to be influenced by it. In our opinion, sugar also should be included. Last September we had a year's supply in hand, but sales went up to a record high and have stayed there ever since, with the result that serious inroads, unevenly and unfairly distributed among the population, have been made into our reserves. In a war of siege and counter-siege, we could learn something from our enemies, who, have not hesitated to enforce the degree of equality of sacrifice which rationing implies.

New Statesman **1939**

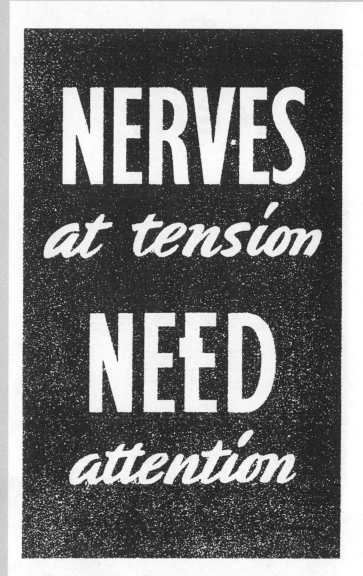

YOU AND YOUR FAMILY NEED

SANATOGEN

NERVE-TONIC FOOD

IN the last war a Cabinet Minister told the House of Commons that " 'Sanatogen' is a national necessity for preserving good nerves." In these days the benefits which 'Sanatogen' can bring are even greater than in 1914-1918. Buy a tin for yourself and your family to-day.

*Obtainable at all chemists
in 19/9 jars (8 weeks' course) and 2/3, 3/3, 5/9 and 10/9 tins.*

Have you tried the new COFFEE FLAVOURED 'Sanatogen'?

The Registered Trade Mark 'SANATOGEN' applied to Nerve-Tonic Food, denotes a brand of casein and sodium glycerophosphate chemically combined by Genatos m Limited, the proprietors of the Trade Mark.

DARK AND DAWN

Sir,—There is another example in our history of how the dark precedes the dawn, comparable to that of the year 1756, of which Sir John Marriott reminds us. I refer to the spring of 1797, when England, left without a single ally, was facing the imminent threat of destruction by a world in arms, led by the victorious legions of France under the supreme military genius of Napoleon. In that dreadful hour the crews of our Fleet rose in revolt at Portsmouth, at Sheerness, off the Dutch coast, and even as far away as the Cape and Porto Rico. A terrible war was raging in Ireland. There had been blunders, miscalculations, and incapacity in high places; everywhere throughout the land poverty, dearth, and misery were rampant. Credit appeared to be at the point of collapse. Discontent seemed to be rising into open rebellion, and it was necessary to employ an armed guard to protect Pitt from the insults and violence of the mob. There is no more thrilling story than that which tells how our dauntless people emerged from that fearful crisis, and surmounting all their difficulties reached victory in the end. It is recounted in words of splendid eloquence by Lord Rosebery in his monograph on Pitt—that intrepid soul—the record of whose inflexible determination and unshakeable courage may well inspire and strengthen us to-day. I am, Sir, &c.,
June 8. H. B. VAISEY.

The Times 1940

HOME NOTES.

WOMEN LAND WORKERS WANTED.

The "grow more food" drive in Britain is hardly out of the "muddle through stage." It is not to be expected that great national movements rendered urgent by the war can be brought at short notice into full efficiency in organisation and working. Many difficulties and prejudices have stood in the way of putting the Women's Land Army on a footing to make good the shortage of agricultural labour. Reports from all over Britain show that on some of the large arable farms only one or two regular farm workers are left. Some of the twenty-year-olds have been called up and many have left the countryside for better paid employments in the building of camps, Government work, munition and other factories. Unless women come forward more freely as workers on the land, as they did in the last war, and adequate facilities are provided for training them, the home production of food will fall far short of what it might be made. The minimum wage of 28/- a week in the Women's Land Army is not great, but skilled labour on the land can command high pay. Women are also wanted for work in forestry for tree planting and felling timber for pit props. It means living a camp life, and hundreds of girls are wanted for this new job in the Women's Land Army.

York Star 1940

Stratford upon Avon Herald **1940**

A milkman takes the Blitz in his stride.

MARGARINE & FATS POOL

ALL U.K. MAKERS

ONE COMPANY FOR THE INDUSTRY

All the margarine and compound cooking-fat manufacturers of the United Kingdom have decided, for the period of the war, to pool their resources, sink their individual identities and give up their brand names.

This was announced last night by the Margarine Manufacturers' Association, which states that the industry will operate as one company under the name of Marcom, Ltd.

Intended as a contribution to the national effort, this co-ordination, it is pointed out, will enable each factory to be utilised to the best possible advantage, and will effect a vast saving in man-power and transport. The new scheme is the industry's contribution to the arrangements for decentralising food manufacture and supply into virtually watertight areas.

FOOD MINISTRY'S AGENT

The new organisation will be appointed selling agents for the Ministry of Food, and will distribute two brands of margarine—Special at 9d per pound, and Standard at 5d per pound. In addition, domestic cooking-fat will be sold at 7d per pound, and margarine for use in bakeries and by confectioners will be supplied in standard grades. All the margarine for household use will be vitaminised with Vitamins A and D.

The margarine industry is largely controlled by Lever Brothers & Unilever, which controls, directly or indirectly, Jurgens, Van den Berghs and Jurgens, English Margarine Works, De Bruyn, Craigmillar Creamery Company, and R. S. Hudson. Products include: Margarine "Blue Band," "Stork," "Echo," "Polo." Cooking-fat — "Cookeen," "Spry."

Other margarine or cooking-fat companies are: Benninga's British Margarine and Produce Company ("Sunni face" and "Green Circle" margarine; "Lardex" for cooking). W. Brandis and Co. Ferguson Shaw and Sons. Hugon and Co. (" Atora" suet and lard). Peter Keevil and Sons. Loders and Nucoline. Southern Oil Company (" Snowdrift " lard).

Financial Times 1940

Food 1941

Food Wasters May Get Two Years' Imprisonment

THE Ministry of Food on Tuesday made an Order, which comes into force next Monday, for preventing waste of food and carrying with it penalties against offenders.

Under the Order it will be an offence to waste food, which is described as "everything used by man for food or drink other than water."

Under the Order it is not forbidden to give meat to dogs, but anyone giving an excessive amount would be liable to prosecution.

Mr. Robert Boothby, Parliamentary Secretary to the Ministry, emphasised that the Order would not be harshly interpreted. It was more in the nature of a warning, and he did not expect a lot of prosecutions.

THE OFFENCES

The penalties will be the same as those provided in the Defence Regulations, with maximums on summary conviction of three months imprisonment or £100 fine or both, and on indictment to two years' imprisonment or £500 fine or both.

Under the Order it will be an offence :—

(1) Where food fit for human consumption is wilfully or negligently damaged or thrown away ;

(2) Where anyone having control or custody of food fails to take reasonable precautions for its preservation ;

(3) Where anyone procures a larger quantity than is reasonably required for his purpose and part becomes unfit for use, and

(4) Where anyone having the disposal of food unreasonably retains it until it becomes unfit for use.

Under this last heading shopkeepers who have food and cannot sell it at a reasonable price are exempted.

When he was asked whether inspectors would be sent to houses to see if the regulations were being carried out, Mr. Boothby said, " Oh no, there are going to be no Boothby snoopers."

On the question of the supply of plums for jam-making expected on the market shortly, Mr. Boothby said that if it should prove to be necessary the Ministry would put a price control on plums.

OUTLOOK FOR WINTER

Describing the food outlook for the winter Mr. Boothby said it was hoped to avoid any further rationing and he expected the Ministry would be able to increase certain rations, particularly tea.

Latest figures show that the national milk scheme is a success. There has been an increase of 600,000 applications in the last week. Milk under the scheme, either free or at 2d. a pint, is now being received by 1,787,849 out of a total of 3,758,000 potential beneficiaries throughout the country. Of the recipients 464,905 are getting free milk and 1,322,944 milk at 2d a pint.

Mr. Boothby stated that the scheme for dealing with the egg problem had not yet been completed, but he hoped it would be ready before the end of the month. Meantime the Ministry were taking steps to purchase as many eggs as possible from abroad.

Western Mail 1940

AN Order in force on January 13 makes it an offence for any manufacturer, wholesaler, retailer or other dealer to sell at a price higher than he charged on December 2, 1940, any of the following foods :— coffee (including coffee essence and coffee chicory); cocoa powder; cocoa butter; chocolate sold for use as a beverage; canned and bottled vegetables; canned pork and beans; honey; meat, fish, poultry and other edible pastes; meat and other edible extracts; shredded suet; dead poultry (other than turkeys); rice, tapioca and sago; macaroni, spaghetti and vermicelli; biscuits, rusks and crispbreads; tinned, bottled and powdered soups; processed cheese; pickles, sauces and relishes; custard and blancmange powders; table jellies; and edible nuts.

LETTERS TO NEW HOMES

POST OFFICE DIRECTIONS

The Postmaster-General desires to help people who have had to leave their homes temporarily or otherwise as a result of air raid damage, or of precautionary measures taken after an air raid, to receive correspondence addressed to them at their former homes.

Those who remain temporarily in the neighbourhood of their home should inquire at a local post office for the point at which they can obtain their correspondence.

Those moved to other districts who have left their former homes unoccupied and who have not made other arrangements for the reception of their correspondence should, as soon as they have settled in more or less permanent quarters, apply at once at a post office for a re-direction card, P 221611. If they follow the instructions on the card their correspondence will be forwarded on to them at their new address. If they were on the telephone they should enter particulars of their former telephone number on the card also.

The same course should be taken by any people remaining in their original neighbourhood when they have taken up fresh quarters there on a permanent or semi-permanent basis.

Salisbury and Winchester Journal 1940

THE MAKING OF MARGARINE

Food Trade Review 1941

AN ACCOUNT of how margarine is made was given by Mr. J. P. Van den Bergh, director of margarine and cooking fats at the Ministry of Food, in the popular radio feature " The World Goes By " in the Home service one evening last month. The talk took the form of an interview between Mr. Van den Bergh and Mr. F. Grisewood, who conducts the feature.

Mr. Van den Bergh said that two main materials went to make margarine. The first was milk and the second was vegetable oils. The oils were obtained in crude form from nuts or seeds, grown largely in British colonies. When they reached this country the crude oil was got out of them by extraction or by crushing and had to be highly refined. Many margarine factories had an oil refinery alongside the factory.

As for milk, the other main raw material, either liquid milk or milk powder could be used. It was pasteurised, and then run into long tanks, where certain cultures were added for the purpose of developing the butter taste in the milk, because it was the milk which gave margarine its flavour.

There remained, continued Mr. Van den Bergh, the question of vitamins. The margarine manufacturers a year ago agreed, in consultation with the Ministry of Food, that vitamins A and D should be incorporated in a fixed proportion in all margarine sold for household use.

WORK OF THE JAM CENTRES

To the Editor.

Sir.—Mrs. Fisher misses the main point of my letter which was and still is that many good windfall apples are lying rotting in country cottage gardens, despite the fact that these can be had for the gathering.

I know at least one village where the President of the Preservation Centre states there are no facilities for making apple jelly. This waste of good food is deplorable. Only a very small percentage of people, if any, would actually allow fruit to waste before selling it. Surely Mrs. Fisher would not dispute this. But you cannot expect elderly people to take small quantities of fruit a distance of several miles in some cases to the jam centres. There is a vast difference between the cost of making rhubarb jam, even with sugar, at manufacturers' price, and the local selling price. Where does the huge profit go? Profiteering is far too rife and encourages waste. I paid 1s. 2d. for carriage on one marrow weighing 10 lbs. from Halesworth to Ipswich, and the Railway Company stated this was the growers' cheap rate. The vegetable marrow cost me twopence. Are marrows to be the next item on the waste list?

JOHN GLASS.
300, Wherstead Road,
Ipswich.

East Anglian Daily Times 1941

THE meeting between President Roosevelt and Mr. Churchill will rank among the most memorable personal encounters in world history. There are few types of event which so readily strike the imagination as meetings between great personalities whom character, position or circumstance invests with a decisive part in moulding human destiny.

Such occasions may be rendered famous by a large variety of conditions. The actual physical setting, the character of the persons concerned, the purpose of policy which brought them together, the issue that hangs on the outcome of their discussion, the ultimate consequences—these are the factors which dramatise the event and cause it to stand out in its epoch.

How far back into history may one not delve for instances of the faith that personal contacts and private conversations between principals are likely to yield results?

Novelty of Aquatic Mise-en-Scène

The mind inevitably ranges back over the pages of history to recall meetings which have made their mark in this sense. To search for " parallels " would be in vain, for the circumstances of each occasion are necessarily unique, and it is indeed the contrasts rather than the similarities that command interest and attention.

One feature—not the most important—which distinguishes the Roosevelt-Churchill meeting from all previous ones of comparable moment is that it took place at sea. It has taken the development of modern science and travel to make the water a suitable rendezvous for political conversations; and in the midst of such a war it could hardly have been expected that negotiators would secure the requisite detachment for their purpose in the Atlantic Ocean.

Daily Telegraph 1941

Rose Hip Syrup

PLANS have been made to harvest the vitamin wealth of Britain's hedgerows in the form of wild rose hips. Rose hips are particularly rich in vitamin C the anti-infective vitamin. Both garden and wild varieties are twenty times richer in this vitamin than oranges. Hitherto, these health-producing fruits have been allowed to go to waste. Now, because of the war-time scarcity of fruit, the Ministry of Health and the Department of Health for Scotland are encouraging a nation-wide drive to collect them so that they can be converted into syrup.

The hips, which must be ripe, can be gathered from wild or cultivated bushes, but they should be free from bits of stem and leaves. Haws, the red berries of the May, are not wanted and care should be taken to avoid picking them. The picking season extends until the end of October.

The various collecting organisations are arranging to supply the rose hips in bulk to a number of firms who have agreed to pay for them at the rate of 2s. for 14 lbs. (minimum 28 lbs.), carriage forward. It is specially requested that small quantities should not be sent direct to the firms but be handed in to a collecting depot.

As a result of the campaign it is hoped that a total of some 500 tons of rose hips will be converted into a tasty, health-fortifying syrup, for the benefit of babies, children, and adults. The syrup will be marketed at a reasonable price.

Food Trade News **1941**

No Grounds for Complaint

A Scots business man mentioned yesterday over lunch that the most delicious coffee he ever tasted was at Kuantan, now prominent in the news from the Far East. It was poured, he explained, by an ancient Malayan from a bully beef tin through a strainer made from somebody's sock!

Scotsman *1942*

POTATO PRICES

The Ministry of Food, after consultations with the agricultural departments and the Treasury, have arrived at a new scheme for paying farmers for their potato crops. Farmers are to be paid £10 per acre for all ground returned as being under potatoes in June of this year. Prices for consumers will be regulated so that they will average 8d. per seven pounds throughout the year.

The cash payment for potatoes will be part compensation for farmers who had bad luck with their early potatoes this year, when prices were disadvantageous, said a Ministry official. "We hope by this scheme to encourage growers to go flat out next season."

ONIONS

There will be no extension of time for people to register for onions. Those who were on holiday during the period for registration can apply to their local food executive officer for permission to register. If the crop of onions improves the reservation of two pounds per head may be increased.

East Anglian Daily Times *1941*

More Girls Bare-Legged This Summer

"Star" Reporter

GIRLS' stockings—or the lack of them—will be more than ever news this summer. Many girls have decided to be bare legged in order to save on their clothes coupons.

What their legs will look like will depend on the cosmetic manufacturers.

Mock stockings, put on out of a bottle, with a seam carefully painted down the back of the legs, are going to be scarce.

Some beauty salons will still be able to give such treatments but the supply of the cheaper sorts of "bottle stockings," formerly sold at the popular stores, is expected to disappear.

"There should be a fair amount of leg make-up available," a representative of a firm of cosmetic manufacturers told me, "but manufacturers are free to choose how they use their quota.

"Most of us have cut out all non-essential lines and concentrate on major needs.

"We are still making the flat leg make-up used by many film stars in Hollywood. This is a 'solid' preparation which is sponged on to the legs to give a matt surface. It is in six shades."

Coupon-savers should be able to give their bare legs a matt appearance by careful use of their cream and powder rations.

Star **1942**

Do you remember when the headlines said—

"No potatoes for this Sunday's joint"

While thousands of housewives enjoyed another little grumble, the wiser families who had dug for victory enjoyed their Sunday joint with all the potatoes and other vegetables they wanted. Learn from experience. To be sure of the family's vegetables, you must grow them yourselves—women and older children as well as men. If you haven't a garden, ask your Local Council for an allotment. Start to

DIG FOR VICTORY NOW!

POST THIS COUPON NOW (Unsealed envelope, 1d. stamp)

TO MINISTRY OF AGRICULTURE, HOTEL LINDUM, ST. ANNES-ON-SEA, LANCS.
Please send me copies of free pictorial leaflets, "How to Dig" and "How to Crop"

NAME ....

ADDRESS ....
                                                                          B.99
I S S U E D   B Y   T H E   M I N I S T R Y   O F   A G R I C U L T U R E

Food 1942

July 23	1435	Sugar Confectionery and Chocolate and Chocolate Confectionery (Distribution) Order, 1942.	Provides for control of the wholesale distribution of sugar confectionery and chocolate and chocolate confectionery during the period from July 27 to September 19.
July 25	1481	Rationing (Personal Points) Order, 1942.	Provides for the rationing of chocolate and chocolate confectionery and of sugar confectionery under the Personal Points Scheme.
August 28	1731	Order amending the Food Control Committees (Local Distribution) Order, 1939, and granting a General Licence thereunder.	Amends the schedule to the Principal Order, as amended, by substituting the item "chocolate and sugar confectionery, including chewing gum" for the item "chocolate and sugar confectionery other than chewing gum." Thus retailers may now be required to obtain a licence to sell chewing gum.

"DRIED EGGS are my eggs — my whole eggs and nothing but my eggs"

Dried eggs are the complete hen's eggs, both the white and the yolk, dried to a powder. Nothing is added. Nothing but moisture and the shell taken away, leaving the eggs themselves as wholesome, as digestible and as full of nourishment and health-protecting value as if you had just taken the eggs new laid from the nest. So put the eggs back into your breakfast menus. And what about a big, creamy omelette for supper? You can have it savoury; or sweet, now that you get extra jam.

DRIED EGGS build you up!

In war-time, the most difficult foods for us to get are the body-builders. Dried eggs build muscle and repair tissue in just the same way as do chops and steaks; and are better for health-protection. So we are particularly lucky to be able to get dried eggs to make up for any shortage of other body-builders such as meat, fish, cheese, milk.

Your allowance of DRIED EGG is equal to 3 eggs a week

You can now get one 12-egg packet (price 1/3) per 4-week rationing period — three fine fresh eggs a week, at the astonishingly low price of 1¼d. each. Children (holders of green ration books) get two packets  each rationing period. You buy your dried eggs at the shop where you are registered for shell eggs; poultry keepers can buy anywhere.
Don't hoard your dried eggs ; use them up — there are plenty more coming!

Note. *Don't make up dried eggs until you are ready to use them; they should not be allowed to stand after they've been mixed with water or other liquid. Use dry when making cakes and so on, and add a little more moisture when mixing.*

FREE — **DRIED EGG LEAFLET** containing many interesting recipes, will be sent on receipt of a postcard addressed to Dept. 627E, Food Advice Service, Ministry of Food, London, W.1.

ISSUED BY THE MINISTRY OF FOOD (S.74)

Home and Country
1942

Herbs for Prisoners of War

An excellent idea, which originated with W.I. members, is that culinary herbs should be included in the parcels of food sent to British prisoners of war by the Red Cross. The idea has spread and many letters have come to HOME AND COUNTRY making local suggestions for despatch. We have got into touch with the Red Cross and they are very willing that a scheme should be arranged.

The simplest scheme is often the best and we suggest that where no scheme is already in operation Institutes should increase their present efforts at collecting culinary herbs and send some of the herbs, either rough dried on the stalk or in powdered form, to the British Red Cross Society Stores, Prisoners of War Stores, Powells Wharf, Pottery Street, Bermondsey Wharf, London, S.E.16. Mr. Duffner, the Red Cross buyer for the Stores, will be delighted to receive any amount at any time. The particular requests he makes are that the packages should be clearly labelled and that the packing throughout should be *very* dry as even in transit herbs can go mouldy.

We are sure that Institutes which have not already considered this idea will be anxious to do anything they can to relieve the monotony of prisoners of war food, even if it means increasing their 2 lbs. target.

The Bread Decision

Food 1942

THE three Statutory Orders made by the Minister of Food on March 12 at long last settle the bread controversy. Whether, or no, the Minister has decided wisely we shall have to wait before reaching a decision. He has certainly cut the knot of discussion that has been raging for months now with one swift stroke. Everybody in the country is immediately affected. Dates have been chosen for the operation of these Orders to assist in the disposal of present stocks.

After March 23 the miller is prohibited from making any white flour, except under specific licence. No white flour may be delivered except to licensed bakers, and then only in the proportion of one part to three parts of National wheatmeal. After the same date the baker is authorised to incorporate not more than 25 per cent. of white flour in the flour content of national wheatmeal, and after April 6 the baker is not permitted to manufacture any bread other than national wheatmeal, or speciality bread, the flour content of which is at least 75 per cent. of 85 per cent. extraction. The biscuit maker and confectioner, after April 20, are prohibited from using white flour unless it is mixed with three times its weight of national wheatmeal flour. The production of flour mixtures, including self-raising flour, from existing stocks of white flour will be permitted for one month, until April 20. Whilst one can be certain that the people of this country would be quite willing to accept brown bread, in spite of its unpopularity, if the responsible authorities were convinced that such a policy is definitely a necessity because of the seriousness of the shipping position, their patriotism does not need to be bolstered up by incorrect claims for nutritional advantages that are still a matter of scientific doubt.

The Times 1943

Tea or Carrots

LORD WOOLTON lately declared minced carrots to be more stimulating than early tea and LADY WOOLTON, hesitating dislike, added, " But not so comforting." There can be no question which side most people will take in this domestic argument; the lady will win with ease. While grateful for the attribution of comfort, votaries of the early cup will never admit that it is not supremely stimulating. Its power of rousing the comatose to action is its outstanding merit. This was clearly the view of a small boy and girl who long ago produced a weekly journal for family consumption. The serial story, its chief feature began with these words: " When " the pretty housemaid brought Lord " Algy his early tea in the morning he " jumped out of bed and rapidly kissed " her five times." Could a minced carrot have done as much ? The only rival in the matter of dispelling swinishness and getting a man out of bed is probably a fixed bayonet. Whether the teacup should immediately precede the fatal hour of rising or should be brought some time before so that the drinker may sink again not into slumber but into an exquisite dreaminess; whether or not it finds its perfect complement in the first cigarette of the day—these are questions of great interest but perhaps something too sybaritic to be freely discussed in wartime. Enough that it is surpassingly " sweet when the morn is grey."

End of Luxury Feeding

The Order now being drafted by the Ministry of Food, designed to regulate restaurant feeding, is much overdue. It is to be hoped that, now the Government has been persuaded of its necessity, the Order will be drastic and effective. Reports suggest that the number of courses will be limited to three; that a strict upper limit will be placed on the cost of meals; and that days without fish, game or poultry will be introduced. It is expected that meals after 11.0 p.m. will be prohibited, except for night workers and hotel residents, and that the holding of unnecessary public luncheons will be discouraged. It has been apparent since the outbreak of war, that the spectacle of luxury feeding was intolerable to a people on whom the need for total sacrifice was being officially impressed. Moreover, the possibility of building up food stocks through stricter regulation of restaurant, café and club meals should have outweighed the consideration that the net saving would be too small to make a perceptible difference to the current domestic ration. It is still not quite clear why, despite the admitted technical difficulties, the Minister of Food does not decide to go the whole way and introduce food rationing in restaurants. Coupons were surrendered in restaurants in the last war, and there has been more surprise than satisfaction that no such scheme has been brought in this time. Even under the new Order, there will be no upper limit, apart from actual physical capacity, on the amount of food which the crawler from eating place to eating place can absorb.

Economist 1942

One-Time 'Fuehrer' Is Out

NO ONE WILL TELL WHERE MOSLEY IS

SIR OSWALD MOSLEY, one-time chief of the British Union of Fascists, and Lady Mosley were released from Holloway Jail soon after seven o'clock yesterday morning.

They drove away in a closed car to a secret destination.

One of the few who know where Sir Oswald has gone is his mother. She said yesterday that she has not even told her other sons where it is.

Baroness Ravensdale, Sir Oswald's sister-in-law through his first marriage, who has been looking after his two eldest children, said she had " no idea where he had gone."

" I imagine that he will be under some form of house arrest,"

said a former member of the British Union of Fascists.

" He was met by a Home Office representative and taken to the place where he will live during his period of liberty. His state of health does not necessarily mean that he will have to have an immediate operation.

" There are periods when he requires treatment, and other periods when he has to lie up."

Sir Oswald, who is believed to be suffering from phlebitis, had been detained under 18B since May, 1940, and his wife since June of that year.

People 1943

Fish is 'Scarce,' Yet London's Wealthy Get It

From ROSE SMITH

LONDON housewives, hunting for something as mid-week dinner, have been sadly disappointed if they expected to get fish instead of the inferior quality meat ends in the shops.

The fish they saw was poor quality stuff and there was very little of it.

West End contrast: waiters assured me that wealthy diners, "always anxious for something light after the heavy Christmas meals," were able to eat good quality fish.

Buyers—in cars—have scoured the London markets to get the fish for them; they have ranged far afield and have brought back fresh salmon, turbot, halibut and Scotch hake.

With a well-lined purse, capable of dropping anything up to £20 a week to salesmen, they come back with well-filled baskets.

DODGE REGULATIONS

Catering workers assure me that a number of methods are adopted to dodge the Government limit of purchase to one pound per 50 persons who take a main meal.

All meals, including breakfasts and light teas, are included for obtaining excessive fish supplies.

Kitchen porters told me that shell fish, not included in the Government order, is used as another device for getting more soft fish.

In addition to supplies of lobsters, prawns, scallops, mussels and oysters, boxes are delivered containing soft fish, but are invoiced as shell fish.

Daily Worker
1944

People
1943

£1,600 For A £700 Home

SPECIAL TO "THE PEOPLE"

LARGE-SCALE racketeering in houses is sending prices sky-high, and is causing much hardship to people who are being compelled by the shortage to buy houses because they cannot rent them.

For the past two years, syndicates of speculators have been buying up large and small properties. Now that the shortage is at its worst, they are beginning to sell them at tremendous profits.

Houses which cost £700 in peace time are now being sold for £1,500 and £1,600.

Cottages which used to be worth £250 are being sold for £600 and more.

Terrace houses which were obtainable at £400 before the war are now fetching £900.

Prediction 1943

Uncanny Movements of Bed

As I lay awake this morning, suddenly I felt the bed move backwards and forwards, then up and down. I called to my husband who was downstairs, and told him of my alarming experience. Possessing some knowledge of Spiritualism he explained to me that someone beyond wishes to communicate with me. At the time of this queer occurrence my husband was having breakfast and was thinking of the next world.—W.E.T., Gloucester.

No intelligent spirit would, in order to attract your attention, so risk shaking you out of your senses. The phenomenon you describe is a common trick of the poltergeist. For example, in the well-known Enniscorthy case a heavy bed with two young men in it was dragged right across the room; on another occasion, with three occupants, it "rose and fell without making any noise." One should not encourage such a type of psychic activity by letting one's thoughts dwell upon it; for, happening often, this sort of thing, although harmful solely to the nerves, might become a decided nuisance.

Housework and men are like petrol and flame—put them together and anything may happen at any time. Here are some drifts of comment overheard recently.

Brilliant woman doctor, reproached by husband for haphazard method of table-laying: " Well, if I can't be an amateur in my own home . . .."

Young Naval Officer (unmarried) : " I'd rather have a charming wife than a perfect housekeeper. There are too many drearily efficient people about."

Husband : " The trouble is you will do things too well. When we are short-staffed in the office we cut down unnecessary work." *Wife* : " Of course, we could have dinner on a trolley every night." *Husband*—very hastily : " No, that's much too uncomfortable."

Bright Young Thing : " The only men I know who do any housework are Canadians—they're marvellous."

Fascinating, blue-eyed stockbroker of our acquaintance : " The thing to do, when asked to wash up, is immediately to drop several plates. Then you're never asked again."

Middle-aged D.S.O. who spends three days weekly training his lawn : " I'll do a bit of coal-humping if it's absolutely necessary, but there it ends."

Harassed mother of three : " My husband's just finished his holiday at home. He *said* he was doing it to help, but you know what it means. . . .."

Magnificent middle-aged lady on a bus : " I tell him I simply cannot even boil an egg—that is if one had an egg, of course."

Good Housekeeping 1943

RECRUITS.

It is a good thing that ringers should interest themselves now in the problems of reconstruction and should talk about what they hope to do when peace comes. It is a good thing that they should discuss, for instance, the best way to secure recruits and how they intend to try to fill the vacancies in the belfry. When the time comes they probably will have to do what they can and what they must, rather than what they would, but that is no reason why they should not make plans and do their best to carry them out.

The future will have to find the solutions of its problems, but in the meanwhile it may be well to consider the question generally, and in the light of past experience.

In themselves, recruits are not desirable. They are only desirable so far as they give promise of becoming sound ringers. As long as they remain recruits they are not only a big tax on the time and the patience of the older men (which is no very great matter), but they usually are the cause of bad ringing, which is a nuisance to the neighbourhood. This is a very important matter. If we could take our learners into some secluded spot and away from the hearing of outsiders as a choirmaster can train his choir in an empty church, all would be well enough. But that we cannot do. The whole parish must hear, though ringers, shut up as they are in a remote belfry, seldom realise it.

Ringing World 1942

Daily Herald
1944

Sirens—And They All Go Out Again

LONDONERS, though denied the blessings of "moonlit" streets, relaxed last night with some contentment in the glow of more brightly lit rooms behind unblacked-out windows.

But early in the hours of the new dim-out the Alert sounded and they had either to switch off their lights or scramble to replace their blackout. The "All Clear" soon followed.

But police and wardens had a busy time warning people to blackout their houses.

One warden said: "Scores of people never heard the Alert because of the noise of their wireless. I quite expected that 'Jerry' would put this one across and we anticipated a busy night.

"A large number of people have destroyed their blackout entirely—a hasty decision because in an Alert they will have to sit in the dark.

"Another thing worrying us is the amount of light which can be displayed. I saw one house with muslin curtains. We could see the occupiers playing cards.

"They certainly put out the light when the Alert sounded but switched it on again before the All Clear had finished.

Daily Worker 1944

Taking Fingerprints is 'Slur on Man's Character'

THE practice of the police taking finger-prints of a person before he is convicted or even committed for trial, is inconsistent with our British presumption of innocence until proof of guilt, and it is natural for it to be regarded as a slur on a man's character, said Lord Justice Scott in the Court of Appeal yesterday.

His Lordship said he believed there was no statutory authority for such treatment, and suggested that the matter deserved serious consideration by the Home Secretary and the Lord Chancellor.

A claim for damages for wrongful arrest and false imprisonment, against three members of the Liverpool City Police, was upheld by the court.

CLAIM DISMISSED

The appellant, Alfred George Dumbell, of Briardale Road, Aigburth, had been arrested and charged with being in unlawful possession of a quantity of soap-flakes, but the magistrates dismissed the charge.

His claim for damages against the police had been dismissed at Liverpool Assizes, and his appeal was against that decision.

The Lord Justice said that the police not only failed to carry out the conditions of the Liverpool Corporation Act, 1921—under which Dumbell had been charged—but they also failed to make such inquiry as would entitle them to think they had reasonable grounds for suspicion.

A new trial was ordered to decide the amount of damages to be paid to Dumbell.

Daily Mail 1944

Britain is Putting On Weight

Warning to Women

By Daily Mail Reporter

LADY, watch your figure. Your weight is going up again.

Back in the winter of 1940-41 we were all down to fighting-weight men and women, Professor Sir Jack Drummond, scientific adviser to the Ministry of Food, told a London audience yesterday.

"During that winter every man and woman lost on an average five to fourteen pounds—and we were all better for it."

Latterly, we have been putting the weight back. Experts have noticed that with a slightly more varied diet we have been tempted to eat more and curves are coming back—not always in the right places.

Heed this warning from Sir Jack: "Putting on weight is not a bad thing if you are under 30. If you are over 30, watch out."

Sir Jack himself is under weight. He is 53, 5ft. 10in. high, and so spare that he weighs only 10st. 7lb. In his university days more than 30 years ago he boxed at welter-weight. He is still in the welter-weight class. The point he made yesterday was "It is so easy to put on weight, so hard to take it off."

The Homes That 750,000 Wives Want

By ALISON SETTLE

WOMEN who have offered their suggestions for ideal homes to Lord Dudley's sub-committee for the designing of houses do not expect them to produce many practical results.

They expressed their ideas in replies to questionnaires issued by women's organisations at the committee's request.

The report on their wishes is to be handed to the Minister of Health next month. They believe, however, that their advice will be whittled down by local authorities until the result of their suggestions is negligible.

Nearly fifty organisations, representing 750,000 women, expressed their views on the best designs and equipment of houses suitable for families with small incomes.

No Standard House

A Ministry of Health official told me yesterday that there is no question of asking the country to accept a standard house.

"Recommendations will probably be included in a housing manual similar to those on which local authorities have based their plans in the past."

The secretary of an important women's organisation said: "We understand that construction of post-war houses on a large scale for people returning from the Forces can only be undertaken if fittings are reduced to a minimum. We feared this would happen.

"Women believe that refrigeration, soundproof walls, well-planned kitchen cupboards, central heating, and hot water on tap are necessities in every home, but they have no real hope of obtaining them.

"Many thousands of homes have no adequate heating arrangements. Thousands of women who answered the questionnaires revealed that they have no water laid on to their houses. They appreciate the statement of Mr. Alfred Bossom that women after the war will have electric potato peelers and washing-up machines, but they feel that he is being unduly optimistic."

Observer 1944

My Home
1945

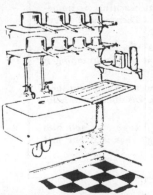

The kitchen in a small flat has no cupboard room for pots and pans. The above arrangement with two shelves over the sink will be found convenient. The small shelf on the right, for soap powders, etc., is especially useful.

A neat arrangement of shelves.

SORRY IT'S SCARCE

—but you'll be glad to find you get as many cups of good coffee from each bottle of 'Camp' as in pre-war days. It is therefore well worth waiting for—and your grocer is doing his best to distribute his limited supplies of 'Camp' fairly among his customers.

'CAMP' COFFEE

FULL STRENGTH FINE FLAVOUR

Dundee Courier 1945

Last March Of Home Guard

By WESLEY CLAPTON

A LONG line of khaki will wind through London's West End on the afternoon of Sunday, December 3.

It will be the same line that stood between Britain and invasion after the dark days of Dunkirk.

The Home Guards will be marching for the last time. They will be honoured in the capital of the country they sprang to defend when the call went out in the hour of danger.

Every unit throughout the country will be represented. Many of the marchers will be veterans of two wars.

There is keen competition for the honour of representing the unit. Some units are deciding by ballot who shall go.

The marchers will carry no arms, but will wear steel helmets and greatcoats.

The route will be Piccadilly, Regent-street, Oxford-street, and back to Hyde Park via Marble Arch.

Daily Herald 1944

POSSESSION OF A LITTLE BELVOIR COTTAGE

At Melton County Court on Friday, Sir Arthur and Lady Pilkington, of Little Belvoir, Wartnaby, were granted possession of a furnished cottage at Little Belvoir, at present tenanted by evacuees, named Pearce.

Lady Pilkington said she required the cottage for a gardener. She used over an acre of garden as a market garden, producing foodstuff, and the gardener was needed to help with this garden.

Mrs. Pearce and her children had come in 1940 from London after their home had been blitzed, but later the husband had joined them.

He was now working as a lorry driver in Melton.

The house had been let to the Pearces fully furnished for ten shillings a week.

Judge Field made an order for possession in two months.

Mr. H. K. Barker represented Sir Arthur and Lady Pilkington.

Melton Mowbray Times 1945

CABBAGE FROM CORNWALL.

Sir,—Would it be possible to find a few people not completely mad among the officials who run our food distribution?

Going to buy some cabbage in Perth to-day, I said I hoped it would be really fresh, as hitherto that had not been the case. "Well," said the girl serving me. "you see all the cabbage we get to sell comes from Cornwall, and it is generally so yellow by the time it gets here people hardly care to buy it!" This at a time when every cottage garden is full of kale!

No wonder the prices charged are quite exorbitant.—Yours, &c., Disgusted. Perth, 17/7/45.

'BRING YOUR EATS'

Says Archdeacon

The Archdeacon of Bath, the Ven. W. Marshall Selwyn, and Mrs. Selwyn announcing "at homes" at Bath Rectory on June 18 and 29, state that "they will be delighted to welcome any members of Bath Abbey congregation and others who care to come, but 'eats' and milk being what they are, it would be safer if guests brought their own!"

Evening News 1945

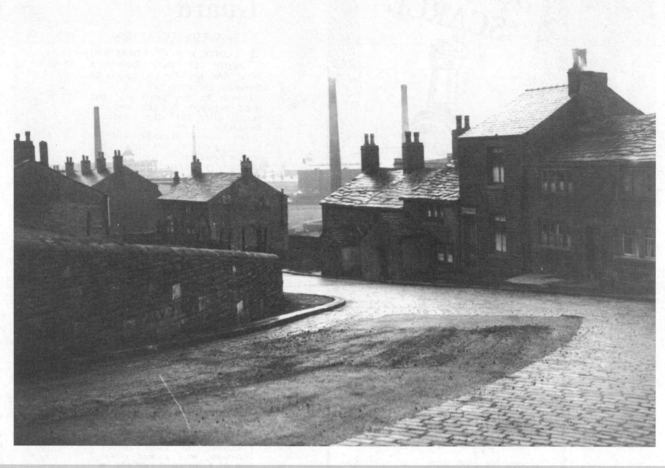

Housing for cotton industry workers in the Shaw Valley, Lancashire, 1946

My Home 1945

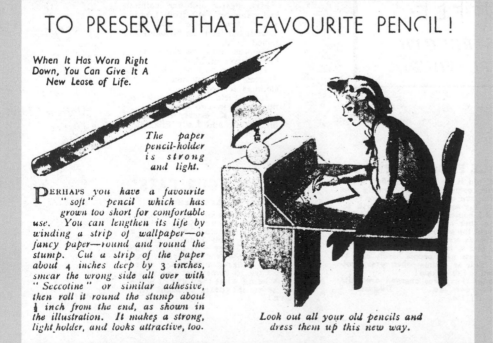

TO PRESERVE THAT FAVOURITE PENCIL!

When It Has Worn Right Down, You Can Give It A New Lease of Life.

The paper pencil-holder is strong and light.

Perhaps you have a favourite "soft" pencil which has grown too short for comfortable use. You can lengthen its life by winding a strip of wallpaper—or fancy paper—round and round the stump. Cut a strip of the paper about 4 inches deep by 3 inches, smear the wrong side all over with "Seccotine" or similar adhesive, then roll it round the stump about ¼ inch from the end, as shown in the illustration. It makes a strong, light holder, and looks attractive, too.

Look out all your old pencils and dress them up this new way.

Daily Sketch 1946

THE PHONE RANG HER WEDDING BELLS

'Daily Sketch' Correspondent

Lorna Kathleen Groves, of Pen-y-lan-road, Llandough, near Cardiff, told me yesterday how she was married by telephone to Chief Petty Officer Murray Lars Petersen, of the U.S. Navy, stationed at Bremerton, Washington.

"I came home from my work at the offices of Penarth electricity works, tired, wet and hungry," she said. "I had tea and the phone rang.

"A voice — my husband's — said: 'Hello, Lorna,' then another voice said: 'This is chaplain Young speaking. If you are willing I will now perform the marriage ceremony.'

"It seemed to be the usual wedding service like that in the Church of England."

Lorna Groves

PILES OF CAKE, MEAT —IN ITALY

'Daily Sketch' Correspondent

MOUNTAINS of cream buns and sweets in confectioners' windows . . . whole carcasses on the butchers' hooks . . . pink hams and cooked meats piled high on delicatessen shop counters pyramids of Parmesan and Gorgonzola cheeses . . . oranges, lemons and tangerines by the ton.

This is no dream. It is the everyday reality of Ventimiglia, on the Italian Riviera, as described by a writer in *La Liberté* (Nice).

Similar displays are seen in other Italian towns where the black market has become the "legal" market; but Ventimiglia is the place where profusion jars most, because hungry France is only five miles away.

Italy Has Rice

French visitors, accustomed to meagre stocks and interminable queueing, stare at Ventimiglia and rub their eyes unbelievingly. "We thought Italy lost the war. We thought we helped to win it," they say.

Here are specimen black market prices from Ventimiglia shops: Good quality, boneless meat 12s. 6d. lb.; Parmesan cheese £2 10s. lb.; rice 2s. lb.; bread 2s. 6d. lb.; popular brands of French and U.S. cigarettes 12s. 6d. and 17s. for 20.

These prices are calculated at the official rate of 400 lire to the pound sterling. The black market rate is 1,400 to the pound.

The wares of Ventimiglia are of little use to the Italian worker who has to keep a family on £13 or £14 a month, but wealthier Italians are revelling in pre-war luxury.

Daily Sketch 1946

FOR FUEL · ECONOMY

"One bag please..."

—and your "Courtier" will burn NIGHT and DAY for a week. Think of having no morning fires to light — no messing about with ashes — always a comfortable room to greet you on a cold morning—then decide upon a "Courtier" Stove.

Civilian supplies are still limited

The Courtier Stove
DAY AND NIGHT

Manufactured solely by

MITCHELL RUSSELL & CO LTD CHATTAN FOUNDRY · BONNYBRIDGE S C O T L A N D

'PENICILLIN No. 2' MAY BE CURE FOR T.B.

A NUMBER of new penicillin-type drugs, which may prove to be the long-sought cure for tuberculosis, are now being experimented with by British scientists.

Dr. J. H. Hartley Williams, Secretary-General of the National Association for the Prevention of Tuberculosis, said in London yesterday that he hoped the drugs would do for tuberculosis patients what penicillin had done in other directions.

Strong and well-planned measures would have to be taken to see that tuberculosis was not neglected, he said. One of the worst aspects of the problem was the shortage of houses.

There was not much prospect of a large number of patients getting new houses in the next few years, and practically nothing could be done for some people if they were crowded together with a tubercular patient among them.

The new drugs are—like penicillin—derived from moulds, writes a DAILY SKETCH correspondent. The initial experimental stages have been passed. Several of the drugs have inhibited the growth of the tubercle bacillus in animal tissue and in live animals.

Daily Sketch 1946

Surrendering coupons for bacon in Sainsbury's.

Bread Ration Cut May Now Be Avoided

By OUR POLITICAL CORRESPONDENT

THE end of the coal strike in the United States should make our food situation considerably easier. When Mr. Strachey made his statement last week he was clearly warning the country of what might happen if the strike were prolonged and the flow of supplies from America dried up altogether. With our reserves already below the safety margin, a cut in the bread ration would have been inevitable.

Unless some new labour trouble occurs, it should be possible to maintain the present ration. The Cabinet would like to do more. The question of doing away with bread rationing had already been discussed, I understand, and the Government was beginning to hope that this might be possible earlier than seemed likely a few months ago. There is, it is true, still a world shortage of cereals of something like 200,000,000 bushels, but Britain has always been in a better position to get her supplies than many other countries. The Cabinet was determined that bread rationing should not go on for a day longer than was absolutely necessary.

News from America suggests that wheat has been piling up at the ports; it remains to be seen how quickly these stocks can be shipped to Europe. There would seem to be no reason why Britain should not get her supplies in time, provided that we are not asked too high a price.

Observer
1946

" We can't seem to get him to shake hands —he insists on that low, sweeping bow "

Woman's Journal 1947

" SQUATTERS " MUST GO BY WINTER

AMENITIES TO BE PROVIDED

Pointing out that some of the Service camps taken over by "squatters" are really unfit for housing accommodation, the Ministry of Health announced yesterday that the camps must be cleared before winter conditions set in.

" That will no doubt very soon become evident to the 'squatters' themselves," the Ministry stated.

Local authorities have been told in the meantime to provide at once and without prejudice to the ultimate use of the camps proper sanitary accommodation, water and light. The various Government departments are reconsidering the use of the camps which have been occupied.

" Wherever possible," the statement said, " camps which have been occupied in considerable numbers and are at all suitable for housing purposes will be taken over by the local authority for housing."

Sunday Times 1946

" My Target will make Washing Day easier !"

" I'm putting all I can into Savings for a washing machine. What with having to do washing for the four of us you can understand what a boon it will be. Small wonder I'm keen on saving ! It's only natural, really, when you've got something worth saving up for — and who hasn't ? "

FOR YOUR OWN SAKE
SAVE

SAVINGS CERTIFICATES . DEFENCE BONDS

SAVINGS BANK DEPOSITS

BRITAIN'S TARGET ● £520 MILLION BY APRIL

Daily Express 1947

The man who popped into No. 11

Express Staff Reporter

EDMUND HAMILTON SUTCLIFFE, 23-year-old unemployed man who is serving a sentence of six months' imprisonment for stealing, is responsible for a shake-up in the Metropolitan Police Force.

It was revealed last night that when Sutcliffe, who lives at Glenfield-road, Betchworth, Surrey, was sentenced by Miss Sybil Campbell at Tower Bridge Magistrates' Court on August 8 one of the offences which he asked to be taken into consideration was the theft of a cigarette box and two letters from 11, Downing-street.

They were the property of Mr. Hugh Dalton, Chancellor of the Exchequer.

Sutcliffe, who stated at the court hearing that he had been drinking, was not able to tell the police how he got into No. 11. That is the fact which is disturbing Scotland Yard.

How was it done?

One way into Number 11.

Daily Worker 1947

Lights Up

Restaurants may now use electricity for lighting during the restricted hours.

Opening for the first time on a Sunday, 11 Birmingham British Restaurants will tomorrow provide meals for customers to take away.

Kitchen Note

Electric - cooking housewives should specially note that tomorrow they can use supplies—if available—from half an hour before the permitted time.

This is a "Sundays only" concession arising from the lowered industrial demand on that day.

ALUMINIUM HOUSES

EMERGENCY aluminium bungalows are rolling off the mills in increasingly large numbers. Though they are only intended as temporary homes, even owners of permanent houses will envy many of the features in them. These include a kitchen unit consisting of cooker, refrigerator, clothes boiler and sink with two draining boards—all in a row, so there will be no unnecessary steps here! Then there is a special broom cupboard and, farther away, on an outside wall, a larder and store cupboard. All this is in aluminium, from the outside walls and windows right through.

Woman's Journal 1947

Sash and bouffant bow of striped taffetas on a coat frock

A barrel shaped jacket and hobble skirt at Balenciaga

The new longer silhouette and pleated skirt at Christian Dior

à Paris

Longer Skirts

PARIS has thrown down the challenge for the return of elegance! Great discrimination is shown in the new fashions between informal and formal dressing. In the one the feeling is for loose, casual sweater tops of the most modern, and in the other the figure is outlined from shoulder to hip with the grace of bustle days.

A new star amongst the Paris *couturiers*, Christian Dior, has sprung into the lead. His most Parisian, most experimental, most delightful collection undoubtedly sets the shape of things ahead. And that shape—what will it be? Certainly longer skirts in all afternoon clothes. Paradoxically in evening dress, other than for the grand occasion, favour settles on the shorter full ballet length skirt.

There are two silhouettes. The hobble line with slanting shoulders—1912 in fact. A fashion difficult to wear, hard to illustrate, but with a chic that is most attractive when you see it well carried. The other choice is the fully pleated skirt reaching halfway down the calf, the small clipped waistline, slightly padded hip, and closely moulded bodice. Shoulders again less squared and smaller. This line is young, graceful and has great distinction.

It is satisfying to find the inclination is towards the feminine. Soft chiffons, tulles, rich taffetas, failles and satins sweep forth for evening wear once again. Afternoon dresses are made especially elegant by draping the material closely across the figure to balloon out at one side of the waist in a big chou, bow or drape and reveal the form divine on the other side. Pleated apron tops, slanting flounces and cross-over lines are other tendencies—in Paris.

Woman's Journal
1947

FOOD PRICE OFFENCES AT DIDCOT.

OVERCHARGES FOR POTATOES AND APPLES.

Fines for selling foodstuff in excess of the controlled price were imposed upon a number of traders at Didcot on Friday.

The Oxford Co-operative Society pleaded "Guilty" to offering potatoes for sale in excess of the maximum price at Didcot, and the manager of the shop, Ronald Webb, of 2, Council Houses, Blewbury, pleaded "Guilty" to a similar offence.

Mr. A. W. Taylor (prosecuting) said a purchaser of 6lb. of potatoes was charged 7½d. instead of 6½d.

For the defendants, it was stated that Webb had no price list. The greengrocery department at Oxford told him that the price was 1¼d. a lb., which was correct, but he was not told that 6lb. would be slightly cheaper.

The charge against Webb was dismissed on payment of 10s. costs, and the Society was fined £1, with £2 12s. 6d. costs.

Local Preacher Fined.

Cyril Moxon, of 90, Broadway, Didcot, pleaded "Not guilty" to a similar offence.

Mr. M. Huckins, a food inspector, of Faringdon, said Moxon was offering for sale Grade "B" Majestic potatoes at 1d. a lb. Moxon claimed that they were best-grade potatoes and that there was no reduction on 7lb., but the price for 7lb. should have been 5½d.

In evidence, Moxon said the potatoes were King Edward and he had paid for them as such. He produced a quantity of potatoes which he said were from the same bag, and said he had been selling them under the correct price and not over.

Recalled, the inspector gave it as his opinion that the potatoes produced were not King Edward.

On being told that he was fined £1, with £1 1s. costs, Moxon said he was a local preacher "and a man out for the truth."

"I don't like my name being put in the paper for people to read who don't know me," he said. "I will pay, but I don't like that."

Harwell Man's Protest.

John Gibb, Meadow View Farm, Harwell, was summoned for selling imported apples at an excess price at Didcot and for failing to exhibit a notice of sale of imported apples at Didcot on 7 February. He pleaded "Not guilty."

Mr. Huckins said that Gibb, when told he should exhibit a notice, put up a notice on which the apples were marked at 9d. a lb., and sold 2lb. to each of two women. When he told Gibb that the price should be 8½d. he said. "You are a snake. Once a policeman, always a policeman."

Gibb, in evidence, protested against the inspector letting him mark the apples at 9d. and then letting him "rob" people.

"I would rather give £5 to charity than be accused of robbing the public," he declared.

He thought the correct price of the apples was 9½d., and decided to charge 9d.

He was fined 5s. in each case. "There is £2," said Gibb, putting the money on the Clerk's table. "You can give the rest to charity."

North Berkshire Herald 1947

Stainless Steel at its brightest

MODEL K.U.210

1. Polished stainless steel sink and drainer in one piece.
2. Soap dishes in stainless steel.
3. Double panelled door on chromium continuous hinge.
4. Ribbed drainer sound deadened.
5. Silent drawers on roller bearings.
6. 2″ toe recess and front structure in stainless steel.

ANDREWS
Elizabeth Ann
KITCHEN UNITS

ANDREWS BROS (BRISTOL) LTD. WALCOT ST. BATH
TELEPHONE: BATH 60251 (5 LINES). TELEGRAMS STAINLESS, BATH

WHAT EXPORTS MEAN TO US

Britain imports over 12,000 tons of tea a month

but all our exports are paying for only three-quarters of everything we buy.

People sometimes ask 'Why send goods abroad when we could do with them at home?' Well, here is part of the answer. If we didn't export, how could we pay for our tea and tobacco? We can't produce them here and no one is going to give them to us for nothing. Do without? Perhaps, but we can't do without cotton, wool, rubber, copper and a hundred other things — including much of our food. We can live on credit for some time, but credit has its limits. *Only exports can pay for the imports we need.* We must go on increasing our exports.

FILL THE SHIPS AND WE SHALL FILL THE SHOPS

ISSUED BY THE BOARD OF TRADE

Only a Dancing Partner

I went dancing one night and a man asked me for a dance; I didn't know it very well, but I accepted and our steps fitted perfectly. He said I was a nice dancer and asked me to go for a cup of coffee but, as he was a stranger and I didn't want to leave my girl-friend, I refused. Every week now he asks me for several dances but has never again asked me to 'sit out' with him. Now I feel I'd like to get to know him better but don't want to make myself cheap.

● *You probably gave him the impression that you looked upon him as a dancing partner only, and now it is up to you to give him a gentle hint that you wouldn't turn down a second invitation to have a drink. It should be possible to indicate that you are thirsty without making yourself look cheap.*

Woman's Own
1948

"SNOOK" NEXT ON YOUR HOME MENU

BY OUR OWN CORRESPONDENT

A NEW variety of "stop-gap" fish is to be introduced into British homes. It is snoek (pronounced "snook"), a South African tinned fish, which, according to Mr. John Strachey, Food Minister, is long and thin and weighs about 18lb.

"I don't know what it tastes like," he confessed at a conference in London yesterday. "When we get it—which won't be until next spring, we shall have to organise a 'tasting' conference"

Experts describe it as "very good, nutritious and palatable."

Snoek is going to take the place of Portuguese sardines,

for which we cannot spare currency.

Ten million tons of tinned snoek is expected next year.

The Ministry has also arranged for supplies of Norwegian tinned brisling.

Early next month the housewife will, too, be able to buy tinned Russian salmon and crab.

BABIES' FOOD

Because milk-based baby food, which is scarce, has been consumed by adults, the Ministry has, from to-day, made it an offence to sell such food except on production of the green ration book of a child of two or under. Retailers are instructed to mark the O coupon on page 13 of the book.

Manufacture of baby food and national dried milk will be maintained during the winter.

There is no question of the Ministry indulging in direct marketing of vegetables. The new Fruit and Vegetable (Marketing and Distribution) Organisation will only make arrangements through local authorities for market space to be made available for that purpose.

JAM

The preserves ration will be increased from 1lb to 2lb for the four-week period beginning next Sunday. The additional 1lb will consist mainly of plum jam. Consumers will not be allowed to take additional sugar instead of the additional preserves.

Asked about prospects of potato supplies and the possibility of rationing, Mr. Strachey said he could not deal in advance with rumours.

"It is not fully known yet," he added. "The main crop has not been lifted."

Birmingham Gazette 1947

Woman's Journal
1947

"Now that I can talk there are a few things I want to get off my chest"

The Times
1948

TO-DAY'S SILVER WEDDING CELEBRATIONS

◆

THANKSGIVING AT ST. PAUL'S: 22-MILE DRIVE THROUGH LONDON

BROADCAST BY THE KING AND QUEEN

The King and Queen returned from Windsor to Buckingham Palace last evening in readiness for to-day's celebrations of their silver wedding anniversary.

The flag-decked route along which their Majesties will drive this morning for the thanksgiving service at St. Paul's attracted many sightseers in the bright sunshine yesterday. If it is fine—and fair or fine weather is forecast—the carriages of the royal procession will be open.

The King and Queen will broadcast to-night after a drive of nearly 22 miles through the streets of the capital.

Princess loved 'penny dreadful'

—AND SISTER INKED HER CURLS

Express Staff Reporter: New York, Thursday

PRINCESS MARGARET once had a taste for "penny dreadfuls." So says her former governess, Marion Crawford, in the first instalment of her book, "The Little Princesses," published here.

The penny dreadful, "a thumbed and torn tale of blood and pirates," she found in an old box at Glamis Castle. It was treasured as "the one book that was all her own."

Both Princesses, Miss Crawford tells readers of the Lady's Home Journal, were fond of Barrie's "Peter Pan," and they liked Lamb's "Tales from Shakespeare," but "Alice in Wonderland" was never asked for. ("They thought it rather stupid.")

Princess Elizabeth's French tutor was an elderly mademoiselle:

"One day Lilibet, goaded by boredom, picked up an ornamental silver inkpot and placed it upside down on her own head.

"She sat there, with ink trickling down her face, and slowly dyeing her golden curls. I never really got to the bottom of what happened."

In the Tube

Miss Crawford writes about the time the Princesses rode in London's Tube.

Lilibet, when she was tiny, had been watching people stream out of the station near her Hyde Park Corner home. "What fun it must be to ride on those trains," she said.

They travelled four stations— now a 2½d. ride—to Tottenham Court-road.

On the escalators Margaret's hand tightened on Crawfie's. Nobody noticed the Duke of York's children.

Crawfie, Ayrshire born, spent 17 years as governess to the Princesses.

Her book may be made into a film.

Daily Express 1949

The Bathless

FORTY-SIX per cent. of the houses in Britain (England, Scotland, and Wales) have no bathrooms, according to Minister of Works Charles Key. As the Ministry of Health consider that there are about 12,000,000 dwellings in Britain, it means that about 5,520,000 dwellings are bathless in this modern atomic age. However, all dwellings built today are required by the Ministry of Health to have bathrooms. Other figures with an indirect bearing on baths show that 44 per cent. of British households have no piped water supply, and that 25 per cent. have to rely on the old-fashioned copper for heating domestic water.

The average daily water consumption per person is 30 gallons in the country, according to figures issued by the British Waterworks Association, while Londoners consume an average of 52 gallons every day. The average bather uses from 25 to 35 gallons in his bath, compared with the 15 gallons of the war-time 5-inch bath.

Leader 1948

A fine bird's-eye tweed makes this brown Harella suit with a slim, new elegance. The back of the jacket is cut to flare below the waist, skirt is straight. About £5 12s. 6d.

Woman's Own 1948

Beverley Nichols

"**What do you do if a barrow boy calls you 'dearie'—smile back at him, or kick up a fuss?**"

"I WON'T be called 'ducks'," she cried angrily. "It's revolting!"

I suggested that it was kindly meant.

"And after that . . . *dearie!* It makes me feel like hitting people!"

With which she flounced out of the room, leaving behind her a trail of expensive perfume, and an echo of the swish of a very New Look skirt.

I hasten to say that it was not I who had aroused the lady's indignation by these terms of endearment. It was a barrow boy, or rather two barrow boys. The first was selling tomatoes. She was in her car, near Covent Garden, and she got out to buy a couple of pounds.

"There you are, 'ducks'," said the barrow boy as he handed her the parcel. (She was a very pretty lady.)

She gave him 'a look,' as they say, and passed on. It was then that she saw the lilies on the other side of the road. And when she had bought a bunch, the barrow boy said, "Mind you cut the ends off the stalks when you get home, dearie."

Which was just too much for her. She felt outraged, humiliated. It positively spoiled her luncheon. The cheek of people—the damned cheek!

And quite a number of pretty ladies in these days are feeling the same way.

Now, I am as fussy as anybody else about nice manners and proper discipline. I think that schoolboys should say 'Sir' to their masters, and that soldiers should salute smartly, and if I am in a restaurant I think I'm entitled to be treated as though I were welcome and not—as in some restaurants—as though I had slunk in to pinch the milk from the kitchen cat.

No insult

BUT I do most violently disagree with, and disapprove of, the young lady who kicked up such a fuss about being called 'ducks' and 'dearie.'

It seems to me more than a little vulgar on *her* part. A woman who is 'sure of her position'—(to use that unpleasantly snobbish phrase)—has no need to be 'madam'd and 'milady'd,' any more than she needs to wear the family jewels in order to convey an air of distinction. A really well-bred woman remains well-bred even when she is standing in a queue, clad in an old mackintosh.

To her, 'ducks' and 'dearie' are not insults; they are pleasant, warm, rather cosy words. Not so very long ago, at times when it was extra cold and dark in the shelter, and when the bombs were falling just a shade too close, there was something very comforting in the sound of such words. Like the thick china cups of strong, over-sweet tea that some kindly old woman always seemed to be able to produce.

But there is another side to it, a much more serious and important side.

The world—to put it very mildly indeed—is in a state of some upheaval. Centuries of privilege are being swept aside overnight, whole classes are being thrown on the scrap-heap, without so much as a by-your-leave. In short, revolution is in the air.

There seems no reason to suppose that we shall ever have a revolution in this country—in the sense of aristocrats hung on lamp-posts, tumbrils rattling through the streets, and castles going up in flames. But we are definitely—(and I think desirably)—moving in the direction of a classless society. And if *that* revolution is going to be accomplished smoothly, and with a minimum of unpleasantness, then the more 'ducks' and 'dearies,' the better.

Woman's Own
1948

AN EMPTY TIN
—costs £500

An empty condensed milk tin thrown down a manhole, blocked the whole drainage system at Amersham, Bucks, it was stated at the council meeting yesterday. It cost more than £500 to repair—borne by ratepayers.

Daily Express
1949

Here is the latest in 'Pyrex' BRAND streamlined casseroles

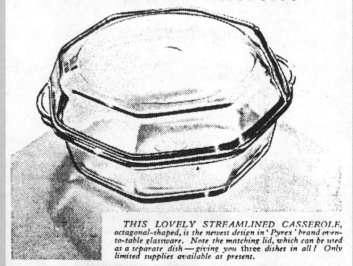

THIS LOVELY STREAMLINED CASSEROLE, octagonal-shaped, is the newest design in 'Pyrex' brand oven-to-table glassware. Note the matching lid, which can be used as a separate dish — giving you three dishes in all! Only limited supplies available at present.

These **9** advantages with 'Pyrex' brand oven-to-table glassware

- Cooks food evenly all through
- Preserves the natural goodness of the food
- Food doesn't get dried up in the oven
- Food tastes better
- Saves washing-up of saucepans
- No waste from dishing-up
- Saves fuel
- Looks lovely on the table
- Keeps food hot at table.

REGD. TRADE MARK **'PYREX'** BRAND **OVEN-TO-TABLE GLASSWARE**

All 'Pyrex' brand ovenware carries a 12 months' free replacement guarantee against breakage by oven-heat. It is made by James A. Jobling & Co. Ltd., Wear Glass Works, Sunderland.

The end of clothes rationing, March 1949.

D. H. Lawrence as I Knew Him

By LADY CYNTHIA ASQUITH

THE first time I ever saw D. H. Lawrence was when Sir Edward Marsh brought him to see my husband and me while we were staying at Kingsgate. Except that he was a poet with a tendency to consumption, we at that time knew nothing whatever about Lawrence; but the moment a slender lithe figure stepped lightly into the room, we both realised, almost with the shock of a collision, that something new and startling had come into our lives.

I do not believe anyone could have been in Lawrence's presence for two minutes without being struck by his difference from other people. It was not a difference of degree, but of kind. Some electric, elemental quality gave him a flickering radiance. You could see that he was preternaturally sensitive and abnormally alive. With his broad, slightly jutting brow and clear, sensitive eyes—very, very wide apart—he looked half faun, half prophet, and very young. He had not yet grown his tawny red beard. He wasted no time—he never did—on small talk, but dived with a clean plunge into some subject that interested him, and he could not fail to make it interest everyone else. Words welled out of him. He spoke in flashing phrases, at times colloquially, almost challengingly so, but often with a startling beauty of utterance. One moment he was lyrically, contagiously joyous; the next sardonic—gibing.

Listener 1949

2oz BIRDS HOLD UP' BIG BEN

Express Staff Reporter

BIG BEN ran nearly five minutes slow last night, because of a flock of starlings.

They flew across from St. James's Park just before 8.45. Then B.B.C. engineers faded out their European Services programme to bring in the chimes on the quarter hour.

But nothing happened.

The starlings were covering the clock's faces and hands. And they were probably in the works.

A starling, on average, weighs 2oz. But their combined weight on the hands and other parts was enough to upset the six-hundredweight pendulum.

Then the clock struck. The noise frightened the starlings and they flew away. Big Ben was put right.

Daily Express **1949**

WHAT'S NEW . . .

Give your home a CHRISTMAS PRESENT

A boon by day and a blessing by night is an apt description of the Sterofeed. Baby's bottle can be prepared in advance and when the 6 o'clock feed is due, all you have to do is to plug it into your bedside lamp and in five minutes the milk is the right temperature. The Sterofeed costs 57s. 6d. and is on sale at most chemists, but if you cannot trace one, Sangers, 258 Euston Road, London, N.W.1, will put you in touch with your nearest stockist.

Cooking dinner in a matter of minutes is possible with a Prestige Pressure Cooker. Three separate foods can be cooked at once by using the aluminium separators. No dishing up is necessary, as a spare lid transforms the cooker into a handsome addition to your dinner table. Priced at 72s. 6d., it makes an ideal Christmas present for a busy housewife. They are on sale at Wylie Hills, Glasgow; D. Evans, Swansea; John Walsh, Sheffield; Brights of Bristol, but The Platers and Stampers, Ltd., Derby, will put you in touch with your nearest retailer.

Specially designed for a bachelor girl or a mother with a baby, this miniature clothes line extends to a length of 30 ft. or less if you wish. It costs about 5s. 3d., and it can be bought in most hardware stores throughout the country, but Taylor Law & Co., Ltd., Rufford Road, Stourbridge, Worcs, will put you in touch with your nearest retailer if you fail to get one locally.

If you enjoy this game as much as we did you will certainly get your 7s. 4d. worth from it! It is called Tic-Tac, and is played with six or less cardboard horses on strings, with the floor as the racecourse. Ideal for Christmas parties, it is available from most toyshops, or by post from F. F. Games, Ltd., Cleeve Road, Goring-on-Thames, Oxon. If ordered by post, please enclose 2d. extra to cover cost of postage.

Daily Graphic
1950

Enough soap for all

Unless there is an abnormal demand when soap is derationed at the end of the week, supplies are expected to be adequate.

Meat ration up in three stages—and 3d. a lb. more

From Our Parliamentary Correspondent, JUSTIN LONG

LARGER meat rations in three fortnightly stages beginning on July 22 at increased prices were announced by Mr. Maurice Webb, the Food Minister, in the House of Commons last night. He also indicated that a forecast he made last week when he said the meat ration would be about double its present size by the end of August, would be implemented by still further increases not yet announced.

This is the buying guide for housewives and caterers, who will also get proportionately more:—

JULY 22.—The existing 10d. ration will go up to about 1s. at present prices, but it will cost 1s. 2d. because the retail price of meat will then be increased by an average of 3d. a lb. The extra ration will be entirely carcase meat.

AUGUST 5.—A second increase will give a meat ration equivalent to about 1s. 2½d. worth a week, but at the new prices it will cost about 1s. 5d. a week.

AUGUST 19.—A third increase to at least 1s. 7d. worth a week is expected. This would be equivalent to 1s. 4d. worth at present prices.

The Minister said the increased prices were necessary because of the higher cost of Argentine meat and other increases to our Dominion and home farmers.

Yorkshire Post 1951

" You're absolutely right, my dear. Now show me how much easier it would be if I had a system "

Woman 1950

NATIONAL RADIO EXHIBITION
By G. HOWARD-SORRELL

Gramophone 1951

My comments last month regarding Moving Coil pick-ups at the show, brought a phone call from **Murphy**, who pointed out that their A172R uses a moving coil pick-up for SP whereas the LP unit is moving iron. Rather a case of hiding a light under a bushel as the leaflet describing this excellent reproducer only mentions this important feature in parenthesis on the back page. Among the range of motors, autochangers and gramophone players shown on the **Collaro** stand was a new pick-up fitted with two needles for SP and LP reproduction, which eliminates the need for changing the head for the two types of discs. There were no less than six different models of the popular "Microgram" on show, three suitable for single speed and three for dual speed discs. **Connoisseur** where recording and reproduction equipment were shown, again exhibited their gramophone motors—famous for steady running with heavy non-ferrous turntables. The pick-up range continues unchanged from last year.

THE CENSUS

ON Sunday next, April 8, a census will be taken of the population in the United Kingdom. The "head of each household"—a phrase that has quite a Biblical flavour, especially as Passover approaches—will be required to record in the schedules that have been distributed information about everybody present in the house at midnight. This census will be carried out in a typically British manner—not by inquisition or cross-questioning, but by getting ordinary people to set down in the privacy of their own homes a few simple facts about themselves. A personal responsibility therefore rests upon every citizen to ensure the successful working of this essentially democratic institution. Owing to the war, it is 20 years since the last census was taken. The simple and straightforward particulars which are now asked are all necessary in order to have facts and figures which are absolutely vital for the common good. At the same time it should be emphasised that all the information given in the schedules must by law be treated as strictly confidential, and that there are very severe penalties for the improper disclosure of any particulars. The personal details derived from the returns will be used in complete and absolute confidence for statistical purposes only, and never in any circumstances to the detriment of the individual concerned. This fundamental principle of the British census must be specially appreciated by Jewish citizens, who cannot be unmindful how the enemies and persecutors of Jewry in other countries have exploited census returns for their own nefarious purposes. In keeping with British practice, no question is asked about religion.

Jewish Chronicle 1951

Reveille 1951

Braces sales are slipping

FALLING sales in braces and ties are worrying a section of the wholesale textile trade.

At a recent meeting of the Wholesale Textile Association it was reported that a committee was to meet the Tie Manufacturers' Association to discuss how to improve sales in medium-priced and cheaper ties.

Self-supporting

The committee was also making an approach to the Belt and Brace Manufacturers' Association following reports of falling sales in accessories.

Said the secretary of the Wholesale Textile Association, Mr. W. T. Caves:

"There is a tendency among the public to copy the American styles of self-supporting garments.

"Some manufacturers and wholesalers are looking askance at the trend, because if it grows it will have a detrimental effect on that part of the trade."

Woman's World 1952

GARDENING WITH THE GUBBINS

A tip from Dad—
PROTECT THE BUDS OF RED CURRANTS AND GOOSEBERRIES FROM BIRDS WITH BLACK COTTON AS SHOWN

Mum says—
COVER CLUMPS OF VIOLETS WITH CLOCHES. IT WILL HELP TO BRING THEM ALONG EARLIER

Jack and Jill—
HAVE REMOVED DECAYING LEAVES FROM PRIMROSES SO THAT THEY DO NOT HARBOUR PESTS

SMOKE LESS

£25 for holidays

CLAMP ON HIRE PURCHASE

Daily Express
1952

ONE THIRD DOWN AND 18 MONTHS TO PAY

MR. R. A. BUTLER, Chancellor of the Exchequer, last night abruptly ended the "Something for nothing" era and told Britain that she must turn to the Empire to solve her problems. "Pay your way or perish," was his theme.

The cuts announced in Parliament last night amount to an emergency operation. The real cure for Britain, said Mr. Butler, is development of the Commonwealth's vast resources. Meanwhile this is the treatment :—

THEY—the Government, that is—will cut the Civil Service and Whitehall's information services.

YOU will have to pay for wigs, teeth, and pills. You will have to smoke less. Your "comforts" like cars, refrigerators, and television sets will be heavily cut—and the "never-never" system of buying them will get a time-limit. Your money for a holiday abroad goes down to £25.

Mr. Butler will bring in his Budget on March 4—before the end of the financial year, March 31. That has not been done since 1900.

DOES it surprise you to know that 60 Russians who bought a fourpenny form and filled it up have become British this year?

It cost each of them a little more than that before becoming one of us, but not enough to discourage any determined would-be Briton.

The Government promise of an independent inquiry into the cure-by-kindness methods of Broadmoor prompts a wider question : "Are the British, besides being the most civilised people the world has ever known, also too soft-hearted for their own good?"

In particular : "Is it too easy to become British?"

Look at the figures. In the first quarter of the year more than 800 aliens were granted certificates of naturalisation.

Since the end of the war in Europe more than 58,000 have sworn the oath of allegiance to the Crown, and have been lost among the mass of Britons.

Most of them, so far as anyone knows, have settled down among us to lead useful, honest lives.

'Wrong 'un'

BUT, now and then, a "wrong 'un" is given the blessing of a British passport and all the rights and privileges which we take for granted.

Their discovery casts doubt upon the usefulness of the fourpenny form and the security check it involves.

Daily Express
1952

WHY DO WOMEN SMOKE?

THREE unnamed women smokers will be questioned by a psychologist in a B.B.C. "Woman's Hour" programme a fortnight today to find out why they started smoking. They will be anonymous, a B.B.C. official said yesterday, because "the reasons why women begin smoking are often closely linked with emotional upset and it may be necessary to ask them very personal questions." Later the psychologist and a doctor will discuss their findings on the air.

Daily Express
1952

THEY PUT YEARS ON YOU
Liverpool's Hospital For The Healthy

VITAL statistics tell us that man is living longer, but do we all live as long as we should, or do many of us die too soon? There are people who would have it that we die when our time is due; that there is more to living and dying than physical health or lack of it.

There is, however, an organisation in Liverpool—it is the only one in this country—holding very

---

By HAROLD ARMSTRONG

---

different views. It also considers it is proving them.

This is the Liverpool Institute of Research for the Prevention of Disease. It has a somewhat dry-sounding title, and the years of war that came shortly after its formation in 1938 seem to have obscured much of its work from the public eye.

35 To 40

But it appears to me that it is time more people knew something about this institute in Liverpool's Grove Street. If the beliefs of Dr. I. Harris, its honorary director, are correct, it might help them to live much longer, and alter the vital statistics still more.

First, Dr. Harris maintains that the majority of illnesses which cripple or kill people over 40 years old usually take root, ten, 20 or 30 years before the victim realises there is anything wrong. Between 35 and 40 is the age when the seeds are largely sown.

An apparently healthy man

collapses and dies from heart failure; this is the culmination of a disease that has been slowly but surely damaging the heart for a long time.

A blood vessel breaks in the brain, and either kills outright or paralyses; the walls of the vessel have been corroding for years. These, and other diseases concerning high blood pressure, brain, kidney and the like, have one characteristic in common.

During the years in which they grow and develop they can remain unrecognised and untreated. Normally, it is only when they have progressed to a certain stage that efforts are made to prevent the often fatal results.

Heredity

So maintains Dr. I. Harris, himself a heart specialist. "A worn-out heart, a worn-out blood vessel cannot be made normal again.

"I fear the public do not often realise the position, and what makes it so poignant is that the fault is not in their stars, but in themselves," he says.

He agrees that heredity plays a part in some instances, and that there are in others some factors beyond control, but in the main the normal span of life is shortened by abnormal wear and tear.

How then can all this be avoided? The institute has been created to reduce abnormal wear and tear to a minimum. Here every organ of the voluntary patient is submitted to a searching examination twice a year.

Exact requirements, weaknesses, and peculiarities of each individual are ascertained, and a code of living suggested which will prevent disease taking root.

This institute is not intended to deal with disease. It might, indeed, be called a hospital for the healthy. When disease is detected, however, it can be dealt with by the patient's own medical attendant. Finding the first sign is the important factor.

Full Check

Carried on voluntarily, the institute is available for any person of 35 and over, but it is not a hospital for the deserving poor. Those availing themselves of its services pay what they feel these are worth.

Naturally, the examination has to be very thorough. Apart from the usual physician's record of history; height, weight, chest and abdominal measurements are taken; blood pressure and pulse recorded.

There are tests for non-protein nitrogen in the blood, and a haemoglobin test is performed.

Cases are examined by physician, surgeon, eye specialist, laryngologist, by those interested in cancer investigation, and by a radiologist.

Analysed

To-day there are between 500 and 600 people on the institute's books. They include doctors, solicitors, architects and other professional people—all of the class that tends most to feel the strain of modern life — the middle-class.

In submitting people to searching examination by a team of specialists, it is claimed that conditions such as cancer and other diseases are bound to be discovered at a much earlier stage than would otherwise be possible; a stage at which treatment has some chance.

Liverpool Echo 1952

First plan to sell council houses

NEWS CHRONICLE REPORTER

News Chronicle
1951

CHESTER is the first town in Britain to hand in plans to Whitehall for the sale of council houses.

Following the new Housing Minister's policy statement, the city council have submitted detailed proposals for the sale of pre-war council houses at prices ranging from £553 to £1,027 apiece.

The Ministry is considering the scheme, I was told yesterday, but the safeguards laid down by Mr. Harold Macmillan will involve detailed inquiry on present market value, the condition of the houses and the status of prospective purchasers.

At a recent Press conference Mr. Macmillan was asked to define prices at which council houses would be sold by local authorities—whether at market value or at sitting tenants' rates—and replied that steps would be taken to ensure that the price was reasonable and fair.

305 OUT OF 326 WOMEN. The great Whiteness Test on washing powders was carried out in London by an impartial authority, the Good Housekeeping Institute. 305 out of 326 women voted the Persil-washed towel the whitest of all!

PERSIL WINS GREAT WASH-DAY WHITENESS TEST!

6 FAMOUS WASHING POWDERS ON TRIAL

MORE than 300 housewives were recently invited to judge a great wash-day whiteness test.

The well-known Good Housekeeping Institute in London carried out the test. They took 6 new white tea-towels, soiled them all equally, then washed them. Six famous washing powders—both well-tried and new—were used, a different one for each towel. The manufacturer's instructions on the packet were carefully followed in each case.

Later, the towels were laid out for inspection.

How the Voting Went

One at a time, the housewives filed past, and each was asked to pick out

> 326 Housewives
> act as judges

the whitest towel. None of the women knew which washing powders had been used. The result? 305 out of the 326 voted for the Persil-washed towel!

Yes, Persil washes whiter—you can *see* it does!

And the secret? Persil's millions of tiny oxygen bubbles! They shift the dirt out as nothing else can. Persil-washed things are white because they're clean.

And don't forget—gentle Persil suds make your coloureds and fine things *brighter, fresher . . .* your woollens *softer.*

Yes, Persil is kind to ALL the wash—and to your hands! You can *feel* it is!

PERSIL washes whiter!

Tiverton Gazette
1952

NATIONAL APPEAL LAUNCHED

THE Lord-Lieutenant of Devon, Earl Fortescue, and the Lord-Lieutenant of Somerset, Lord Hylton, have launched a North Devon and West Somerset Relief Appeal. They write:

"We invite not only the people of the Westcountry, but everyone who has known and loved Lynmouth and the quiet villages of North Devon and West Somerset, which have suffered so grievously in this disaster, to contribute to a fund for the relief of all who have suffered.

"These villages have been overwhelmed by a tragedy terrible in its suddenness and completeness. Homes have been swept away with whole families. Others are bereaved, or homeless, or have nothing left. In the darkness of a single night part of the town of Lynmouth itself has disappeared for ever.

THE British Commonwealth stood still when its young Queen spoke for the first time on Christmas Day to each of the many millions in her great family.

In London and the big towns of Britain no one moved out of doors. The streets were empty, desolate. The villages were silent.

EVERYONE WHO COULD BE WAS WITHIN EARSHOT OF A RADIO SET TO LISTEN TO THE YOUNG MOTHER WHO IS THE SYMBOLIC HEAD OF ALL THEIR ACTIONS.

In Britain the silence seemed deeper even than in the Two Minutes Silence on November 11, which for so long has been the most solemn moment in the year.

Daily Graphic
1953

Daily Express 1952

HUSBAND MANIA

Wives rush in to tell how men annoy

By CHAPMAN PINCHER

HUSBANDS, too, are afflicted with near-pathological habits so irritating that they cause chronic domestic disturbance, 600 angry wives complain today.

These women, stung by my last week's list of feminine failings, have reported on the masculine maladjustments which annoy them most.

From their long list I select 20 which seem to be the most prevalent :—

Gastro Energitis.—Patient appears to be in a coma until a meal is announced, whereupon he immediately leaps to his feet and rushes off to finish a half-done job.

Pool-iomyelitis.—Attacks its victim first post on Monday morning, giving rise to a high fever by mid-week, and reaching the "crisis" stage by Saturday, evening, when entire household is compelled to silence during the reading of the sports results. In 999 cases out of 1,000, deep depression follows.

Dishpepsia.—A complaint which gives the patient such overwhelming self-satisfaction from giving his wife a hand with the dishes that he considers himself automatically absolved from any other jobs.

Ashtigmatism

So like a man . . .

Housemaid's Knee.—The one not reserved for his typist.

Posterior Fire-brositis.—A winter complaint in which the victim appears to feel the cold in only one part of his anatomy.

Lowbar Pneumonia.—Internal dampness due to exposure to too many draughts in low pubs.

Not-sleeping Sickness.—A morbid desire to sleep in trains and armchairs, accompanied by a delusion that the patient " only shut his eyes for a moment."

Collar-Blindness.—The patient seems unable to see things which have been put in the proper place, in particular, collars, socks and handkerchiefs.

Skirtsophrenia.—Obsession with hemlines, waistlines, and plunging necklines.

Club Foot.—An impelling irritation of the feet, necessitating frequent absence for treatment at a club bar.

Manner-allergy.—The patient divests himself of his good manners along with his overcoat when entering his own home.

Posterior fire-brositis

Delusion of Man-deur.

Fish prices: a reply to housewives

Losses on trawling

From our Hull staff

Housewives may become angry when they read that fish is being sold on the quaysides at Hull and Grimsby for 4d. a lb. and yet find their fishmonger is charging 1s. 6d. or more for a fillet of cod.

Leading members of the fishing industries of the two ports went to great trouble yesterday to explain to a Press conference at St. Andrew's fish dock, Hull, that nobody in the fish business was making colossal profits.

Last year Hull trawler owners with 20 fleets ranging from one to 25 vessels lost an aggregate of £590,000, said Mr. Douglas Dunn, head of the Economic Investigation Department of the Hull trawling industry.

The present glut of fish, combined with an unaccountable drop in demand, meant that many trawlers, without allowing for depreciation or interest on capital, were not covering the expenses of their trip.

Yorkshire Post 1953

The Background To Liverpool's 'Colour' Problem

Liverpool Echo
1952

AMONG the 800,000 population of Liverpool live 18,000 coloured people, a community which has grown over the years and now presents an extremely difficult problem.

Are these people to be made part of the social fabric of the city—or are they to be segregated? The decision has to be made, for it is not one that can be left to time.

In South Africa the colour question, aggravated by internal politics has assumed ugly proportions. In the Southern United States of America, despite tremendous effort by social organisations, the colour bar is still prominent.

Criticism is often levelled, justifiably or otherwise, at these countries for their attitude to the negro. But Britain herself has to give serious thought to the question.

Liverpool, more than any other provincial centre, has been for many years the focal point of research and discussion on "colour-consciousness."

Investigations

It is hoped in the very near future that proposals will go before the City Council "that greater interest should be taken in the welfare of coloured people in Liverpool."

The 18,000 coloured population includes Africans, West Indians, Chinese, Indians, Arabs, Malayans, and other groups.

No exact figures can be given. Neither the Colonial Office nor the Home Office keep any record, for instance, of the large numbers who arrive here from Africa and the West Indies. They are British subjects and travel on British passports.

Taking the lowest estimate only half are recent migrants—the others are Liverpool-born citizens. The first group comprises about 2,350 Africans, 600 West Indians, and 50 from other colonies.

TV worried by 'horror' serial

By JAMES THOMAS

SQUEAMISH viewers and children are being warned by the B.B.C. not to watch Saturday's last instalment of the TV rocket ship serial "The Quatermass Experiment." The reason: It is too "horrific."

And now TV is worried that there may be an outcry from people who grew interested in the serial, particularly from parents whose children are now advised not to follow it through.

The 'Thing'

TV said yesterday: It was a mistake not to have announced the trend of things at the beginning. We are sorry we realised it a bit late."

The serial began to reach the "horrific" stage two weeks ago when the survivor of a trio of space explorers began to grow cactus out of his hand.

Last Saturday the man developed into a "thing" which was seen to turn vegetable. That instalment carried a "not suitable for children" warning.

News Chronicle
1953

Daily Mail
1953

New TV tube is 27 inches —at £200 a set

Daily Mail Science Reporter J. STUBBS WALKER

THE biggest television tube ever put on the market in Britain, giving a direct-viewing picture measuring 27in. from corner to corner is to be shown for the first time at the National Television and Radio Show at Earls Court, London, tomorrow.

The new viewing tube was announced as a last-minute surprise last night by the Pye organisation. It is six inches bigger than the previous largest tube in commercial use and gives a picture about 24in. wide.

Price of the tube will not be announced until tomorrow, but it is likely to be not far short of £45, including purchase tax, and will be so valuable that the firm is to institute a scheme for repairing the tubes in the event of failure.

The new Pye receiver to use the giant tube has not yet been officially announced but the indications are that it will cost more than £200.

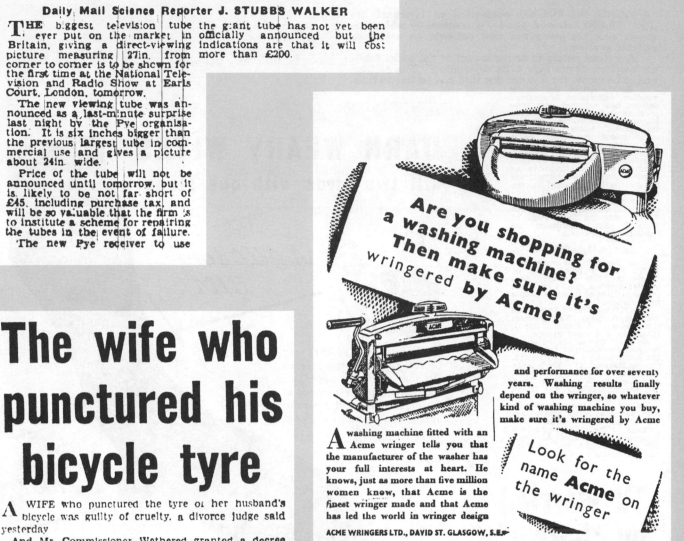

Are you shopping for a washing machine? Then make sure it's wringered by Acme!

A washing machine fitted with an Acme wringer tells you that the manufacturer of the washer has your full interests at heart. He knows, just as more than five million women know, that Acme is the finest wringer made and that Acme has led the world in wringer design and performance for over seventy years. Washing results finally depend on the wringer, so whatever kind of washing machine you buy, make sure it's wringered by Acme

Look for the name **Acme** on the wringer

ACME WRINGERS LTD., DAVID ST. GLASGOW, S.E.

The wife who punctured his bicycle tyre

A WIFE who punctured the tyre of her husband's bicycle was guilty of cruelty, a divorce judge said yesterday

And Mr. Commissioner Wethered granted a decree nisi at Bristol to Ronald Alfred Scaddig, of Park-close, Clifton, Bristol, against his wife Wilhelmina Scaddig, with the comment: "Love has died completely between them."

In 1952, six years after the couple were married, "some very curious things happened" in their life together, said the commissioner.

Repaired It—15 Times

The wife on various pretexts punctured her husband's bicycle tyre. In all there were fifteen repaired punctures in the inner tube which was produced in court. The wife admitted responsibility in two cases.

In the first case, he said, she threatened to puncture the tyre after an argument over housekeeping money, and her husband replied: "You wouldn't dare."

The second occasion followed an accident to her husband on an icy road. She claimed she had punctured the tyre so that he could not use the bicycle and risk having another accident.

Daily Mirror
1953

Fog blanket over England: Traffic halted

DENSE fog came down over much of England to-day, delaying road traffic, holding up trains and river traffic, and completely stopping the air lines.

The Air Ministry forecast gave little hope of improvement. Fog is expected to develop widely to-night, becoming dense in many places, and clearing only very slowly to-morrow.

VISIBILITY A FEW FEET

In many parts of the north visibility was down to 10 yards, in London it varied between 30 and 100 yards, and near the Surrey—Sussex borders it was only a few feet.

Northern cities and towns were plunged into gloom, street lighting was switched on, and neon signs pierced the darkness.

In London National Health Service smog masks were in the shops, but there was no rush to buy them.

*Lancashire
Evening Post*
1953

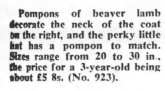

Pompons of beaver lamb decorate the neck of the coat on the right, and the perky little hat has a pompon to match. Sizes range from 20 to 30 in., the price for a 3-year-old being about £5 8s. (No. 923).

Buttons are not always the easiest things to manage on a wriggling toddler; here is the answer—a zip at the back of the coat. The front is smocked and has a little Peter Pan collar with a tiny edging of a contrasting colour. The bonnet has a face-framing frill of crêpe de chine below the brim. The new "snugglies," in which the seat has a lining of batiste, complete the set, which costs from around £5 for sizes 14, 16 and 18 in. Bonnet and coat can be had without the leggings (No. 911).

Nursery World 1953

It's fun to own a Hohner

easy to play with the FREE 5-minute tutor

Give a Hohner for Christmas and give pleasure throughout the year!

Everyone enjoys a tune — and with a Hohner harmonica you've a tune in your pocket every day of the year. Hohners are *real* musical instruments — played by the stars of radio and TV. It's a happy Christmas for everyone if you pop a Hohner in the children's stocking and hang a few on the tree for the grown-ups. There are many popular models at prices from 2/6 to 35/9, and more advanced self-tutors by Tommy Reilly and other harmonica experts at 1/- and 2/- from all music dealers.

HOHNER HARMONICAS
AND ACCORDIONS
M. HOHNER LTD., 9 FARRINGDON ROAD, LONDON, E.C.1

Daily Mail
1954

TV WEATHER —NEW STYLE

Wives are told: Put washing out early

Townswoman 1954

The Costly Egg

" It would be a patriotic gesture, if something could be done to bring the nutritious egg, which is so important a part of our diet, within the reach of all consumers," said Mrs. G. A. Scholey, Vice-Chairman of the Chesterfield and Sheffield Federation, when she spoke from "The Consumer's Angle" at the Conference of the Poultry Farmers' Association of Great Britain held at Chesterfield.

" How many people today," she asked, " are able to have an egg with their bacon every morning ? I find it's more the usual procedure to scramble two eggs and share them out to four persons." Since November, when the Conference was held, the price of eggs has fallen, but not, of course, to the point where eggs can be cooked and used *ad lib*, than which, said Mrs. Scholey, "there is nothing a housewife enjoys more."

Mr. GEORGE COWLING describes the path of a rain belt across Britain. This is how viewers saw him with his chart in television's new-style weather forecasts which opened last night.

Mr. Cowling, of the Meteorological Office, had a chatty way of dealing with the weather " If you didn't get your washing dried today," he told housewives, "get it out early tomorrow."

But he had good news about tomorrow—F.A. Cup replay day. " We don't expect any frost, though there may be some rain."

Herald 1954

End of tell-tale kisses

THEY'VE found it at last . . . a really kissproof lipstick writes WINIFRED MUNDAY. It is a Scandinavian idea. In London yesterday I watched a model try it out on a cigarette and coffee cup. Not a trace of red on either. Then she gave it the severest test of all. She planted a firm kiss on the cheek of Armand Hauge, managing director of the firm which is marketing the lipstick in England. *Not a smudge.*

It tried it myself and no amount of kissing, tea drinking, or eating would remove a smear. The secret of the new formula lies in the soluble dyes which merge with the skin.

Too Many Models?

ARE manufacturers defeating their own ends by the rapidity with which one improved model follows on another ? The housewife may well hesitate to lay out twenty or more pounds on an up-to-date appliance when she realises that the same firm has produced two or three models during as many years, and that the last or last but one version has depreciated in price in the shopwindows and is of but little value when offered in part exchange for the latest model. If, she may well argue, I wait a month or two, I can buy this very desirable new product for less money or, alternatively, I shall get a more efficient machine for the same amount.

It may be argued that the manufacturer is right to adopt every improvement made possible by research and practical experience, and to make it available at the earliest possible moment to ease the housewife's burden in these servantless days. In that case, could not some means be found to form a central exchange mart where former models could be disposed of at a price commensurate with the initial outlay less depreciation for fair wear and tear, thus giving the less well-off user an opportunity gradually to lighten *her* work and running costs ?

For instance, the latest gas cookers, with their battery lighters and safety switches, would surely be far more in demand if the housewife knew that her still quite serviceable older model could be offered for sale in a secondhand department of the local showrooms. Or again, the housewife, who sees and covets a steam electric iron, might willingly part with the four or five pounds that it costs if she could be assured that the two or three pounds invested in her well-preserved, thermostatically controlled model would not have to be consigned as a dead loss to a cupboard shelf.

In this way much needed relief from household drudgery could be spread far more widely throughout the population—for this is not a plea for calling a halt to the application of scientific knowledge to the home. Great credit and thanks are due to the manufacturers who during the comparatively few years since the war have restored many pre-1939 amenities to lighten and brighten the housewife's task.

Townswoman 1954

To become a citizen of the United States—or of Britain?
That was one young man's problem. And here he tells—

WHY I CHOOSE TO BE BRITISH

A FEW years ago I wrote an article asking "Briton or American—which shall I be?" I had the choice because I was a dual-national, born in this country of American parents. The mail-bag I received was enormous, and left me more confused than ever.

Most of it was abusive—"Get out and stay out, we have no need of you here." Some advised me to leave—"You're lucky to have the chance. If I was a young man I wouldn't hesitate, England is finished." And a few letters told me to stay, saying there was no country like it in the world.

Soon after this I enlisted in the American Air Corps. Never once, in two years, was it held against me that I spoke with an English accent, and I found in the American Army a system of democracy and good common sense which I cannot believe exists in our own Services.

But this was in Germany, far away from the pressure of American life. I returned to England, studying at Cambridge under the wonderfully generous G.I. Bill of Rights, and have made it my base ever since.

Thankful choice

NOW I have finally made up my mind. It is not a good thing to belong to two countries, even if one is able to, and I choose Britain thankfully.

I am writing this by the coast, looking on to a wild stretch of sand, with a group of gulls sitting disconsolately by the water's edge, all facing the same way, and sunlight picking out the colours of the headland. I know of no country that has such a feeling of peace or where the people seem more untroubled.

The grass seems fresher, the villages happier. The weather provides a variety that most countries envy. I remember when I was in Canada that I caught a bad cold and had to spend a day in bed : when I got out again I discovered I had missed the spring and that after a blinding white winter I was already in a blinding white summer.

I like to wander in Lon-

"... the grass seems fresher, the villages happier ... I can no longer conceive of a town without a pub. ..."

don, through the sprawling elegance of Hyde Park, the quiet, dignified crescents and squares, the bustle of the docks, the colour of Soho, the cheerfulness of the East End. I even like the tatty brightness of Piccadilly-circus and Leicester-square.

New York, in comparison, seems heartless.

I can no longer conceive of a town without a pub, so different from the American bars with their disillusioned solitary drinkers.

I was arrested the other day, which is another reason for my choosing Britain. I have a strong, possibly pathetic, belief in British justice. The idea of an English judge or member of Parliament being corruptible strikes me as absurd. I feel safe over here ; if I was in trouble I'd expect fair treatment, but I'd be scared as hell in the States.

After a party

I COULD not live happily in any country where I had to watch my thoughts or words, and I should certainly have to watch them there.

I was arrested because I was causing a disturbance. It was after a party, and, walking down the street, I saw one of the girls who had been there held in the grip of two young and rather worried - looking policemen. I arrived on the scene and joined the rapidly growing crowd that had, for some reason, maybe because the girl was young and beautiful, taken sides against the two policemen. One of the crowd shouted : "Gestapo !" and I capped this with "Police State !"

Chastened

IN a few moments several police cars drew up, the crowd was dispersed, my two friends were driven away, and I was put in a Black Maria for the first time in my life.

Considerably chastened, I arrived at the police station and was charged.

The next morning I arrived at Bow-street. The policemen I had met the night before greeted me cordially, and the atmosphere of the court, astonishingly enough, seemed to have the good spirits of an American musical.

My turn came, and in the distance a small man pronounced judgment. I paid my 20s. and emerged, after warm handshakes with the police, a free man.

But what impressed me so forcibly was that I had been a free man all along, treated with honesty and pleasantness. I had been in the wrong, I had been punished. I should hate to be in the hands of the American police, however innocent I might be.

But these—the feelings of beauty, safety, and friendship—though they are the most important, are abstract reasons for remaining here.

In my first article I spoke gloomily of the lack of incentive, of the restrictions to start with and the heavy taxes to finish with. These objections do largely remain, but how different England is from the depressed, apathetic state of a few years ago.

Many of the restrictions that drove one of my best friends, also a dual-national, to leave the country with his wife and children for the American Middle-West have been removed, and he writes miserably that he is now existing a living death. I cannot honestly complain of the food here, and it is cheaper than in France and America.

Pet hates

THERE are many things I detest—British Railways, B.B.C. programmes over Christmas, closing time at eleven, forms and regulations—but they are not hard to bear and one must feel angry over something.

There are so many things I like—the staggering good humour of bus conductors when they must be dropping on their feet, rich Cockney wit, fish-and-chips, brown-and-mild, the hatreds of the Hyde Park orators, the national delight over Boko, the telegrams of congratulation from Parliament to the Bermudan Negro who laid out his coat before the Queen, the judge who refused to evict a family before Christmas because of the children, the campaign against myxomatosis when it's being given artificially to rabbits in Australia.

I like the outrage of the British public when it feels that injustice is being done, regardless of how trivial the case may be. I like its toughness, which makes it pander to no master, no witch-hunt or trend.

Above all, I like the warm good humour, the strongest asset any nation can have, which even justifies the British in their insufferable superiority complex.

D. N. F.

***Daily Mail* 1954**

WHAT goes on inside those tins today? Presented here is our panel of eight Tinned Food Tasters who were summoned by us to take part in an emergency Cooks' Conference.

THE EIGHT EXPERTS met round a table

¶ *THE JUDGES were people to whom time and trouble in cooking are no object: expert cooks who have each made their name in a different field.*

M. Saulnier, who wrote the classic encyclopedia of cookery which is known as the "Chefs' Bible";

Bruce Blunt, Daily Express writer, a connoisseur of good living, good food, and good wine;

Elizabeth David, the woman whose books made Provençal cooking popular with London housewives;

Mme. Prunier, the French-woman who runs the famous sea-food restaurants in Paris and London;

Helen Burke, the Scottish author of many cookbooks, who writes a cookery column in the Evening Standard;

M. Pierre Toulemon, the chef at the Connaught Hotel, whose family have been chefs for five generations;

Elizabeth Craig, a cookery writer for 20 years and author of dozens of books on all kinds of cooking; and

Mr. John Chandos, professional gourmet who specialises in books on wine.

The points we put to them were these:—

● ALTHOUGH fresh food has improved daily in quality the food in tins is still mainly what it was 10 years ago.

● WHAT was meant to be a quick, delicious meal ready to serve is now so often taste-less that it takes quite as much time and trouble as fresh food to make it palatable.

● ALTHOUGH pork is off the ration you cannot always find it in the baked beans.

● ALTHOUGH vegetables could be tinned young and delicately cooked, they are usually overcooked and far too large.

● ALTHOUGH good tomato sauce is freely available, you rarely get it in the spaghetti.

● ONCE you could find recognisable pieces of mush-room or chicken in the soup; now you seldom do.

● CALIFORNIAN tinned peaches have a thick, sweet syrup, but the kind we get here have a thinner, more tasteless syrup.

● AND there are certain foods which seem to lose flavour when they get inside a tin — like ham and tongue and steak.

● MANY housewives keep a pile of tins stored for an emergency. But often, when it comes to the point, they feel a lot safer dishing up some eggs.

So the eight judges were asked to give their verdict on what is going on inside our tins—on grounds of taste and quality alone. And the general verdict was this: A lot of tinned food is not palatable as it stands.

WHY BOTHER?

The real controversy was about whether it was worth while dickering about with it.

The specialists in good, plain economical cookery, Elizabeth Craig and Helen Burke, insisted that tinned food wasn't as bad as it looked, and that it could be made palatable if you took a little trouble and added seasonings.

The connoisseurs like M. Toulemon, the chef, M. Saulnier, Bruce Blunt, and John Chandos felt that if a dish has made a bad start it isn't worth trying to improve on it.

Daily Express
1954

REGENT PACKS PUNCH

The LIVELIEST PERFORMANCE of any petrol

You can feel the increased power of Regent T.T., *the* premium petrol. Its unfaltering punch and splendid acceleration at all speeds is a joy to experience. High octane is a *natural* property of the crude oils from which T.T. Petrol is refined. Engine knock is eliminated by the high octane in T.T., so you can stay in top longer and get maximum miles per gallon.

T.T. PETROL

ALSO
REGENT BENZOLE MIXTURE
(PREMIUM GRADE BLEND)

It's laughter all along the Line!

with ARTHUR ASKEY in

THE LOVE MATCH

HIS LATEST FILM

Full Steam Ahead with Arthur at the

REGAL, ABERDEEN

Soon

Daily Express
1954

In a cauliflower—

A lark's nest with four eggs was found in a cauliflower by Mrs. L Sandall, of Hereward - street Bourne, Lincs, as she was about to cut up the cauliflower for lunch. The lark is now hatching its young still in the cauliflower.

RATE YOUR ESCORT . . .

Mr. A, Mr. B, or Mr. C?

HOW few men there are who are always the perfect companion. He may be a wow in some ways but he is probably a wash-out in others. Rate your escort on the questionnaire below—*TEN marks for each A answer, FIVE for a B, NOTHING for a C*—then check his total with the answer chart at the foot.

SCORE HERE

★ **AT NIGHT CLUBS**
A. He stays as late as you like and dances all the time....
B. You have to make him dance.........................
C. He goes under protest and sulks....................

★ **ON WET WEEK-ENDS**
A. He makes you laugh on a hill in the rain............
B. He grumbles about the weather......................
C. He sits indoors and reads..........................

★ **AT DINNER PARTIES**
A. He's a smash hit with your hosts...................
B. He's a reliable asset who you know will behave well....
C. Nobody remembers his name.........................

★ **ON EVENINGS AT HOME**
A. You can't imagine why anyone ever wants to go out....
B. You feel you have to make an effort to entertain him...
C. He's restless and bored...........................

★ **WITH HIS FRIENDS**
A. He knows you'll be a riot.........................
B. He doesn't care whether you meet them or not........
C. He's sure you wouldn't fit in with them...........

★ **WITH YOUR FRIENDS**
A. He's anxious for them to like him—and they do.........
B. He puts up with them..............................
C. He makes it plain he thinks they're a waste of time......

★ **AT TENNIS PARTIES**
A. He plays well himself but doesn't mind if you don't......
B. He starts grumbling after the first set...........
C. He snaps every time you lose a point.............

★ **ON HOLIDAYS**
A. He makes Brighton seem like the South of France.......
B. He does what you want to do, but after a battle.......
C. He makes the South of France seem like Brighton......

★ **WITH PRETTY GIRLS ABOUT**
A. They all try to grab him after one look.............
B. They'd like him if he wasn't yours already..........
C. They're happy to let you keep him.................

★ **ABOUT YOUR WORK**
A. He asks you the right questions...................
B. He treats it as a joke............................
C. You have to keep telling him what it is...........

TOTAL

— STUDY THE TOTAL—and LOOK BELOW

WHAT HIS SCORE MEANS			WHAT YOU THINK OF HIM
80—100	He doesn't exist.	or	You're so in love you can't see straight.
60— 80	He *must* be married already.	or	You're in love, all right.
40— 60	He's worth hanging on to.	or	You're not sure about him.
20— 40	Try for something better.	or	You're definitely not in love.
0— 20	..................JUST YOUR LUCK..................		

Daily Express
1954

Toothpaste row leads to decree

A HUSBAND slapped his wife's face because she squeezed a tube of toothpaste from the middle instead of the bottom, said a Judge yesterday.

He slapped her, too, when he found cobwebs behind a picture and when she opened a new pot of marmalade before the old one was finished.

The quarrel over toothpaste was one of the most serious of a series of such incidents, the judge said, because the husband did it in the presence of his little boy. After the slap the wife ran from the house.

Mr. Justice Barnard, at Nottingham Assizes, described the husband, Geoffrey Rutherford Morris, of Salfield, Gloucestershire, as "a most plausible gentleman."

He granted a decree nisi and the custody of the child to Mrs. Marion Pacifica Morris, of Anlaby-road, Hull, on the ground of cruelty, which the husband denied.

Daily Mail
1954

The Farmer in Parliament

By DENYS BULLARD, M.P.

Farmer's Weekly
1954

THE ORDER PAPER OF THE House of Commons is always very quick to be affected by what is going on in the outside world, and there have been plenty of questions about the effects of decontrolling meat.

All of them so far have been concerned with the rise in price in some cuts of beef in some shops. These questions began on Monday week, almost before the new systems had started, and they continued this week.

Mr. Shinwell asked the Minister of Food whether he would re-impose price control, "in view of the increases in price which have occurred since de-rationing."

Dr. Charles Hill told him that meat prices had already fallen substantially from the levels reached under the naturally uncertain conditions prevailing in the first day or two of free trade and were still tending to fall. There was plenty of meat about, he said, and there were many signs that the shopping public and responsible traders were seeing to it that it was sold at reasonable prices. It was not intended to re-impose control.

TV CuMMERCIALS

They're the bits of advertising you'll be seeing at the beginning and end of each ITA programme. JAMES THOMAS, first reporter to sample what promises to be TV's biggest controversy, tells what's in store for viewers

News Chronicle 1955

BOYLE, toothpaste ; LESTOCQ, soft drink

Tainting of food impossible.
At Grocers, Stores, Ironmongers,
Trade inquiries to Shipley, Yorks.

WAIT for it, children. I have just seen your television uncle Humphrey Lestocq joyously waving a bottle of Blank's orange juice and exhorting cordial enthusiasts large and small to drink the *real* stuff.

Anything can happen now. Britain's first TV "commercials" have arrived, though it is easier to get into the Bank of England vaults than it is to get yourself a seat in the little private West End theatres where they are being shown.

Don your false beard, adjust your wig, try to look like an eccentric but prosperous adver- tiser, and slink with me into this elegant doorway. Ignore those gilt-and-ivory offices, don't gape at the chandeliers, stop fiddling with the golden tassels—this is the hall of the advertising kings.

Daily Sketch 1955

Daily Sketch Reporters

VILLAGERS of Uck- field, Sussex, were talking last night about the most fan- tastic week-end they have known.

Even after Princess Margaret and Group- Captain Peter Townsend had returned separately to London police stayed on duty at all known entrances to Uckfield House.

During the two days and three nights the couple stayed there the staff there, I am told, were threatened with instant dismissal if they spoke of what they saw or heard.

STRICT ORDER

Normally most em- ployees and staff on the estate and at the house live out, but during the week-end everybody except the bailiff was ordered to live in.

Lord Rupert Nevill keeps a staff of gardeners for his nursery work—he sends flowers to market.

All outside staff were warned not to step beyond a perimeter surrounding the house.

At the same time all in- side staff were ordered not to leave the house.

Ten minutes before Prin- cess Margaret left for Lon- don in her black Rolls- Royce police ordered all re- porters, photographers and members of the public to the other side of the main road.

The effect was that no one could get to within half a mile of the mansion itself, or within a quarter of a mile of the grounds.

By HUGH PILCHER   Parliamentary Correspondent

HEROIN, the pain-killing drug, is not after all to be banned. The Government last night suddenly surrendered under pressure from lawyers, doctors, MPs and Peers.

It announced a year's postponement of the ban, during which heroin may still be made, exported and imported.

There are already two years' stocks in Britain. So patients needing heroin to relieve pain are sure of three years' grace.

The Government news came as a shock in the House of Lords at the end of a long, bitter debate in which doctor Peers disagreed.

Daily Herald
1955

Dundee Courier and Advertiser 1954

WE CAN THROW AWAY THOSE RATION BOOKS NOW

Butchers still to fix new meat prices

After today meat—the last rationed commodity —is freed. All except children entitled to free milk can tear up their ration books.

Farmers, butchers and slaughterhouse men are working overtime to have a first-class display in the shops on Monday. Women intend to celebrate today with a rally in Trafalgar Square.

Lord Woolton, who for three and a half years watched over Britain's larder during the war, said last night:—

" It was necessary in war-time. I always disliked it. When we returned to power we said that we would end it. We have done it."

An unofficial estimate of the increase to take place in beef on Monday was given yesterday at from 8d to 1s per 1 lb.

Nothing definite, however, will be known until butchers meet over the week-end to fix the new prices.

They will have to make deductions for hides, tallow, offal, &c.; then add to the cost of the carcase their usual gross profit.

Only when they have arrived at that figure will they be able to fix prices for the various cuts. Naturally, those in greatest demand will cost the most.

At Forfar yesterday cattle sold at up to £2 per cwt. more than the control price. On the other hand pigs and sheep were considerably cheaper.

Farmers termed it a grand sale for cattle, but said the Government would have to make pretty heavy deficiency payments for sheep and pigs.

THAT PORTRAIT of Sir Winston Churchill which was causing a nation - wide artistic storm a month ago stood yesterday in the dark back room of an empty house.

THAT PORTRAIT, the gift of M.P.s and peers on Sir Winston's 80th birthday and the target of Lord Hailsham's remarks, "Disgusting, ill-mannered, terrible," stood on a lonely easel among sparse furniture. And nobody knew yesterday if or when it will leave the dark back room of No. 28, Hyde Park-gate, Kensington, which is the Prime Minister's private London home.

The controversial portrait which shocked televiewers when unveiled in Westminster Hall *was* taken to No. 10, Downing-street.

SILENCE . . .

BUT within a few days it was moved to No. 28, Hyde Park-gate, which has been empty since a tenant, the Cuban Ambassador, moved out in September.

Daily Express 1955

Crowley's gardener

I was very interested in your articles on Aleister Crowley, as my uncle (who is still alive) worked for him at Boleskine for a year, laying out his gardens. Crowley called himself Lord Boleskine. One day when he was out shooting rabbits, my uncle got in the way, and had the heel of his boot shot at. The local people were very dubious about Crowley's sanity, and kept away from him. He had a room built like a temple, where he used to pray to a dummy which was suspended from the roof.

G. F. URQUHART,
INVERNESS.

WHEN YOU'RE NEW TO GARDENING

COMMON SENSE— EXPERT ADVICE

By JOHN NORTH

MANY men marry and start life afresh in homes of their own with gardens already cultivated to some extent.

Some may look forward with keen delight to keeping that garden in order. Others find gardening a bore, and do not know how to begin. This should not prove difficult if common sense is allied to expert advice. The use of the term expert in this case refers to the local nurseryman. He will be a practical person with a knowledge of the local soil, and can give sound advice on what to grow in the new garden. Plants bought from the local nursery are just as good as more expensive varieties purchased elsewhere.

A complete range of gardening tools will be needed. The best advice is to buy the best you can afford, bearing in mind that a shoddy product may prove to be the dearest in the long run.

IDENTIFYING STOCK

The new gardener will need a spade, a fork, a rake, and a hand trowel. A strong penknife with at least one sharp blade is a " must," and will have a thousand and one uses in the garden.

In the early part of the year there is usually no way for the beginner to tell one shrub or perennial from another. Do not let this worry you. Transfer all the plants to one part of the flower bed, making sure they are all firmly planted against the wind.

This will enable the beginner to free the rest of the garden, which can then be planned from scratch incorporating his ideas. Later, when the plants which have been transplanted have flowered and been identified, they can be thrown away or incorporated in the final border layout of the garden.

Exeter Express and Echo 1955

Picture Post 1956

WHO'S U?

by RIGOLETTO

Now that Christmas is over and the last servants, if any, given their tips, if any, let us lay (or lie?) back and have a *véritable snob*. Are you or are you not really U? For those who have not or could not read *Encounter* during the past few months it should be explained that Nancy Mitford and A. N. Other have greatly upset the English-speaking world by suggesting that one can after all divide the sheep from the goats, the U from the Non-U (upper class), the top-drawers from the note quate-quates.

Nobody believes himself in the lower bracket so, to find one's favourite usage, such as milk in first, or happiest qualifying locution, 'to my mind', branded as Non-U naturally raises the hackles.

The following is a short test paper, to which additions can be made *ad lib*.

1. What is wrong with envelopes addressed as follows:
   The honourable Mrs Nancy Mitford.
   Mr Evelyn Waugh, Esq?
2. Put into U:
   'Kindly touch the bell, ducks, if you haven't the requisite.'
3. Put i to Non-U:
   'A re lly delightful man came about the wi eless.'
4. Put into Queen's English:
   'It has been a great privilege for my husband and I to visit you in your own homes.'
5. Put into official English:
   'Whatever did you choose this book to be read out of to for?'
6. Pick the U synonyms for a child from the following:
   Poor little soul, ditto mite, lovely little kiddy, brat, infant, offspring, youngster, nipper, junior.

7. For which of the following would you be (a) delighted, (b) dismayed, to be mistaken by a (tele)phone caller?
   Dr Charles Hill, Rose Macaulay, Malcolm Muggeridge, Peter de Francia, Angus Wilson.
8. Have you ever used a fish knife (if so—for what); a napkin and/or serviette ring; a made-up bow tie (except on the stage)?
9. Distinguish between:
   That's 'snough: that will be sufficient thanks.

   Really rather: ever so.
   Having to complain: not half creating.
   Illness: complaint.
   Taken ill: gone home queer.
   Magazine: book.
10. Try for U-ness the following names in the news:
    Guy Burgess, Lady Docker, Dr Sitwell, Freddie Mills, Aneurin Bevan, Dr Fisher, Raymond Mortimer, the entire What's My Line? panel and all your friends (if you have any left).

My Weekly 1956

BARBARA Replies to Your Letters

IT'S good to have someone to confide in when you are worried about something. That's why I am here. To help you with your problems, big or small, to discuss them with you and do my best to find a solution.

So if you've something on your mind, please don't hesitate to write to me about it. I shall be only too pleased to try to help. My address is—Barbara, " My Weekly," 186 Fleet Street, London, E.C.1. If you'd like a prompt, personal reply, please enclose a stamped addressed envelope with your letter, and for a reply in my column, let me have a pen-name I can use.

RUSTY.—Frankly, my dear, your chances are pretty slim of being able to work your passage to Canada. You might try getting in touch with one of the shipping companies and asking if there are any available jobs, but it's hardly likely you'll be signed on for one voyage. Most companies would require you to sign on for a certain period. Again, there's just a chance you might be able to get a paid passage as companion to a child or an old lady, but it's extremely remote. If, however, you're considering emigrating for a few years, you might qualify for a partially paid passage; if you're interested in doing the journey in this way you should write to Canada House, London, for particulars. But, you know, a single fare to Canada (tourist) is not really very expensive. So if you're going to emigrate for a period, I'm sure you would be able to afford single fare, then you could take a job over there for a few years; you'd easily be able to save up for your return fare. Good luck!

FOOLISH GIRL.—You are. And I think you yourself will understand why I say so.

OLD AGE PENSIONER.—I'm afraid your friends are right, Mrs M. You won't qualify for the old age pension until your husband is 65.

TOO OLD FOR LOVE?—My dear, of course I don't think you're too old at 45 to get married. Lots of people far older than you get married, you know. I do think you'd be wise to take this chance of happiness—you and this man sound ideally suited to each other. Naturally you can't expect to know the starry-eyed rapture of youth's first love, for you are two mature people with life and experience behind you. What you will have is something deeper and richer, a mature, understanding love and companionship and trust—the foundation, in fact, for every worth-while marriage. Good luck, my dear—and please don't let thoughts of age or regrets for what you may have missed in the past spoil your happiness.

MAID OF HONOUR.—It is usual nowadays, due to the expense, for bridesmaids to provide their own dresses, although traditionally the bride pays. However, although she no longer pays for them, the bride still has the privilege of choosing the colours and styles to fit in with her own, bearing in mind, however, the requirements of her attendants. Your flowers will be provided by the groom. As chief bridesmaid you will help the bride to dress, and be waiting at the church door to help rearrange the veil. Then you will walk down the aisle behind the bride and her father. At the altar you stand slightly behind her and to the left, and when the ring is about to be placed on her finger you will take her bouquet. Later, in the vestry, you will sign the register after the best man. At the reception your duties will be similar to those of the best man—to see that the guests are mixing and enjoying themselves. Then you help the bride to dress in her going-away outfit and deal with any last-minute details that may crop up. I hope you have a lovely time at the wedding.

FIRST DATE.—No, my dear, I most certainly would not suggest going " Dutch " on your first date with this boy. Far from appreciating it as a kind offer, he'll probably be insulted. He would never have asked you out in the first place if he hadn't been able to afford it. Time enough to suggest going " Dutch " when you know him a lot better and have been going out with him regularly for some time.

HOPEFUL.—You are certainly not too old at 34 to remedy a figure fault and much can be done to improve a sagging bust by exercise and support. If you care to write to me again enclosing a stamped, addressed envelope, I shall be very pleased to send you one of my leaflets on exercises for improving the figure and also go fully into the problem of proper support.

Smoking and cancer link now 'definite'

By JOSEPH TOBIN

THE Cabinet were considering today whether they should warn the public of the dangers of a link between smoking and lung cancer.

The Government will announce on Thursday that they have been told by their medical advisers that there is now much more evidence of a link between smoking and lung cancer.

At the same time as the statement is made in the Commons by the Minister of Health, Mr. Denis Vosper, the reports by the Medical Research Council will be presented.

At a head

It is suggested that this report states that there is a definite link between heavy smoking and lung cancer.

The Prime Minister, Mr. Harold Macmillan, held two Cabinet meetings today to take important decisions before the opening of the Commonwealth Premiers' Conference on Wednesday and the reassembly of Parliament tomorrow.

The Medical Research Council's report on smoking brings to a head the government's difficulties in recent years.

Ministers have held off making any definite pronouncement until they were absolutely sure.

They have not wished to be accused of starting a public scare without more proof from their medical experts.

Newcastle-upon-Tyne Evening Chronicle 1957

MR. PAUL RAYMOND is 26. His theatrical ventures are packing in audiences throughout the country. These enterprises range from " Paris After Dark " to " Piccadilly Peepshow," which is now delighting family audiences at Margate.

Family audiences? Mr. Raymond assures me that children, rising from infancy to the teens, are taken to his shows by their doting elders.

The shows are billed in lurid terms.

" Paris After Dark " is subtitled " The Web of Desire." Raymond's Harlem Nudes perform the " taunting, scantily-clad " Native Mating Dance in " stark naked reality."

In " Folies Parisiennes," Mr. Raymond features the " Only Moving Nudes."

There is a law against presenting mobile nudes on any stage in this country.

Mr. Raymond explains: " They're static, really. But I present them on revolving stages."

In the same show, Mr. Raymond's " Eurasian Voodoo Dance " is described as " A Raging Torrent of Emotion that even Nature cannot control"; and the performer of the " Banned Reefer Dance " is heralded as the Dangerous Girl with the Low Neckline.

Daily Herald 1954

MIDLANDS
IDEAL HOME EXHIBITION

OPEN

Birmingham Post 1956

MAKING THE PEOPLE 'TEETH CONSCIOUS'

Birmingham Dental Health Drive

"An apple three times a day prevents dental decay" might well be the slogan for the first dental health campaign to be sponsored by a local authority which opened in Birmingham yesterday. It will last a month.

This was one of the points stressed by Mr. F. J. H. Hastilow, the corporation's senior dental officer.

Pointing out that the major cause of dental decay and pyorrhœa (disease of the gums) was our high content sugar and carbohydrate soft diet that did not require chewing and which produced acid and with it dental decay, he advised after-meal brushing, chewing a piece of apple or washing out the mouth vigorously with water.

At a time of the year when apples are scarce or expensive, he did, however, suggest celery or even raw carrot as an alternative.

Sugar Chief Danger

Though sugar—and especially refined sugar—was the chief danger to teeth, Mr. Hastilow added that eating sweets between meals was even more harmful.

More than 98 per cent of Birmingham's population suffer from dental disease, he said. Nine out of every ten two-year-olds had sound teeth, but by the time they reached the age of nine, they had decayed teeth. But more and more parents were appreciating the importance of having their children's first teeth filled.

Under the National Health Service, 200,000 courses of dental treatment at a cost of nearly £1,000,000 a year were provided in Birmingham each year. And yet, Mr. Hastilow went on, though the city's dental services were now almost fully occupied, only one in four of the population visited a dentist every year.

Teaching People

Dr. Jean Mackintosh, of the Public Health Department, said: "We are more interested in prevention than cure. This is partly because it is the philosophy of this department and also because we have to look facts in the face. Dentists are scarce and if we want to get quick results we must teach people to prevent decay."

3.45 MUSIC WHILE YOU WORK
Harry Leader and his Band

4.30   News Summary
MRS. DALE'S DIARY
(BBC recording)
Repeated on Tuesday at 11.15 a.m.
Richard Fulton told the Dales he would pay all expenses for a holiday for Sally when she left the nursing-home. They decided she should go to Mrs. Dale's villa in Italy, accompanied by Violet Hichens. Sally appeared to be getting better. Mrs. McGussie's son, Roy, went to King's Acre to try and persuade her to return home, but without success. Dr. Claughton had supper with the Dales and she and Mrs. Dale became more friendly.

Mrs. Dale	Ellis Powell
Dr. Dale	James Dale
Sally Lane	Margaret Ward
Mrs. Freeman	Dorothy Lane
Bob Dale	Leslie Heritage
Jenny Dale	Valerie Gaunt
Mrs. Maggs	Grace Allardyce
Alec Dale	Stuart Nichol
Janet Dale	Lois McLean
Henry Freeman	Preston Lockwood
Richard Fulton	Norman Chidgey
Fickling	Robert Webber
Rachel Guest	Joan Hart
Mrs. Leathers	Hattie Jacques
Dr. Fenimore	Martin Lewis
Dr. Claughton	Molly Rankin
Tony Coppard	Nicholas Stuart
Vicky Clare	Lydia Sherwood
Miss Smith	June Tobin
Serena Sutcliffe	Sheila Manahan
Mr. Brewster	Harold Reese
Freda	Beryl Calder
Matron	Ella Milne
Sister	Sheila Manahan

Productions this week by
Betty Davies and Wyn Knowles

Radio Times 1958

THE SHOW HOUSE—Work of *Midland Craftsmen*

THE brick-built house which is the centrepiece of the exhibition provides an example of the fine workmanship of Midland craftsmen and manufacturers. Both in the construction of the house and in the interior decorative and furnishing schemes, the emphasis has been on Midland products.

Four local builders have co-operated in its construction under the supervision of the Birmingham firm of estate agents Jones, Mackay and Croxford. They are Coleman and Parkin, of Aston; H. J. Egginson, Ltd., of Small Heath; William Vaughan Ltd., of Selly Oak; and Alfred Walker and Son, Ltd., of Coleshill.

The house itself has three bedrooms, a through lounge with dining recess and a large kitchen, and is typical of the new type of houses now being developed.

Floor-warming

Costing about £3,000, which includes electrical floor warming—which is used for the first time in a house of this type—a refrigerator and immersion heater, it covers a total area of about 1,300 superficial feet.

Sand-faced facing bricks made by the Bickenhill firm of Jackson's (Warwickshire) Brickworks Ltd. have been used for the exterior walls, and the attractive mansard roof with dormer windows is of brown Marley tiles. Leaded lights have been used in the front windows; the back windows all have a two-feet width.

Several new features are incorporated in its design. The stairs, for instance, instead of being in the hall have been placed at the side of the house behind the garage and are lit by a large window at the top.

The kitchen, which measures 13ft. 4½in. by 9ft. 9in., has a meals corner to take a table and four chairs and a serving hatch to the dining recess. A double-drainer sink unit in porcelain enamel incorporates a built-in refrigerator with Formica top, and there are broom and food cupboards with sliding doors and a floor-to-ceiling cupboard fitment. An extractor fan over the cooker instead of an air brick has been used to take away cooking fumes.

A novel feature of the kitchen is the door from the hall which, facing the front door, has been fitted with glazed portholes to give an improved effect on entering the house.

The three bedrooms are all double rooms with built-in hanging cupboards. The bathroom is half-tiled in grey and has a heated towel rail and large airing cupboard.

Birmingham Post 1956

And, by Gas, that's easily cooked grub too! For with Gas you can always *see* what you're doing. You can *see* whether the heat is too high, too low, or just right. Gas takes the guesswork out of cooking. There's a tremendous variety of Gas Cookers on the market, from little fellows suitable for small bed-sitting-rooms to great shining giants big enough to take the largest of turkeys. You'll find just the type and size you need at your own Gas showrooms—and you'll also find you can get it on easy terms.

All the latest Gas Cookers— simple to use, lovely to look at, easy to keep spotless—are on show at your own Gas showrooms.

Mr THERM - mother's daily help

THE GAS INDUSTRY MAKES THE BEST USE OF THE NATION'S COAL *Issued by the Gas Council*

A DIFFERENT OUTLOOK

I have been married for over ten years and my husband has never once succeeded in remembering my birthday.

He says, if I remind him of the date well in advance, he will buy me a present but I tell him that to me there would be no pleasure in receiving a gift which I had to ask for. Do other wives of forgetful husbands feel the same, I wonder?

The pleasant fuss and excitement which surrounds a child's birthday makes the date so memorable and so looked forward to, that this feeling gets carried on into later life.

A birthday, even in middle life, is a special day, and even the most sensible wife cannot help a sense of disappointment that it should apparently mean so little to her life-partner.

It must be accepted, though, as one of the differences in the outlook of the sexes, that dates mean very little to husbands. Wedding anniversaries and birthdays alike pass unnoticed, except by the rare few men who have that kind of memory. It is understandable you should not like to have to prod in advance but bring philosophy to bear, and realise that, because your man fails to remember one day in the year, this does not mean he forgets to love and appreciate you on all the other three hundred and sixty-four.

Woman and Home 1957

UNBECOMING SHYNESS

I have managed to bring up my daughter to take her part in conversation, and not to be shy. Yet now I hear from various people that she is considered forward and precocious. Surely I am right in my idea?

An old-fashioned notion still lingers on that shyness is becoming in the young, but nevertheless you have done your daughter a great service by cutting out those awkward years when a girl first takes her place as a grown-up and is quite unable to hold her own in conversation.

Of course, she will grow up to her manner and in a few years' time will be admired as a young woman who has poise and is an asset to any social gathering. Then she will be grateful to you, for your helpful way of bringing her out and dispelling that youthful shyness which can be such a handicap in life, if it persists. A mother who sees the advantage of practice in meeting and talking to people of all ages without embarrassment can be of the greatest help to a girl.

Woman and Home 1957

Actress uses Pifco Hairdryer to cut drying time by more than half

When this actress unpins her golden blonde hair it measures 26 inches long. You can imagine the time she used to spend drying it, crouched in front of the fire! Now, she uses a Pifco Electric Hairdryer. Drying time for her is cut down by more than half.

For you too this light efficient Hairdryer can save time and trouble. Flicks on instantly to a stream of hot or cool air. T.V. and Radio suppressed, 100% shockproof—and like all Pifco products, made to last a very long time. In its attractive box the Pifco Electric Hairdryer makes a delightful present. Fully guaranteed. From chemists, stores and electrical shops, 76/9.

PIFCO

Electric Hairdryers are so dependable

Makers of the famous Pifco Vibratory Massager, Intra-Red and Sun Lamps

EAT YOUR WAY TO BEAUTY

VITAMINS. MINERALS. PROTEIN. Don't dismiss those words as dry-and-dusty scientific terms. *They are the most important in the vocabulary of beauty.* Ask the top models. Ask your beauty editor. Ask your doctor.

Your skin, eyes and hair *cannot* look at their best if you are not getting enough vitamins, minerals and protein. And that is why you should take Bemax every day.

Bemax is stabilized wheat germ— the richest natural vitamin-protein-mineral supplement. It supplies you with all the 'beauty nutrients' which are so often lacking in present day diets.

Plain or chocolate-flavoured Bemax from all chemists, price 3/-. Plain also 1/9 or 5/6.

For a FREE booklet on eating for health and beauty send a post-card to the address below.

SPRINKLE BEMAX ON YOUR FOOD

VITAMINS LIMITED (DEPT. WO 6.), UPPER MALL, LONDON, W.6

Woman and Home
1957

HOW THEY KEEP THEIR GRAMOPHONE RECORDS

Owner of one of the finest private collections in the country, Mr. Dudley Scholte has specially adapted fitments for housing his treasures.

The combined radiogram and television set is concealed in a backless, pickled-pine cabinet. Portraits of Marlene Dietrich can be seen inside the doors.

★

DUDLEY SCHOLTE, a great patron of the arts, has a collection of records numbering about two thousand, which includes many valuable early recordings of famous singers.

These he stores in attractive, specially-built pieces of furniture.

He keeps the main part of his collection in the hall of his elegant London flat. A long, white-painted fitment made like an open bookcase, with two rows of shelves, holds books of opera and ballet works, and long-playing records. Further along the wall is a white and gold cabinet that contains the musical comedy and revue records. This was a modern piece of furniture painted white with the simple beading and panelling picked out in gold. Another cabinet has neatly arranged shelves of continental records and all Mr. Scholte's tape-recordings.

The cabinet closed.

'Ernie', the electronic machine which selected the prizewinning numbers in the first Premium Bond draw last weekend at Lytham St. Annes, Lancashire

Listener
1957

He frowned when he noticed . . .

. . . he'd seen my hands. Seen how dry and chapped they were. I'd tried everything, but nothing seemed to do any good. Then he told me about CARE, the wonderful new lanolin hand-cream the doctors at the hospital use. CARE has a special antiseptic called Octaphen. I tried CARE and it really worked. You should just see how smooth and lovely my hands are now.

CARE is perfumed with French Moss, and costs 1/9, by Field's of Bond Street, London.

CARE
for your hands

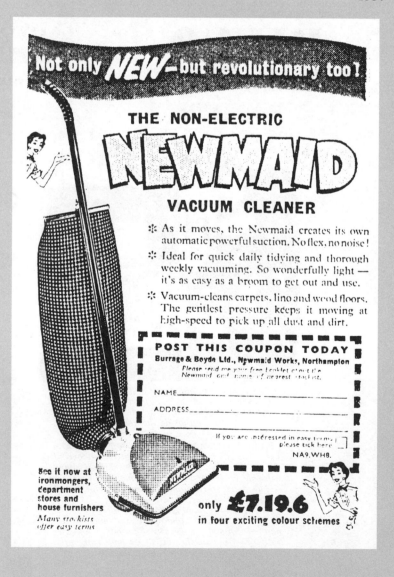

Not only *NEW* — but revolutionary too!

THE NON-ELECTRIC
NEWMAID
VACUUM CLEANER

❊ As it moves, the Newmaid creates its own automatic powerful suction. No flex, no noise!

❊ Ideal for quick daily tidying and thorough weekly vacuuming. So wonderfully light — it's as easy as a broom to get out and use.

❊ Vacuum-cleans carpets, lino and wood floors. The gentlest pressure keeps it moving at high-speed to pick up all dust and dirt.

POST THIS COUPON TODAY
Burrage & Boyde Ltd., Newmaid Works, Northampton

Please send me your free leaflet about the Newmaid and name of nearest stockist.

NAME_____

ADDRESS_____

If you are interested in easy terms please tick here

NA9.WH8.

See it now at ironmongers, department stores and house furnishers
Many stockists offer easy terms

only **£7.19.6**
in four exciting colour schemes

A <u>new</u> MAIN advantage!

High-level grill

Quick, labour-saving, easy to watch—the high-level grill is just one of the striking new features of the Main Super-Century. The new 'glide-over' pan supports permit the free movement of pans over the hotplate. The 'keep-cool' hob prevents spillage from burning-on; is easy and quick to clean. The grill pan has a special cool-type handle. Boiling burners (all with push-in safety taps), have pre-set positions for simmering. The oven is roomy, lit from the front by flash ignition tube.

Cash Price £39.0.0

FIXING EXTRA
HIRE PURCHASE TERMS AVAILABLE

Ask for details of the Super-Century at your local gas board showrooms.

Colour choice: white with blue or green, cream with blue or green; all white or all cream (with red grill cover if preferred).

SUPER-CENTURY
GAS COOKER

Φ19   R & A MAIN LIMITED

Note the name–made by MAIN

STOKES TABLE FOUNTAINS

Illuminated electric fountains. No mains water. Also garden models. Write for brochure

STOKES FOUNTAINS LTD.
(Dept. H.J.1), 185, London Road, Croydon, Surrey
Tel: CRO 6316

Which? 1957

What are The Snags?

In C R's opinion, rather too much is claimed. 'No-iron' usually really means a good deal less-iron, though, of course, it does depend on your standards and on how much of the shirt, for instance, is going to show. When a waistcoat is worn, only the collar and cuffs and the strip of front are visible. Sticklers for perfection may want a sharper finish on a shirt to be worn with a two-piece suit but even so, there is much less ironing to do than with a normal shirt. That is, so long as the shirt is fairly new.

Dress by Susan Small

Suddenly... excitingly...
the most glamorous you!

Playtex LIVING BRA

LIKE A DREAM come true! You put on your Playtex Living Bra and suddenly you're beautiful... poised... glamorous. It divides so divinely, supports so superbly, moulding you to the *lifted*, rounded, oh-so-feminine American look.

And such blissful freedom —wonderful comfort! The Playtex Living Bra never rides up, never gapes, cuts or binds, self-adjusts to every movement. Playtex Living Bra fits and feels as if fashioned for *you* alone.

Tailored, white elastic and nylon. Sizes 32 to 40, Cups A, B and C in most sizes. 27/6 For fashion's smooth, *long* look —the Playtex Long-Line Living Bra with the all-elastic *magic midriff*. 42/-

MADE AT PLAYTEX PARK, PORT GLASGOW, SCOTLAND   ©1958
LONDON OFFICE: 17 STRATTON STREET, LONDON, W.1   * TRADE MARK

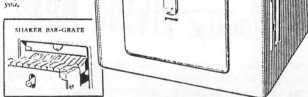

Britain's Mr. and Mrs. Music
Pearl Carr and Teddy Johnson
send this eve-of-marriage advice to
EDNA and TERRY

HOW can two top-line singers combine successful careers with happy marriage? What advice would two who have found the secret pass on to others who—like Terry Dene and Edna Savage—are about to join their ranks?

I called on Mr. and Mrs. Music, Teddy Johnson and Pearl Carr, in their dressing room at the Royal Aquarium, Great Yarmouth, to ask why their marriage had been happy and their joint career so successful.

Last month they celebrated their third wedding anniversary by "rehearsing like mad all day" for Tom Arnold's revue, "Ace High," in which they are now playing.

"There is no band call or rehearsal for marriage," said Teddy. "It becomes the most important thing in your life. You must be prepared to make mistakes, be understanding and to rectify them.

"And the partners must never lose respect for each other. Like an act, it should get better and

In an interview with PETER BAGSHAW

better as the years go by."

"And it should have a long run," added Pearl brightly.

Teddy looked at her and gave her an affectionate hug. "I love this little woman more now than when I married her," he said. "I mean that sincerely. That is the secret. A marriage should progress.

"Ours has, despite the fact that sometimes we have terrible argu-ments about our work."

"That," Pearl pointed out, "is because we were single acts for so long and we are bound to have a clash of ideas now and again.

"But we never hold a grievance. Teddy taught me that and we never allow an argument over our work to intrude into our domestic life."

"Supposing such a disagreement did develop into something really big and threatened to disrupt everything?" I asked.

Teddy was adamant in his reply: "If it came to the point where we could not get on at work, I would say, without any hesitation, that we would cease being Teddy Johnson and Pearl Carr and become plain Mr. and Mrs. Johnson. Marriage matters much more than the act."

New Musical Express
1958

SIX POINTS FOR HAPPINESS IN THE HOME

1. That every housewife should be able to keep simple accounts for housekeeping and other expenditure, and know the current prices she pays for every-day commodities, as this avoids overspending and running into debt.

2. That every practical woman should be able to measure and make curtains and suchlike things for the home, even if she cannot fix them. Generally speaking, men do not want to be bothered with soft furnishings, but usually foot the bill providing the good lady does not go to the extreme.

3. Home Nursing is a thing that every woman should be qualified to undertake, yet how many can remove a grit from one's eye, or bandage a cut finger? Simple nursing is a thing very necessary in any home and nobody but a woman can do it with patience and care, and a cheery word and a kindly face goes a long way.

4. Don't be overproud or fussy, for home above any other place should have a comfortable sound. If things are left about sometimes, remember that the home is not a show-place, but somewhere to live in and be happy. Have interests of your own apart from just running the home and where possible share your man's interests if you can, but don't bother him with details of his work as soon as he returns home; *wait until he has had his meal* and he will talk if he wants to.

5. The kitchen is usually regarded as the woman's preserve, but there may be times when the good man wants to rinse his hands under the tap or draw some water for his garden. *Don't look "daggers" at him*, he has a perfect right to intrude sometimes. And if he is capable of doing little jobs about the house, do not get into the habit of finding fault, otherwise he may lose interest.

6. Whatever you do, don't "nag" or expect to always have your own way. Remember we all make mistakes, so try to see each others' point of view; in other words "give and take". *Avoid arguments over trivial things*, and don't raise your voice, for it is said that "a soft answer turneth away wrath"; and whatever you do don't go to bed in a sulk or in tears, for there is nothing a man dislikes so much as a crying woman.

Home and Country 1959

Courtesy: Daily Telegraph

A happy W.I. family. Mrs. P. T. S. Brown of Broxton and Bickerton (Cheshire) might well be the perfect W.I. wife. She and her husband won the Happy Partners Competition of a national daily newspaper after answering six searching questions about marriage and a final personal interview with the judges. Their prize was a delightful holiday in the Bahamas during which they were able to visit the daughter of Lady Howarth, Cheshire Federation Chairman. Mrs. Brown bakes the family bread, bottles their fruit and makes all her children's clothes (except those they make themselves)

Townswoman 1958

Grumbling

Housing: (1) There should be more women architects. (2) Each self-contained flat should have a bathroom and every "family" its own lavatory. (3) All pipes should be placed on the south side of the house. (4) Too little cupboard space was provided. (5) Larders were sometimes not provided or were in a wrong situation, *e.g.*, near lavatory or drains. (6) Central heating should be provided for all, especially in newly constructed houses. (7) Windows were often ill fitting. Sash windows were considered more successful than dormer. (8) Electric light and gas meters should be concealed. (9) More skilful use of blending of colours (exterior of houses) was desirable.

Clothing and Dress for Women: There should be (1) better lining in chip straw hats; (2) more fashionable outsize clothes designed for the younger woman; (3) longer stockings for taller women; (4) more half sizes in cheaper shoes; (5) more durable underclothing; (6) fewer sling-back sandals; (7) at least six suspenders on corset belts; and (8) slacks should only be worn when the job requires them.

In view of the above criticisms and suggestions it would be interesting to know the feelings of other Guild members. If opinions were strong enough, could not something concrete be done to improve the defects, some very small?

Which? 1959

LAVATORY PAPER

Lavatory paper is not a gay subject, nor one much discussed in polite society. Even the people who make and advertise it avoid, if they can, using the actual words in large type. They stress the 'Softness that you never had before' (ANDREX), 'Comfort women long for' (SCOT-TISSUE), 'You know you can trust' (IZAL). But, mentioned or not, it has to be bought.

Apart from personal comfort, CA thinks that a lavatory paper should be strong, and should give the greatest possible protection against the penetration of bacteria. Which type of paper is the best—the absorbent, still fairly new in the UK and bought only by one family in every five, or the long-established smooth finish type? What is the advantage of an 'hygienic' or 'medicated' paper? How many sheets do you get for your money? Is crêpe paper, sold at about 6d. a roll, in fact the most economical?

Home and Country 1959

CHIEF MEDICAL OFFICER REVIEWS 1957
Views on latest drug introductions

SOME of the developments of modern science became increasingly operative during 1957. Sir John Charles (Chief Medical Officer, Ministry of Health) states in his review for 1957, published by the Stationery Office (13s.). Examples he gives are the extension of vaccination against poliomyelitis "of which the effects are still only partially apparent," and the potential risks of the peaceful use of atomic energy manifested in the Windscale incident. There were three noteworthy outbreaks during the year caused by smallpox, tetanus and influenza.

As in each year since 1943 the number of notifications of diphtheria fell to a new low level, only thirty-seven and the deaths from that cause, only six. Seventy local health authorities were able to report that they had been free of diphtheria for at least five years. The year was notable for a pandemic of influenza, associated with a new variant of influenza virus A, which affected England and Wales in common with the rest of the world. The incidence of poliomyelitis in 1957 was 10·8 per 100,000, a figure exceeded in 1947 (18·3), 1949 (13·7), 1950 (17·7) and 1955 (14·2). The lowest rate recorded since 1948 was 4·4 in 1954. During the year 137 (182 in 1956) cases of malaria were notified including one indigenous case, the first recorded since 1953. There was a further steep rise in the number of new cases of gonorrhoea. "It is now apparent that penicillin, effective though it has been, cannot by itself make a lasting impression on the incidence of this disease." The dramatic decline in tuberculosis mortality continued during the year. The decline was of 11 per cent., compared with 17 per cent. in 1956.

'Tranquillisers,' for example, seem to have been used on an extensive—perhaps too extensive — scale, but their limitations and dangers have become more apparent and their lack of advantage in many instances over some of the older established measures has become obvious. . . . This has not deterred the pharmaceutical industry from devising further variations upon the 'tranquilliser' theme. The pity is that the energetic sales promotion devoted to the marketing of these agents is not always matched by adequate clinical trials of their use in practice."

Chemist and Druggist 1958

Which? 1959

Insect Repellents

For some people, a holiday, or a day in the country can be ruined by biting insects or swarms of flies. They may try to protect themselves with one of half a dozen proprietary insect repellents. Do any of them really work? If they do, is one better than another, or are they all much the same? Do some keep off some insects, not others? Do some last longer than others?

To find the answer, CA used chemical analysis, laboratory tests, and field trials. The results are summarized under CONCLUSIONS and VALUE FOR MONEY at the end of this report.

Radio Receivers

OUTSTANDING development in radio receivers has been the advance made in transistor models during the year. Advance is most marked in portables, but several table models are shown at Earls Court which could in time replace the mains-operated set. Transistors firmly established in hybrid-type car radio equipments, but no really small transistor portable is announced by a British manufacturer. Car radio aerial socket is becoming standardized on portables. In mains receivers A.M./F.M. are now the standard pattern. There are a few F.M.-only models also, but A.M.-only receivers are few and low-priced except in the portable and car radio field.

Wireless and Electronic Trader 1959

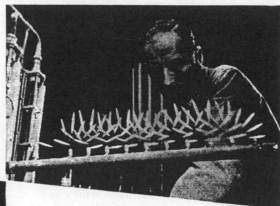

1960 ★ 1970

L.C.C.s EIGHT CONDITIONS FOR HIGH BUILDINGS

DESIGNS MUST BLEND WITH SKYLINE GROUPS

EIGHT conditions which high building projects in London will have to fulfil to obtain approval were disclosed yesterday in a report presented to Parliament. They have been designed by the London County Council.

Mr. Brooke, Minister of Housing and Local Government, has approved the L.C.C.s approach. Developments in 1959 have shown that the appearance of London and other large cities is likely to be changed by the erection of more high buildings.

The general Government policy is that each proposal for a high building is to be considered on its own merits. These include not only the proposed design of the building itself, but the characteristics of the area.

DISRUPTION FEAR
Size of Sites

The eight tests to be applied by the L.C.C. are:

1—Would it disrupt the pattern of existing development or obtrude on the skyline to the detriment of existing architectural groups?

2—Would it have a positive visual or civic significance?

3—Would the site be large enough to permit a base of lower buildings or open space?

4—Would it overshadow adjoining areas and stifle good development there?

5—Would it be better than a lower building and relate satisfactorily to other buildings nearby?

6—Would its design and materials be of high quality?

7—Would it relate satisfactorily to open spaces and the Thames?

8—Would its illumination at night detract from London's night scene?

The Shell building on the South Bank of the Thames is nearing completion. Permission has been granted for other high buildings at Millbank and on Euston Road. The L.C.C. is building high blocks of flats in Tidey Street, Stepney and at the Elephant and Castle.

Daily Telegraph
1960

NOW A SMALLER PENNY?

AT midnight to-night the farthing, having been called in and demonetised, ceases to be a current coin.

The end of the farthing has come suddenly. During the last war the numbers issued were the highest on record and it was struck until 1956. So why the hurry to demonetise it?

The real reason probably is that, once the farthing has gone, the way will be open for a smaller halfpenny and after that, a smaller penny.

Our present penny is the largest coin of its value in Europe and it is an open secret that the Royal Mint would welcome a reduction in its size.

Evening News and Star 1960

For many years this giant knife and fork have been an eye-catching feature over the entrance to the ironmongery premises of Messrs. William Thorne, Ltd., at the corner of Bampton Street and Gold Street, Tiverton. Now Messrs. Thorne's have closed down and the premises are to be occupied by Messrs. Rossiters (Pharmacies), Ltd. The knife and fork are to be sold at next Friday's auction, organised by Tiverton Rotary Club in aid of the World Refugee Year, on condition that the purchaser displays them prominently or presents them to Tiverton Museum.

Crediton Gazette, East Devon Herald and County Press 1960

Instrumentals are becoming hits

BUT 'LITTLE DONKEY' REMAINS AT THE TOP

HERE come the instrumentals ! " Man of Mystery," latest number by the British " Shadows," and " Perfidia " by the Ventures, are the new discs to watch among the Christmas best selling records. Still top seller in Louth is " Little Donkey " by Nina and Frederick.

Last week's tip for the top. "Poetry in Motion" by Johnny Tillotson has jumped into fourth place on this week's chart. He is preceded by Cliff Richard with his teenage romance-rocker "I Love You."

This week's tip is called "Stay" by Maurice Williams This record is number one in the United States. and the same version is to be released over here.

Louth Standard
1960

Four of a kind

Royal thrones of kings? Not quite. In fact, four bridge chairs which even though they do absolutely nothing to improve your game are bound to make you the envy of your opponents—and with luck this may adversely affect their play. The kings are colourfully hand painted and the seats are designed to be comfortable throughout the longest rubber. A choice of tables is available to match.

A gay departure by Lablanc, but in the same tradition of excellence that distinguishes their famous classical designs.

PRICES:
Chairs from £75 each.
Tables from ...... £108.

THE SECRET OF PLANTING FOR YOUR TABLE

GARDENING.

IT is at this season of the year that we really appreciate having a part of the garden for vegetables or an allotment. The young, fresh vegetables and salads are sweeter than at any time throughout the 12 months.

How nice it is to have the first new potatoes of our own growing, with so much more flavour than those we have been buying, and spring onions, young carrots, peas, and really crisp lettuce.

As we clear the ground of potatoes and pull up the rows of peas when gathering is finished, we must sow and plant more crops for use during the autumn and winter.

By following one crop with another we are making full use of the ground, getting full value for any manure and fertilisers we have used, and a just reward for our labours.

By PERCY THROWER

Sunday Dispatch
1961

You can see Lablanc furniture in our showrooms:

Lablanc Ltd., 251-6, Tottenham Ct. Rd., London, W.1.
Tel.: Museum 3113.
Selected stockists throughout the country.

Well kept wild gardens

All those concerned with garden grass cutting in general should know of the numerous and extremely efficient cutters made by Hayters, Spellbrook, Bishops Stortford, Herts. In addition to mowing lawns, these very versatile machines will cheerfully tackle tougher jobs which might otherwise prove difficult.

Some people are lucky enough to have wild gardens—by design! Here, amongst trees and shrubs and naturalised bulb plantings, grass is often allowed to grow roughly and an ordinary mower would be less suitable. Hayters offer several machines for keeping things in order and preventing the wild garden from becoming rampant.

The hand propelled 18-in 'Hayterette' is one. Apart from its general ornamental work it will also tackle rougher areas. It is light, handles easily, and the cut can be adjusted from ¾ in to 3¾ in. Hinged cutter blades are designed to swing back on contact with solid objects and this prevents the machine being damaged. It is powered by a Briggs and Stratton four-stroke engine, with a recoil starter, and costs £33.

As well as a 24-in hand-propelled rotary scythe there is also a 26-in self-propelled model for more extensive areas. This is powered by a four-stroke engine with a three-speed gear-box. The cutting height is easily adjustable from 6 in down to ground level which suits the machine for fine lawn cutting too. The price is £119 10s and trailer seats are available, if required, either roller or wheeled, varying in price from £14 10s to £19 10s.

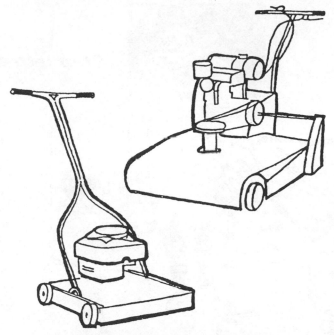

Left: 18-in 'Hayterette'. Right: 26-in rotary scythe

House and Garden 1961

A visit to the Regents Park home of Mr John Profumo, MP, and Mrs Profumo (Valerie Hobson)

House and Garden 1961

QUESTION TIME

Birth-control Pills

Mr. NICHOLAS RIDLEY asked the Minister of Health whether birth-control pills could be prescribed under the National Health Service.—Mr. POWELL replied: Yes. Mr. RIDLEY: Can the Minister confirm or deny that these pills can cost up to 17s. a month if prescribed? In view of this, will he not lay down and publish very careful instructions as to when they may be used, since the prescribing of these pills could cost a lot of money if not controlled on medical grounds? Mr. POWELL: It is not for me to indicate to doctors what they should decide, for medical reasons, to prescribe for their patients.

Mr. MARCUS LIPTON: Is it left to the doctor to decide whether these pills shall be prescribed both for married and single women? Mr. POWELL: It is always for the individual doctor to decide in each case what are the medical requirements.

Lancet 1961

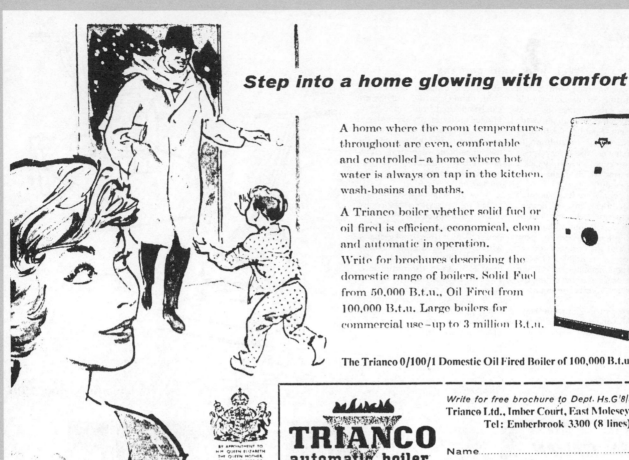
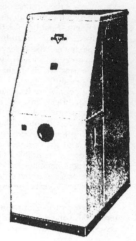
THE NEW BIBLE IS A BEST-SELLER

The worst Bible territory in England. That's what Bible publishers thought of Hampstead—until this week, when local bookshops sold hundreds of copies of the rewritten version of the New Testament, which appeared on Tuesday.

"We sold 120 in three days," said Mr. Ian Norrie, manager of the High Hill Bookshop, Hampstead High Street. "We never expected such a rush. It was almost as big as that for Lady Chatterley's Lover."

He added: "One of the publisher's representatives told me Hampstead has been the worst Bible territory in England for years. He's probably right. If we sell three dozen a year it's a lot."

Collet's, Haverstock Hill, sold 170 copies. "We've already had two deliveries," said manager Peter Chalk. "In terms of money it's running neck and neck with Lady Chatterley."

Melted away

At W. H. Smith's in Harben Parade, Swiss Cottage, manager W. G. Clark said: "We had a window full of them and they've melted away." And at Smith's Golders Green branch, Mr. S. H. Tadd reported: "We've had two deliveries — 400 copies in all — and are still going strong."

Local vicars welcomed the new version. "I think it is excellent and I shall certainly use it," said the Rev. J. Dover Wellman, vicar of Emmanuel, West Hampstead.

Hampstead's rural dean, the Rev. G. B. Timms, vicar of St. Mary's, Primrose Hill, said: "I welcome it. The revisers seem to have done their work sufficiently well for it to be worthy to be read in church. The unfamiliarity arrests attention, and the absence of obscurities will help the reader understand it more clearly."

At St. Michael's, Highgate, the Rev. Harry Edwards commented: "It doesn't compare with the old Bible, but it is a piece of work that needed to be done. It speaks to the people in the language they understand."

But one vicar disagreed. . The Rev. Thomas Jupp, of St. Peter's, Belsize Square, Hampstead, said: "I have only read extracts, but judging from them I think the new Bible is only a paraphrase of the old. It is a loss rather than a gain."

Hampstead and Highgate Express 1961

AROUND THE HOUSE

House and Garden 1961

Spring-clean for carpets

All through the winter months, without your realizing it, grubby marks have been accumulating on your precious carpets, safely hidden by the kindly lights of winter. Suddenly spring comes to show them up and shame you. Obviously it would be a costly business to have these carpets taken up and shampooed by the professionals every time a mark appeared—just as obvious as the fact that professional cleaning must be done from time to time in order to prolong the life of the carpet. To get down on one's hands and knees and rub at the mark with a cloth is now as old-fashioned as the open grate for cooking. Here is a carpet shampooer with little or no bending down involved, because the handle is long enough for comfort and yet short enough for the correct pressure to be put on the working end. The principle is simple: coarse plastic prongs comb the carpet and separate the tufts, a Polyestre foam roller applies the shampoo (fed through by an adjustable valve from the tank above) and a stiff-bristled brush behind the roller finishes the job. By Glamorene, 29s 6d. Refill shampoos, 7s 6d.

'Prints for Pleasure'

There is an awful lot of snob talked about reproductions of paintings, 'If I can't have the real thing, I'll do without', is the most usual. But prints should give the pleasure of being able to have lots of them; to change them as the mood takes you, and 'Prints for Pleasure' is the apt name of some of the best reproductions we have seen. The absence of that usual picture-postcard high-gloss finish is particularly refreshing.

At 10s 6d each, you can happily buy as many as you wish at 33 Park Lane. Out-of-Towners will find displays at large stores.

Special note. Please look at the prints for children. Here is a collection of extremely well-drawn, charming nursery scenes that are not inducive to nightmares for small tots. A box of 6 prints with a whitewood frame costs 1 gn.

Folding plate-rack

After the washing-up is finished, drained, wiped and stacked, what do you do with the plate-rack? Do you leave it standing in all its utilitarian glory on the draining-board, or try to find space in a cupboard? By giving the subject a little fresh, constructive thought, Wireweld Ltd, 4 Elthruda Rd, S E 13, have come up with the patently obvious answer—fold it away neatly so that it will occupy the least possible shelf area.

The rack comes in four colours —red, white, blue or yellow—and it costs 15s 9d from Harrods.

Memory jogger

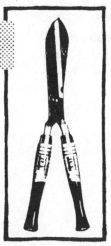

Motorist or pedestrian will find the 'Memopark', by Venner Ltd, a gentle jar to their memory. Although this neat little gadget was originally designed to take the have-I-over-run-my-time-on-that-meter anxiety out of busy lives, the 'Memopark' will quickly repay its cost of 29s 3d in a multitude of uses at home and work.

Basically, the 'Memopark' has a Swiss precision watch movement which can be set to intervals of 5 minutes, up to an hour. At the end of the selected time a persistent, but non-aggressive (certainly not embarassingly loud) buzzer is heard to warn that time is up.

The alarum is easily set by twisting the centre, coloured face until the arrow points to the time —shown on the calibrated dial— when you want it to sound, and if you have to change the timing, this is the easiest movement in the world.

The case is opaque plastic with a red, ivory, blue, black or green centre, or in clear plastic.

Decorated oven-ware

From Phoenix, who make such very high quality glass ovenware, comes an entrée dish with a very intriguingly designed vegetable motif in gay colours on a pearly white ground. An eternally useful utensil to have, especially when it incorporates a warming stand with two small candles, to make sure that food stays hot for second helpings. 35s from good stores.

Also from Phoenix, in the same style, is a very pretty butter dish decorated with a red rose. This costs 7s 6d.

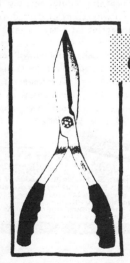
His best suit was on a stranger

When Mr. Leslie Catchpole went home to Maiden-road, Surbiton, one afternoon he found a stranger in the living room—wearing Mr. Catchpole's best suit, his shirt and shoes, and drinking his whisky.

Stephen Shippen, porter, no fixed address, was remanded at Kingston, Surrey, sessions yesterday, for stealing and breaking-in. He was said to have made 50 bombing raids during the war.

Daily Express 1962

ALL DONE BY MIRRORS!

A PLEASANT speaking voice is an asset, we all agree, and for the girl anxious to cultivate one there's a trick worth knowing. It has been practised with success by many people who charm in public, from starlets upwards.

The trick is to take a good "look" at your voice just as you do at your lipstick. It is just as easy, and is done with the same tool—a mirror! For voice "looking," though, next time you decide to ring up your best friend, hang your mirror near the telephone so that you can watch your voice while you chat. The expression on your face, you will soon discover, gives the key to the attractiveness of your voice. When you frown or pout, your voice sounds peevish or disagreeable. A winning smile on your face will put a winning smile in your voice.

In this way the mirror points the way to the cultivation of an appealing voice and facial expression too. Both are assets every girl wishes to possess, and what you practise when telephoning will soon become your natural mode all the time.

People's Friend 1962

There's Nothing Quite Like . . .

The SCOTS MAGAZINE

Each month its colourful pages bring Scotland before you in a way that is completely unmatched.

In the JUNE Issue you will find

"Her zest for life was keen, and there was her wayward only daughter to look after. If only 'the lassie' (then nearly forty) would go to bed at a decent hour—the hour specified being 8 p.m.!"

HELEN B. CRUICKSHANK tells of the humours of life in Edinburgh when her seventy-year-old mother came from the Angus countryside to live with her.

" It used to be said that 'Stoury Feet,' or incomers, had to live for three generations before being accepted as ' Falkland Folk.' "

COLIN GIBSON talks to an old lady whose memories of this corner of Fife range back over eighty years.

These are only two of the many fine articles.

The SCOTS MAGAZINE

JUNE ISSUE NOW ON SALE   Price 1/6d

The Scots Magazine, Bank Street, Dundee.

Fur and Feather
1962

MY LIFE'S TREASURES
PERCY ASHLEY

HERE we are once again in the Christmas festive season. This is my 73rd, but of course I cannot remember all these. I can just about recollect about 65 of them, and I have spent every one of these 65 among livestock of one kind or another.

How pleasant it is when one is piling up the years to relax among one's stock and go through one's memories. What a wonderful thing is this thing we call " The Fancy," and the fanciers in it. The friendship one makes, and the ones that have been broken by the death of someone we hold dear as a fancier friend.

Over the years one encounters many fancier friends whom one would not have met without our Fancy, whose friendship stands the test of time.

At the other end are the new friends one makes.

I have made friends in the rabbit, cavy and mouse Fancies and hold them as some of life's treasures.

Again what joy it gives one to dispense the knowledge one has gained over the years to the beginners. True, many of these fall by the wayside but what matters, so long as one gains a few new friends each year.

I spent a few days this year with the fanciers in Germany. Country or language are no barriers to friendship. I was treated as one of them and I gave them as much of my personal knowledge as I had time for. The German fanciers want me to visit them again in 1963.

I offered to fix them up with stock. I have already sent Dwarf rabbits and a trio of mice and I have made arrangements to forward, by plane, before Christmas three more trios of mice. As soon as I asked my fancier friends for help it was given as friends to a friend. They sent me three lots of mice for sending to Germany.

Where else would you find this spirit outside our Fancy

These German people are my latest friends and by our friendship to them we are helping to open up the Fancy in Germany.

What joy it is to receive letters from friends to whom one has given advice or started off in our Fancy.

If this spirit could only be fostered in the political life of countries, gone would be the threat of war, and we would all live in perfect peace.

I would like to make a list of all my many friends but it would take all of FUR AND FEATHER to put them down.

How often do we read of people retiring, or of younger people who do not know what to with their time. If they were in the Fancy, they would have no such worries. They could visit other fanciers or spend a few hours with their stock. Something which I was taught in early life is that I pass this way but once, and any little good I can do, let me do it now, tomorrow maybe too late.

One point that has struck me many times is how true fanciers can disagree with others on a particular topic, yet remain true friends. Some of my oldest friends and I have had some heated arguments on various Fancy topics, but we are still firm friends. Fancier friendships do not necessarily mean that one has to be a "yes" person. At times, it seems good to disagree on some particular point. One then gets a true view of one's friend's personality.

House and Garden 1961

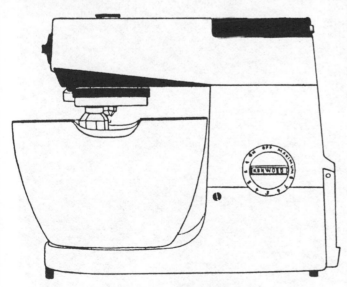

Good mixer
Kenwood's 'Chef' mixer,
beautifully designed and extremely efficient,
has attachments for liquidising,
grinding, mincing and juice extracting.
Most big stores. From £28 17s 6d

Which? 1963

HOME FREEZERS

Most home freezers, on the other hand, are designed to freeze fresh food down to 0°F within 24 hours and keep it at that temperature, and only need defrosting once or twice a year. This means that fresh or cooked or already frozen food can be stored, safely and without losing its flavour, for several months. (See Diagram.)

Freezers are obviously useful for people who live in the country and grow their own fruit and vegetables, or can get hold of more poultry than they can use at once. They may also be useful for town-dwellers with large families, who want to organise their shopping and baking so as to do it less often; to have a supply of frozen foods always on hand for entertaining; and to vary the eternal apples with last year's raspberries.

Slum housing in East Kilbride, Scotland, 1963.

Dustbins and lavatories
outside the front doors in
Count Abby Street, Rochdale,
Lancashire.

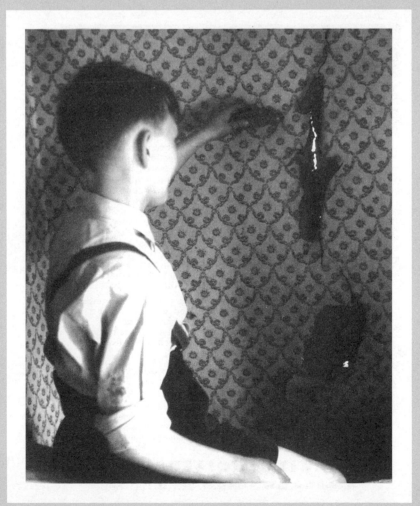

A toy car shows the
scale of cracks in a
wall in Hulme, Manchester.

The extended curving sofas are taking the place of the traditional three-piece suit. Harrison Gibsons' four-seater corner unit is part of their teak underframed Calypso range, from 87 gns. G-Plan's compact Baby K'ang sofas have several decorative permutations. Left and right-hand curved sofas (below) will seat six — £57 15s. each. Adding a corner unit will make room for eight

Ideal Home 1963

Perkins Boilers

FOR AUTOMATIC – PRECISION-CONTROLLED – OIL, GAS AND ELECTRIC CENTRAL HEATING

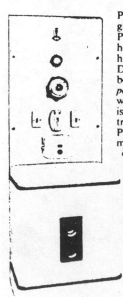

Perkins' long experience enables them to give you a wider selection at lower cost. Perkins offer you a boiler to suit your house *and* pocket, which will operate at high efficiency with or without a chimney. Do you realise that if you use an oil-fired boiler correctly, you must use *fifteen pounds weight* of air for every pound weight of oil? This is a scientific fact. Air is cheap enough—but it can only be controlled if you have the 'know-how'. Perkins have invested a very large sum of money in the development of combustion control and offer you *free* advice.

More and more installation engineers are being trained with the benefits of Perkins technical knowledge.
Perkins boilers are in constant use on land and sea in each of the five continents of the world.

IT WILL PAY YOU TO LET PERKINS HELP YOU.

For the boiler of the future that is available today, please send for copies of our Advisory Service Bulletin and 16 page booklet of the fabulous Perkins Mini-Boiler.

PERKINS BOILERS LTD

Mansfield Road, Derby · Telephone: Derby 48235 (5 lines)

Potato Crisps

Mary Queen of Scots is supposed to have enjoyed marmalade, Pitt, on his deathbed, to have called for one of Bellamy's veal pies. More recently, Mr Khrushchev has said, 'When we were flying around America . . . we sat there in the plane talking and munching with pleasure factory-made potato crisps. . . .'

On average the Americans eat twice the weight of crisps that the British do, but at present crisp manufacturers here are vigorously trying to expand their sales.

If you are buying a packet of crisps, you will want to know what weight of crisps you can expect to get. You may want to know which of the packages will keep the crisps crispest, and the missing twist of salt is a perennial talking-point.

We did tests to answer these questions.

A 4d. packet of crisps contains approximately 140 calories, about the same number as in two slices of bread. Roughly speaking, an office worker could, if he was so minded, get all the calories he needed by eating 18 4d. packets of crisps a day.

Which? 1963

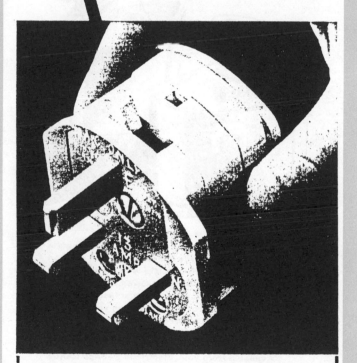

Antique Collector 1964

For Collectors of Caddy-spoons

IT is always welcome news to hear of a new society for collectors of antiques. The latest—and we admit we were surprised at the subject—is the Society of Caddy-spoon Collectors. There must be more enthusiasts for these delightful and varied miniature spoons than we had imagined. The Society's headed paper reproduces one of the well-known eagle-feather spoons. Many other subjects are to be found, including shells, jockey caps, and leaves of the vine and other plants. The hey-day of the caddy-spoon was late 18th century.

The aims of the Society are: To research into the history of the caddy-spoon, to assist those who collect examples, and to compile a fully-illustrated text-book in which it is hoped that members will participate. A regular newsletter is issued with articles by members, and it is hoped to arrange exhibitions. The membership subscription is 2 gns. a year for English members, 1 gn. a year for corresponding members. Meetings are to be held in London twice or three times a year, with possibly occasional meetings in a provincial city. The Hon. Secretary of the Society is Captain John D. Norie, 43 Pine Avenue, Gravesend, Kent.

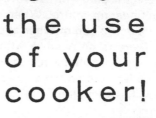

A FAMOUS COUNTRY HOUSE!

A POLICE sergeant stands by a partly-dug pit in the back garden of the House of Secrets—the most publicised house in Britain this week at Leatherslade Farm, Oakley. It's an isolated farmhouse standing in about two acres of land and was used by the mail gang as their hideout.

Curtains the gang used to cover up their movements inside their hideout are still drawn across some of the windows.

On the left of the picture is the brick extension which was built to make it into a three- or four-bedroomed house. Beans grow in part of the garden but the rest is overgrown.

The house is about a third of a mile along a rough track from the B4011 Thame to Bicester-road. Another track leads off in the opposite direction to the Long Crendon to Brill road. The house is about 20 miles from the scene of the crime at Sears Crossing.

Police and scientists have been going over the house piece by piece in their methodical search for any clue, however small, that will give them more leads to the identity of the gang which carried out the biggest train robbery in history.

Leatherslade Farm was recently sold for £5,500. Police know the name of the buyer but have not released it.—16577.

Buckinghamshire Advertiser and Aylesbury News 1963

Topless? It's just not on

THE topless dress has been tried and found guilty. The law has spoken. And now, women—in London, at any rate—wear them at their peril. The verdict was that of Mr. Anthony Babington, the Bow-street magistrate.

News of the World 1964

Norman Hartnell
The famous fashion consultant makes his personal choice only for Great Universal.

Cathy McGowan
has her own swinging Boutique in the brand new Great Universal Catalogue.

George Best
adds more exciting colourful style to make the Great Universal menswear range truly international.

3 great names that help to make Great Universal great!

Great names, great fashions, great service. The greatest! The same outstanding service on every one of more than 23,000 items in the new Great Universal colour catalogue. All guaranteed top quality. When your friends shop through the catalogue, Great Universal give you another great service — 2/- in the £ commission on every single purchase.

CLAIM YOUR GREAT FREE OFFER NOW

Somerset Maugham dead

From Daily Mail Correspondent

NICE, Thursday

AUTHOR Somerset Maugham died in a Nice hospital early today, aged 91.

He had rallied slightly during the night but there was little hope that he would recover from the blockage of blood circulation to his brain that put him in a coma on Saturday.

Mr. Maugham was taken ill on Friday when he fell in his villa at St. Jean Cap Ferrat. He fell again later the same day.

Mr. Alan Searle, his secretary, said Mr. Maugham would be cremated in Marseilles. His remains would be taken to London after Christmas.

"I hope they can rest in Canterbury Cathedral, as he always hoped," said Mr. Searle.

Somerset Maugham wrote 20 novels. The best known were *The Moon and Sixpence, Of Human Bondage, Liza of Lambeth* and *Cakes and Ale.*

He was a superb story-teller who believed in strong plots and disliked obscure novels. He was a supreme writer of short stories and also had four plays on the London stage in one year.

See Page ELEVEN.

Daily Mail 1965

Servicing and repairs

In an emergency

If you have even the slightest suspicion that there is a gas leak in your house, you should telephone the local Gas Board's emergency service immediately.

You can call them at any time, 24 hours a day. The Gas Boards say that you should have a gas fitter arriving within an hour to deal with the leak.

Routine service

For routine servicing there are three possible arrangements:

- *Contract Maintenance Scheme,* where the servicing and repairs are done so many times a year at a fixed annual cost.
- *Regular servicing,* where you arrange in advance for servicing and repairs to be done so many times a year, but pay for whatever work is done, not a fixed price.
- *Occasional servicing and repairs,* where you arrange for the servicing and repairs to be done when you think they are needed, and pay for whatever work is done.

Regular servicing can be disregarded. Very few of our members used this method and the Gas Boards told us it was most unusual.

Which? 1965

Listener
1965

The new elephant and rhinoceros house at the London Zoo (architects, Casson, Conder and Partners)

Brides **1966**

Small chest, £2: paint a bright colour and cover the top with ceramic tiles (we show design CPR 623, Carters). Fit ceramic handles. Placed in the bathroom, you could stick tiles to match, round the bath. Larger chest, 35s.; paint diminishing rect-angles on top, sides and front, in say, fawn, yellow and orange.

NEW! Modern design on a budget

Brianco introduce a greatly increased range of metal ladder units which enable you to plan exciting interiors at remarkably low cost. Our catalogue gives details of these together with shelves cabinets etc. Whether just filling an alcove or designing a large room setting, Brianco provides the answer. We also have a range of square section metal legs and frames for making your own coffee or dining tables.

BRIANCO
Book Shelves Coffee Tables Record Cabinets
Room Dividers Desks Chairs Slatted Benches
Drink Cupboards Bureaux Chests Book Cases

ORDER BY POST.
Write or call for illustrated catalogue at our showrooms.
Brianco Limited,
Dept. I.H.4,
16 Norton Folgate,
Bishopsgate,
London, E.1.
Only 4 minutes from
Liverpool St. Station.

*Baker
and Confectioner*
1965

Nothing Like It

ALTHOUGH modern mothers tend to buy sliced bread and wrapped bread for convenience sake, there is nothing like the oven-fresh loaf, and during the year it was shown still to be in demand, from the queues one sees in fresh-smelling bakery shops.

Many people do, in fact, travel out of their way in order to buy this sort of bread.

It is a shame, however, that customers by and large out of sheer apathy and laziness, accept bread that they do not really like.

90

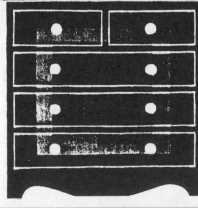

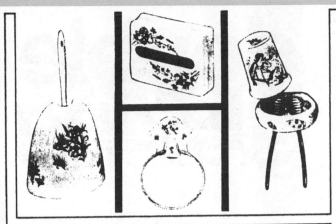

Heating and Ventilating Engineer 1966

An oil-fired small-bore system has been installed

A HOUSEBOAT with a difference is moored in a wharf near Kew Bridge in London. From the outside it looks like any other similar craft, but inside it is equipped with a modern central heating system.

It is owned by Dr. J. W. Moggoch, a consultant anaesthetist, and his wife, Miss Betty Marsden, the well-known actress and radio personality. It is now their permanent home. The hull, which was originally an 80 ft coal barge, was rebuilt and converted in a Chelsea boat-yard to their designs.

A new upper structure was built on to the barge, the roof being specially reinforced to provide a sun deck, and the hold was converted into sleeping quarters. Externally, the houseboat does not convey the spaciousness of its interior, which comprises a combined dining-room and lounge over 35 ft long, commodious kitchen, one huge bedroom, three smaller ones and a study playroom for the Moggoch's two children. There are two bathrooms, a utility-cum-laundry room and endless storage space.

The idea of installing central heating was something of an innovation at the Chelsea yard where the work was done, and it is the first time a boat of this kind has been equipped with an oil system.

HEATHERLEY MAKES THE PERFECT GIFT FOR EVERY BRIDE!

Heatherley bathroom accessories are the ideal gift. Gorgeous designs on lovely background colours—Primrose, Coral, Sky-blue, Turquoise or White. Heatherley porcelain bathroom accessories add a note of elegance and distinction. Available from all good stores or write for fully illustrated literature and name of nearest stockist to Dept. 34, Charwell House, Hook Road, Chessington, Surrey.

Heatherley Fine China Ltd.

NEW!
'GROW' GLAMOROUS LONG NAILS
-in minutes!

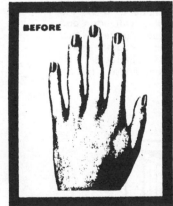

BEFORE AFTER

New from Nailform of New York—most amazing beauty product in years! LIQUID NAILS turn ugly, broken, split nails into hard, long, lovely nails—**in minutes! NOT** a weak paste, but an incredibly strong substance that brushes on easily. Can be trimmed, filed and beautifully polished—will never break or split—stays on until your own nails grow out. **Stops nail biting.** USED BY MILLIONS IN AMERICA.

SPECIAL MONEY-BACK BARGAIN OFFER 17/6 pack for only **13/6,** Limited introductory offer. **Orders and enquiries by mail only.**

SEND NOW! **13/6.** plus 6d. postage and packing, to:

Dept. 259 Honorhouse Products Ltd · 276 Cranbrook Rd., Ilford · Essex

Q. Margaret T. (Sheffield). *I am engaged to be married to a charming boy but he smokes a pipe. You may think me queer but I can't stand the smell, and he admits he lights his pipe even when he first gets up. I've told him how I feel, but he begs me not to make it an issue because it has become such a strong habit with him. Do you advise me to give him up?*

A. If you want the blunt truth, my dear, I'd advise *him* to give *you* up! You're being much too intolerant. I do assure you that a pipe can not only become a habit but a real comfort to a man. To force him to give it up—even if he agreed—would be foolish, because he would only go back to it in the end and then there'd be real trouble between you. It is such a harmless habit, surely you could learn to put up with it and open all the windows wide after he has gone out? As a compromise, you might suggest he doesn't smoke the pipe the whole time you are sitting together. But don't wait till *after* you're married to say so!

She 1966

double double
glazing glazing

'Cuts heat loss by as much as 50%'
'Double windows will reduce your fuel bill by about one-third'
'Heat loss through the window can be cut by 65%'

These are exciting sounding claims. But do not be too excited. It's true enough that double-glazing can cut down the amount of heat you lose through your windows by one-half or even more. But how much does this matter?

In a typical semi-detached house, perhaps one-fifth of all your heat will be lost through the windows. So double-glazing will save only about a tenth of your heat — the rest will go out through the roof, up the chimneys, through the walls and so on. To have a typical semi-detached double-glazed professionally might cost £200. If your annual heating bill was £80, it would take you a long time at £8 to £10 a year to get the money you spent back.

Of course, it also depends on how big your windows are and how much of your wall area they take up. But to save a third of your heating costs, you would have to live in the sort of house in which it would be unwise to throw stones.

Which? 1966

Milton Keynes New Town

The Minister of Housing and Local Government has decided to designate an area of about 22,000 acres as the site of the proposed new town in North Buckinghamshire. The area includes the existing towns of Bletchley, Wolverton and Stony Stratford but the new town will take its name from Milton Keynes, a small village within the area.

Milton Keynes will be the largest town so far designated under the New Towns Acts. Over the next 20 years it will receive about 150,000 London overspill; together with the existing population and natural growth this is expected to produce a total population of about 250,000 by the end of the century.

In his official decision letter, the Minister says that a large and complex area on the scale envisaged must have a structure providing opportunities for growth at the pace required, and the capacity to adapt to new needs as these are recognised. It must also avoid dependence on a single centre, which is at the root of so many of the problems of existing towns. The Minister also says that the site should be defined with sufficient latitude to allow the existing towns of Bletchley, Wolverton and Stony Stratford to be incorporated within the new development in a manner which preserves rather than obliterates their strength and independent sense of local community.

Building *1967*

How to give him his morning tea

{ and still play the sleeping beauty }

Lucky's the girl who gets a Goblin Teasmade—and ten extra minutes in bed every day of her life!

Think of fresh-brewed tea or instant coffee very first thing—it's the most effortless way we've heard of to spoil a husband (or wife!)

All you do is set the Teasmade at night. Then at the chosen moment, presto: a call to wake you, a soft light, and tea is ready to pour.

The Goblin Teasmade is so much more than a superb

tea-maker—it's also a bedside light and electric clock in a conveniently space-saving combination.

Prices range from £13.7.2 for the Popular Teasmade shown left (it comes without bulb and shade), to £29.11.2 for the 'Queen Anne' Gift Pack illustrated above, which comes complete with china and teapot. Goblin Teasmades are available from all leading electrical suppliers. Please write to us for further details.

GOBLIN TEASMADE

GOBLIN ELECTRIC APPLIANCES LTD · LEATHERHEAD · SURREY

M.P. SAYS HE OPPOSES A LOTTERY

'Encouraging a vice'

THOUGH pleased that suggestions he made personally to the Chancellor of the Exchequer that the gambling tax should be increased had been adopted in the Budget, Mr. Alistair Macdonald, M.P. for Chislehurst, is less pleased that the Chancellor proposes a State lottery might be organised.

In a 25-minute speech on the Finance Bill in the House of Commons, Mr. Macdonald said: " I am all in favour of taxing gambling, but it seems to me that there is all the difference in the world between raising revenue from taxes on gambling and running a lottery."

Mr. Macdonald added: " To tax people's vices is one thing. To encourage the practice of those vices is another, and I regret that we are now at the beginning of a course which will cause the social services, the amenities, and indeed the defence of this country to depend on the proceeds of a lottery.

" I thing that if we want these things we should pay for them. If we do not want to pay for them, we should do without them."

Eltham and Kentish Times 1968

Organ Transplantation

IN a statement to the House of Commons on May 6, Mr. ROBINSON, the Minister of Health, said that the requirements of the Human Tissue Act, 1961, in regard to the removal of the donor's heart which was transplanted at the National Heart Hospital on May 3, were fully complied with. The brother of the dead man had given permission acting for the family, since the widow was herself in hospital and unable to be consulted owing to her own serious condition. His department had recently advised hospitals about the demand for news coverage because of Press and public interest in advanced surgery. He wished to protect the interests of the patient and his relatives and those of the donor, and to ensure that no names should be disclosed without the free consent of those concerned. The National Heart Hospital had acted in accordance with this advice, but names had been revealed to the Press from sources other than the hospitals concerned. No observers had been present at the operation and only the normal clinical photographs had been taken and these would not be released. He admitted that there was bound to be conflict between the desire of the Press to get maximum information about such an event and the traditional reticence of the medical profession. He thought that how this conflict was resolved was very much a matter of personal taste. He confessed that he regretted some aspects of the publicity associated with this.

Lancet 1968

Cambridge News 1968

EIGHTY FAMILIES IN TOWER FLATS HORROR

Two men and a woman were found dead in the debris after a corner of a 22-storey block of flats had crashed in Butcher's Road in the East End of London today. Seven people remained unaccounted for and 80 families were made homeless in the disaster, which struck while many of the block's 260 occupants were still in bed.

Throughout the morning, emergency services with bulldozers and cranes, assisted by workers from the nearby Royal Group of Docks, toiled in the rubble, searching for anybody still trapped. Rescue operations were later suspended because of the dangerous situation in which the men were working. It was not thought likely that anyone was left alive.

Officials were working on the theory that there had been an explosion before the crash. A fire officer said there were definite signs of an explosion on the 18th floor.

Part of the roof and walls of the collapsed flats being pulled down.

When he falls down just as the kettle boils: Kiss him better.

The Russell Hobbs Rapide switches _itself_ off.

No other kettle can do that.

THE RUSSELL HOBBS boils 3 pints in a hurry. Then its exclusive switch-off control clicks it off automatically. No rush across the kitchen. No getting the wall steamed up. No wasted electricity. No flat water. No boiling dry. (Switch on empty and a safety cut-out prevents the element from burning out).

And when he's smiling again, click the red reset switch and the water's back to the boil in no time (even after an hour).

There's a new stainless steel Rapide with matt satin finish or there's the familiar model in gleaming chrome on copper (illustrated). Both cost £6.19.6.* And both are approved by the British Electrical Approvals Board and carry a full year's guarantee. So make sure you get a Russell Hobbs, the kettle that watches itself. Unless you're willing to make do with second best, of course.   *Recommended Price*

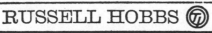

RUSSELL HOBBS

Tube Investments Ltd. an advanced engineering group

Woodware by MALLOD — so right in your home!

Mallod products are made of wood and there's nothing more natural—more *right* in your home. There's nothing tougher either: take Mallod Hods for instance—surprisingly sturdy, completely unaffected by the harsh acids found in solid fuel, absolutely rustproof and incredibly light. Fully guaranteed, they'll last you for years. There's a choice of three types for your lounge and two for use with your boiler, all in a wide range of finishes to go with your decor.

Mallod trays are made of resin-bonded wood covered with attractive heat and stain resistant melamine surfaces. They are strong, hard wearing and completely rigid. Offered in three sizes and a wide choice of wood-grain patterns, plain colours and floral designs.

MINOR
FOR YOUR KITCHEN

MAJOR
FOR YOUR LOUNGE

To William Mallinson & Sons (Mfg.) Ltd., Thames Road, Crayford, Kent.
Please send me (without obligation) your leaflets illustrated in colour.

Name

Address

CMMA50A

Brand-new 1967 three-programme 19" set. Gets BBC1, ITV, BBC2. Transistorised to give even greater sensitivity, clearer picture, better sound. Extra power on picture tube for brightest picture yet. Smooth, dust-free cabinet lines, diamond-finished controls, silver-trimmed facia. Matching legs available.

What every bride should know about colour TV

Only spendthrifts buy TV sets. Prudent girls rent from Radio Rentals on the Single Payment Discount Rental Plan.

Colour TV starts in just a few months now. Swinging new life for the home screen. But a big disappointment to the unwary couple who've just bought – yes, *bought* – a black-and-white set that's suddenly become completely old hat.

We say buying costs too much

In the first year alone, Government controls can make you pay out £50 or more for a 19" set if you buy on hire purchase. You've possible service bills to face, however you buy. And if you pay cash you can lock up a lot of money on a set that you'll soon want to change to colour TV.

There's only one perfect solution

Rent a brand-new 1967 black-and-white set now from Radio Rentals. Choose the Single Payment Discount Rental Plan. For the 19" Model 662, illustrated here, you make just one payment of £22.2.0, and nothing more for a full year. This includes

installation, darn good service – even if we say it ourselves – and insurance against fire and theft. Quite a package for so little money.

You'll be able to change from black-and-white to colour TV with every confidence, because of our years of research and practical experience. Our service staff have already learned colour techniques in our laboratories – so they won't have to learn in your home.

So why don't you give us a call now?

We have about 750 showrooms and about 7,000 trained staff waiting to switch you on to TV viewing the way it should be. Ring or drop in at your nearest showroom and ask for a no-cost trial in your own home. Most of our branches have 24-hour phone facilities. If you live in the London area, phone HUNter 5271 up to 10 p.m.

Go on. Do it now.

RELIABLE
RADIO RENTALS

Punch 1968

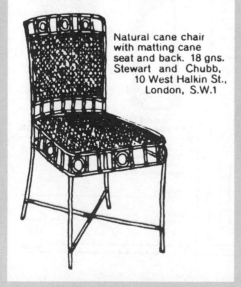

Natural cane chair with matting cane seat and back. 18 gns. Stewart and Chubb, 10 West Halkin St., London, S.W.1

Woman's Home Journal 1968

"—and, of course, another great attraction of the property is hunting with the Quorn."

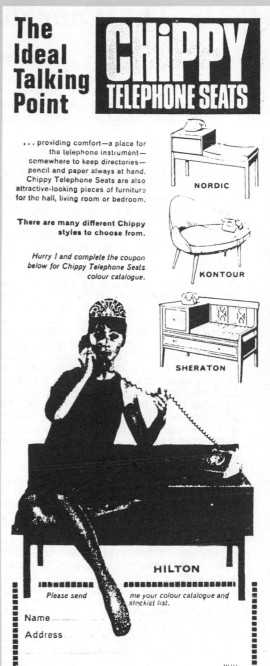

Tablet 1969

The Cannabis Controversy

Seymour Spencer

The Home Secretary's Advisory Committee on Drug Dependence published its findings last week and has created widespread discussion. Its implications are here examined by a specialist on the subject

THE SO-CALLED Wootton Committee was, it must be understood, the Hallucinogens Sub-Committee—under Lady Wootton's chairmanship and now preparing a report on LSD—of the Home Office Advisory Committee on Drug Dependence, whose chairman, Sir Edward Wayne, formally submitted the document to the Home Secretary. But it was, felicitously, more than just this sub-committee: it had co-opted onto it the Emeritus Professor of Psychiatry of London University. It was rumoured that his retirement from the Institute of Psychiatry had not left Sir Aubrey Lewis idle. Ephemeral as may be the Report itself,[1] his Appendix 1, a detailed review of the revelant medical literature, makes the purchase of the document a " must " for serious clinical students of the subject.[2] Likewise, Appendix 2, on the History of the Development of International Control of the drug from 1912 to 1968, with its outline of the important four decisions and four schedules of the Conference for Adoption of Single Convention on Narcotic Drugs, places the whole report in its world-perspective. It is only in relation to these two appendices, especially Lewis's, that the report can be seriously reviewed.

They make it plain how hard it still is, on the evidence of either the literature or witnesses, to " place " cannabis accurately. Basically, it comes between alcohol and the LSD group of hallucinogens. It can, like alcohol, but without alcohol's tendency to physical dependency, tolerance and withdrawal symptoms, afford relaxation and well-being (paras. 26 and 45). These effects, witnesses asserted, have produced a group of *responsible* inhalers of the smoke of cannabis resin (" hash ") in both the professional and unskilled workers' classes, otherwise law-abiding and normal in personality, capable of adjusting accurately their dosage " to achieve the effect they seek " (para. 24), and aiming at no more than a once—or twice—weekly " high " of two to three hours (para. 44). Were these the sole effects, there could be no more moral issue in the use of cannabis than in that of regular, moderate alcohol (except that the very taste of alcoholic beverages affords an aesthetic pleasure denied to cannabis): it was, one assumes, in deference to the needs of

these responsible, moderate, regular " smokers " that the possibility of the ultimate legalisation of cannabis arose in the mind of the sub-committee. The implication of para. 72 is that opinion on this issue was divided, even given the preliminary *desiderata*: control of importation, distribution and standards ; definition of intoxication with methods of detection ; protection of minors and against adulteration ; licensing of synthetic homologues.

[1] *Cannabis: Report by the Advisory Committee on Drug Dependence.* (London, H.M.S.O., 1968, price 7s. 6d.) The paragraphs referred to are those of the report.
[2] More then the pity that the extensive bibliography of nearly 150 references is not cited even by the use of directing numerals in the text: so that, for instance, one has to infer that the 1965 experiment at Lexington and Fort Worth was that of Ball and his colleagues.

Queen 1968

SEX AND THE BRITISH BLUE-BLOOD

The fact that the British aristocracy has lasted so long is not by chance. It has worked out its survival to a T. As sex is fundamental to survival, there has always been a kind of policy platform on how to handle the sex instinct. The rough plan, although not so far formally published, would read something like this:

Article 1—sex is plainly very much there, but socially, in aristocratic circles, it is better to pretend that it is *not* there. In other circles, let fly in a big way.

Article 2—sex is always better when had with someone of a lower social order than yourself, or with a foreigner, because then you can behave as you like without losing your social dignity and poise.

Article 3—homosexuality saves a lot of problems, but should be practised with members of the same social order as yourself, never below you, as you would then be open to blackmail. Or if you *must* practise your predilection with the lower classes, remember you can sleep with other ranks but you can't dine with them.

Article 4—men can marry women of a lower social order than themselves to provide new, strong, *red* corpuscles for the veins of the next generation's blue-bloods. But blue-blooded women should never *marry* red-blooded men of a lower social order, unless the women are princesses – when the red-bloods are created princes or earls and become 'instant blue-bloods'.

Article 5—adultery.

(*a*) by blue-blooded wives. This can be practised openly with one blue-blooded male at a time, but, with more than one, it becomes socially dangerous. With red-bloods (as many as you like), it must be kept *sub rosa* until after the affair is over, when it can be flagrantly publicised and the chauffeur, butler or groom can receive an appropriate monetary reward. And the wife can be thanked for strengthening her husband's line.

(*b*) by blue-blooded husbands. This can be practised with as many women, blue- or red-blooded, as is physically possible, as long as it does not get into the newspaper columns and as long as any children produced by the red-blooded females are fully provided for (in the Good Old Days, they were given the surname of the father with the prefix Fitz) and any children produced by the blue-blooded females are disowned by the real father out of social deference to the blue-blooded female's blue-blooded husband. To wise him up to the situation would definitely not be cricket. And, anyway, he is probably having exactly the same problems with another red-blooded female, who is producing lots of children who would have once been called Fitz-something, and with another blue-blooded wife, whose blue-blooded husband is being kept unaware that his apparently blue-blooded children are not really his . . . If you follow me.

Squatters ousted by police commando

The Times 1969

Showered by a barrage of missiles, police yesterday " invaded " the 100-room Piccadilly mansion occupied by hundreds of squatters since last Monday.

In a spectacular three-minute action they stormed a makeshift drawbridge protruding from a ground-floor window, and within a few minutes a waving constable signalled from the roof that all was under control.

Supported by cheers from 2,000 sightseers, about 50 young police officers formed the first assault party.

Water-filled plastic balls—one broke a woman's collar bone on Saturday night—ricocheted from their helmets; roof slates whizzed dangerously past their heads; stones, pieces of wood and iron bars hit them as they ran to make a bridgehead for a supporting column of police waiting in Hamilton Place near by.

The 200 squatters, remnants of about 700 who had spent the night in the four-storey building at the corner of Park Lane, seemed determined to fight. They had promised the police a hot reception, particularly from squads of Hell's Angels armed with pick shafts, crowbars, rocks, flick knives and at least one pikestaff.

OVERSEAS DEVELOPMENTS

Exotic fashions from faraway places have been appearing in the shops more and more, adding a touch of exquisite colour, elaborate embroidery and unusual style. Ancient, traditional designs are preserved in the heavily-patterned scarves, dresses, bags, metal and leather work from such places as Greece, Russia, Morocco and—in the mystic East—India, Pakistan and Afghanistan. Suzanne Grey shows you here some of the most exciting of the faraway fashions that are available in the shops now

Right: from Pakistan —a traditional hand-made printed cotton dress known as a Kurtas. Simply styled, its gay print achieves eye catching effect. In sizes 10-14, 22s. 6d. from The Souk, 477 Oxford Street, London, W1.

Above: from the small Greek island of Crete—a hand-woven wool on cotton rucksack, the newest way of carrying round all your odds and ends. In vivid colours, 84s. from The Greek Shop, 29 Charlotte St., London W1.

Left: from the Ukraine in Russia—a richly printed fringed scarf makes an ideal shawl for wearing over a plain dress. Traditionally it's worn by folk dancers. Price 49s. 6d. from the Russian Shop, 278 High Holborn, London WC1.

Below: from India—a fine multi-strand Indian silver belt painted with a delicate filigree design and fastened with an ornately worked clasp. It costs 42s. from The Souk, 477 Oxford Street, London W1.

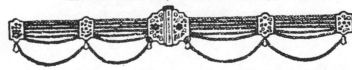

Woman's Own 1969

Daily Mirror
1969

MAN WHO EXPOSED RACHMAN IS DEAD

By RICHARD STOTT

LABOUR MP Ben Parkin, the man who forced the racketeering "twilight area" landlords into the open, died yesterday.

He collapsed sitting in his car while his wife watched their son playing tennis at St. Paul's preparatory school in Barnes.

His body was found by Mrs. Parkin.

Mr. Parkin, 63, became MP for Paddington North in 1953. Earlier he had represented Stroud, Glos. from 1945 to 1950.

For the next ten years he fought to clear Paddington of landlords who charged their tenants sky-high rents to live in appalling conditions.

His crusade came to a head in 1963 when he exposed property magnate Peter Rachman.

At one time Rachman owned nearly 1,000 broken-down houses for which he charged huge rents—and sent in thugs to force his tenants into paying.

The Rachman revelations were the direct reason for the Government taking a long look at landlord and tenant relations.

Threats

For many of Mr. Parkin's constituents, the 1965 Rent Act meant a better deal.

But the threats and war of nerves against him by the landlords took their toll.

Mr. Parkin had been ill for several years with heart trouble. Six months ago, after a series of disputes with his constituency party, he announced that he would retire at the next election.

His death leaves Labour with another marginal seat to contest in a by-election.

At the 1966 General Election Mr. Parkin's majority was 6,464 in a three-cornered fight.

On present voting trends the seat would seem to be a certain win for the Tories.

Arbroath Herald 1969

The Half-Crown Disappears

The half-crown goes out of circulation after December 31. It will then no longer be legal tender. So check savings and collecting boxes and other places where you might have put half-crowns. Use them or take them to the bank before the end of December. Remember, after Hogmanay, half-crowns cannot be used as money.

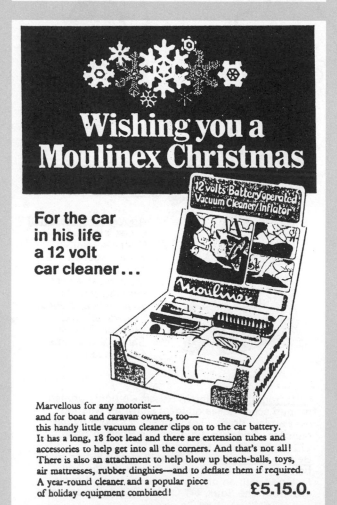
Meet the boys— Matt and Gloss

By Daily Mail Reporter

TWO youngsters settled down to a spot of painting when their mother slipped out for a moment.

Matthew, three, and his brother, Andrew, two, happily sploshed away with white paint from half-gallon tins — all over themselves.

Two ghost-like figures greeted their mother, Mrs Vida Stanley, of High Street, Sheerness, Kent, when she arrived home with icecreams for the boys.

Mrs Stanley phoned for help. Ambulancemen wrapped the boys in paper towelling, slipped them into two large pillowcases and carried them off to Sheppey General Hospital.

Shining

Nurses in the outpatients' department set to with a large bottle of turpentine, another of linseed oil and a great deal of effort.

Fortunately, the mopping up operation showed that Matthew and Andrew had not swallowed paint or put any in their eyes.

After a few hours the youngsters emerged from the hospital shining and clean. But they left their mark: A rather unusual patients' record-book entry reading 'Matthew, covered in undercoat, and Andrew covered in gloss.'

An ambulanceman said: 'I have never seen anything like it before. They looked just like two tiny ghosts.'

All cleaned up : Matthew, three (top), and Andrew, two

Daily Mail
1969